The President's Bib
John Edward Bunch II
Black Dragon
Lifer
National President Retired
Mighty Black Sabbath Motorcycle
Club Nation
A Breed Apart
Since 1974 and Still Strong...........///
www.bikerliberty.com
Host Black Dragon Biker TV YouTube
Host Black Dragon Biker Facebook
Host The Dragon's Lair Motorcycle
Chaos Podcast –

Sales/Advertising 404.692.0336
blackdragon@blacksabbathmc.com
Bunch Media Group
P.O. 931792
Norcross, Ga 30003

**Love, Honor, Perseverance,
Duty, Courage, Loyalty,
Ethics**

Edited by
- Christin Chapman

First Edition, First Printing August 2021

President's Bible Chronicle I Principles of Motorcycle Club Leadership

By, John Edward Bunch II 'Black Dragon' BSFFBS

◊◊◊

President's Bible Chronicle I Principles of Motorcycle Club Leadership is the fifth book of the Motorcycle Club Bible series. Chronicle I is anual that teaches motorcycle club presidents the principles of motorcycle club leadership.

Bunch Media Group
Motorcycle Club Education Division

Library of Congress Control Number: **9780997432237**
International Standard Book Number: **978-0-9974322-3-7**
◊◊◊

For information about special discounts for bulk purchases or club purchases please contact Bunch Media Group at 404.692.0336 or blackdragon@blacksabbathmc.com.

Black Dragon can speak at your live event, host your annual, teach at your MC protocol training sessions, or host your life events. For more information or to book an event contact Bunch Media Group at 404.692.0336 or blackdragon@blacksabbathmc.com.
Black Dragon Biker TV - Instagram
Black Dragon Biker TV - YouTube
Black Dragon Biker – Facebook
The Dragon's Lair Motorcycle Chaos Podcast
www.bikerliberty.com

◊◊◊

Dedication

Above all, I thank God. To Him be all the glory.

To my editor, Christin Chapman, thanks so much for hanging strong on with me on this one! I cannot believe it, we did it again! Could not have done it without you, but then again you know that.

To my beloved mother and best friend who is now deceased Anese Yvonne Bunch 1942 – 1997, I wish you could have lived to see all of this you created in me manifest. Thank you for making sure my English was always on par.

To my dearly loved and now deceased Pitt/Labrador whom I still cannot seem to let go from my heart, Hope Magda Charity Warragal, Mighty Dogg of Dogs the Benevolent, Great Magnificent Conqueror the Lion Hearted, Bunch I, Conquering Dog of the Tribe of Judah, Elect of God! lived up to every bit of that name. 2004 - 2013 RIP Daddy never stops thinking of you.

To my love Tahmehrah 'Tia' Purdue. No man can stand like a king without the backing of a queen. You have been she for some time now.

To The Father of the Mighty Black Sabbath MC Nation Paul 'Pep' Perry. It is for you that I ever attempted to accomplish anything. I never had a father, no man to say—"I'm proud of this one I raised." You became he.

To my two new dogs Braveheart the Wanderer Fearer of None, and Brutus Bartholomew Lucifer Maximus Bunch the Conqueror, your companionship is most delightful.

To the Mighty Black Sabbath Motorcycle Club Nation, extended family and supports. Thank you for believing and allowing me to serve you as a President and eventually a National President, and now as a Lifer.

Figure 1 Father Paul Pep Perry (left) Advising John E. 'Black Dragon' Bunch II (circa 2015)

I have always felt privileged to have the counsel of the Original 7 Founder of the Mighty Black Sabbath MC Nation Father Paul 'Pep' Perry. As a young man who did not have a dad, I searched for many years for someone I could just make proud of me and give me somewhere to belong. When there were many who would not believe in me there was always one who did. He was the man who told everyone that there was nothing I couldn't do. He instilled in me a sense of purpose and always demanded that I considered the club first where it was appropriate. He constantly admonished me to stop saying, "I, I, I, me, me, me, mine, mine, mine, and to start saying We!" This was his litany he repeated like a piece of software stuck in an endless loop. In 2008 he assigned me the mission of building our brotherhood into a mighty MC nation with chapters from coast to coast across the United States. I accepted that challenge knowing that I would finally get a chance to make him proud for taking the time to care about and believe in me. For me this was a good reason to be a national president. For him, for it is from him that I learned how to be WE! #WeMC

Every man must know his strengths, weaknesses, and limitations. When I set out to build the Black Sabbath MC into a national club, I realized I lacked command experience. I could not let my pride get in the way by convincing myself that I could do it all when such was not the case. I enlisted former Mother Chapter President, Submarine Command Master Chief (C.O.B.) Tommy 'Hog Man' Lewis to come out of Black Sabbath retirement and help me lead the buildup of the nation. Master Chief Lewis had Submarine Navy

Figure 2 Tommy 'Hog Man' Lewis with John E. 'Black Dragon Bunch II (circa 2012)

experience in leadership at the highest level. He was a living legend and became a fire battalion chief after he retired. I called daily for nearly a year asking him to come back out of retirement. At first, he would laugh at me with big guffaws. He would say, "I'm glad to hear from you John, let's talk about something else." And we would talk. But I would always come back to saying, "You know we have your home for you right here whenever you are ready to come back." He would laugh again and say, "Goodbye John." Then, one day to my surprise he said, "Okay, I'll do it." Without Hog Man I could never have built the Black Sabbath MC into a national club. A president must never be too proud to seek help and guidance. The Master Chief was glad to lead from behind while I was the face out front.

Foreword

The Genesis of this Material

I heavily borrowed from many US Navy and US Marine Corps military manuals when adopting the core principles, I believe necessary for development of a President of a motorcycle club (MC), that I will present to you in Chronicle I of this President's Bible series that I plan to include six books.

MCs would be better served if they have highly trained leaders to guide them, and though many of them do have good leaders, it seems as though this occurs more by accident or a sheer stroke of luck than it does by the direct intention of the brotherhood through training, molding, and development of its potential leaders. One reason is that there are no MC training academies, correspondence courses, or universities. Club members falsely believe that everything a brother needs to know should be gleaned from within the brotherhood in mouth-to-mouth spoken tradition, handed down from one generation to another. They shun any outside learning and scoff at the idea of gaining MC knowledge from books, social media, or independent research. Tragically, when there is a break in the chain of that method of traditional inner-organizational training years of knowledge and experience are lost. The MC reverts backward losing its forward momentum perhaps for decades or even generations. Any society without written information, records, documentation, training, and education will evaporate from history, leaving no evidence of its existence. Thus, it is essential that MCs learn to document their history and standardize their training and education so that every leader is trained equally in the skills necessary to direct the brotherhood in the way that it should go.

That stated, there is still the obstacle that even if MC leaders are receptive to availing themselves of the hundreds of thousands of books written about leadership, often they will not because those essays do not teach leadership as it relates to MC protocol, making them seem irrelevant and unworthy of study or application. Therefore, I have written this Chronicle I of the President's Bible exclusively targeted toward the discussion of Motorcycle Club Leadership on the ever-evolving landscape of the international biker set. It is purposely written as a study in leadership principles, integrity, couth, and ethics of and for motorcycle club nations mighty and small worldwide. Glean from it your path forward to recreating yourself as an imperial MC leader of the highest caliber and endeavor to be a greater you than you have ever been before, for the sake of the MC, for the sake of the extended family, and for the sake of the brotherhood!

I opted to refer to leadership manuals from the U.S. Navy and the U.S. Marine Corps because I spent a great deal of my adult life in the United States Navy Submarine force. Thus, it is of naval leadership of which I am most familiar. It is in the adaptation of these naval leadership skills I have directly applied in my leadership of the Mighty Black Sabbath Motorcycle Club Nation and to which I will be sharing these skills in this book with you. I think MCs will find familiarity with references in this book, as most traditional MCs follow a paramilitary-like structure. This is due in large part to the fact that modern MC history is sourced directly to returning war vets who helped to shape the club structure and culture we know today. MCs run more efficiently when certain aspects of military culture are exercised throughout the brotherhood.

I want to take the time to point out that just because I am relying on my Naval military leadership experience to write this instruction manual this is by no means intended to convey any disrespect towards any of the other outstanding branches of the United States or any other branches of military throughout the world. In fact, I am confident that if you have come from any of those other services you will recognize much of what I am illustrating in this manual as all branches of the military practice similar doctrine because we ultimately are all about accomplishing victory in much the same ways.

Why I wrote This Book

This is my book, and these are my thoughts. I wrote it to help those who wish to read it. It does not pertain to every president's situation. But for some of you it may help to provide great insight to becoming better at leading men in an MC as President.

For those of you who were wondering, I do not think I am some kind of expert or anything. No one died and made me the king f MC protocol or any such silliness I have ever heard come from my detractors. I am merely a guy who wrote a book, nothing more. And I make no apologies for the contents within. They are accumulated from my experiences of things I have lived, seen, thought, witnessed, and heard during my tenure as an Original 7 founding brother, President of the Atlanta chapter, and eventually National President of the Mighty Black Sabbath Motorcycle Club Nation, established in San Diego, California in the year of our Lord nineteen hundred seventy-four — and as of the writing of this book, STILL STRONG!

If you feel a different way about how things should be configured in this book—from the title to the bibliography—then follow your first mind and intuition! You are a better steward of your own destination than I could ever be.

I also encourage all to write your own thoughts and experiences. There are not enough of these kinds of books written to help our young brothers who are starting, founding, and expanding mighty Motorcycle Club Nations around the world. Do not hesitate to add your own, speak your truth, share your experiences, and if you want, I will even publish your book for you. I designed the Bunch Media Group publishing company's Motorcycle Education Division to spread MC knowledge and protocol around the world. Hit me Up! 404.292.0336 or send an email to blackdragon@blacksabbathmc.com.

I am proud of my contributions to my MC Nation. I brought more to it than I took from it. And that is all we can hope for from any one of our members. You should also strive to make your club a better place.

My grandmother and mother taught me this important concept when I was still a five-year-old bad child. "John John, leave things better than when you found them, now go and help little Tommy clean his room!" Even then, I remember thinking, "You have got to be kidding me! Clean up this clown's filthy room? It does not look like he has ever cleaned this pigsty not even once in all his five years! Are y'all serious grandma and mamma? Good Lord Jesus in Heaven, God, somebody send those two generations of wayward parents a clue please!"

But alas, they were NOT kidding, and they made sure I learned this important principle. I carried it with me from my mother's house to the Navy, where I volunteered for the all-volunteer Submarine Navy. Funny thing was, you could volunteer into the Silent Service, but you could not volunteer out of it. I remember when STSCS SS Nelson told me that we had to "police the brass" at the Army's shooting range, I looked at him incredulously. "You have got to be kidding me Senior Chief! This gun range belongs to the Army! It was filthy, with brass everywhere, before we ever even got here. Now you want us to clean it up?

"You are damned right I do Bunch so round up some of your shipmates, police this area, and make it look so much better after we leave that those ground-pounding fox hole dwellers say, 'Hell yes! The U.S. Submarine service must have been here using this firing range because the place smells like Brasso and spit shine!' " And so, it was.

This is the requirement of a true leader: President, Founder, or Visionary of any mighty MC Nation. As a brotherhood, WE stand as one in the face of adversity so that WE can spread our way of life across this great country from the Pacific Ocean toward the Gulf of

Mexico to the Atlantic Ocean, from the South to the North, making the lives of our brothers and sisters better when we leave them than they were before we found them!

As I have said before, the technical portions of this book about leadership were heavily borrowed from Navy and Marine Corps leadership manuals because the military has mastered the art of building strong leaders. And many of these skills carry over into the successful operation of an MC. The Navy's Master Training Specialist program built me into the public speaker, technical writer, teacher, master trainer, and instructor I am today.

I felt it was important to give MC Presidents (the "P") a book that taught the formal basics in leadership, as this is the first book ever written to train an MC President to run a motorcycle club using the basic principles of military leadership. I felt it important to include technical training on leadership, logistics, discipline, and morale/team building. There are many folks who will find themselves in the position of "P" during their MC careers who have never been anything more than a stocking clerk or having even obtained any education higher than a high school diploma. Despite the fact that many will not have the formal training, experience, or skill before obtaining "P" nothing hinders anyone from 'back-filling' and getting themselves quickly up to speed with self-study in applications of the scientific principles of leadership available to all those who seek this knowledge. It does not take a college degree to lead men. It takes heart, discipline, strength of character, and leadership by example. It is not about what or who you were, it is about the trust the men have in who you are and what you can become. Learn the leadership principles the Naval service uses to teach leaders, as I have presented them in this book then excel! Being an MC President is an enormous challenge and may be the highest rank you ever achieve in life. Learn to do it well. Your MC will benefit if you do, and you will leave it better than you found it when you became a leader.

◊◊◊

"The best parts of any organization are Respect, Communication, and Participation." – Shaggy 1%er Invaders MC Nation via Tombstone 1%er

Who Should Read this Book?

It should be read by MC members and officers who are interested in the advancement of their motorcycle careers to the position of President of their Motorcycle Club Nations, or those members who are interested in how I think the President should do his job and conduct himself.

- MC Presidents
- MC Vice Presidents
- MC Secretaries
- MC Business Managers
- MC Sgt at Arms
- MC Founders
- Full Patched Members

The President is the Face of the MC! Upon his shoulders our direction falls. If he fails, we fail; if he succeeds, we succeed! Long live the President of our Mighty MC Nation!

◊◊◊

When to Use this Book

Use this book as a reference manual to help you develop your leadership skills. In these chapters you will find principles of leadership that should guide you in your MC presidential career! Good luck!

Where there is no competent
leadership chaos will prevail...

JBII

Table of Contents

CHAPTER ONE
The Practice of Brotherhood Does Not Always Pay a Dividend

The practice of brotherhood does not always pay a dividend. You do what is right because it is right, you do not always get a reward in the end, in fact, often your good deeds will go unnoticed, and sometimes may get you punished.

Most folks do not understand that the practice of brotherhood does not always yield an expected result. We often think that if we give our all and our best to the brotherhood, that it will return to our bosom expanded tenfold! Unfortunately, the usual case is that your sacrifices will go unnoticed, and worse, often unrewarded.

When I was a young National President, I met this girl on the internet who was on the biker set. We shared intimate emails and chats for the next couple of years. She was as fine as a summer day is long and I daydreamed of rendezvous with her answering all my fantasies in intricate detail.

We spent many days speaking over the phone but because she was in one state, and I was in another our love affair never really got a chance to take off. But we agreed that should we ever get an opportunity to be together that we absolutely would.

A few years later I was approached by a man who had been following my YouTube channel (Black Dragon Biker TV) and he expressed a blazing desire to join my motorcycle club because he was such a loyal follower. He knew that being involved in the Black Sabbath MC Nation as a member would be the answer to his dreams of brotherhood and family, and that he wanted to follow me and the way he knew that I would handle an MC as National President. He also had several friends who would join with him so that was cool, he brought enough folks to actually start a chapter — it does not get much better than that.

So, I accepted him into the MC and began the dance with the local dominant motorcycle clubs to get the chapter started in that state. And everything went smoothly. We got the chapter up and running. Subsequently he became the President.

Later I was absolutely blown away to find out that his woman was the girl I had been trading emails with for the past several years – even before they got together, we were talking. And when she found out he was coming into our MC she had been very quiet about it. I saw their picture together on her Facebook page and I asked her about the situation, and she told me that she had been talking to me for years before they got together and that she still wanted to continue our friendship. I felt uncomfortable about it, but I did not see any harm in speaking with her over emails and occasionally over the phone since our talks had not been sexual in a few years. But then he started cheating on her, again and again, so she started talking to me a little more often and the chats started to head back to the way they were before.

I asked her if she thought we should be talking about such things when she was clearly now the woman of my club brother and we both knew that this line of conversation could lead to no good place. She then informed me that she was leaving him and that we could finally be together after all this time. There was a huge club party happening in a state between ours which we would all be attending, but he would not be because he was working. So, she let me know that during that celebration would be the perfect time for us to be together romantically for the first time.

Now I must tell you the temptation here was so great that I had an internal struggle the likes of which I am at a loss for words to explain. Suffice it to say that when I arrived in town, I still had not made up my mind as to what it was that I was going to do. Here was this goddess on Earth whom I had desired above all others for many years. And here I was presented the opportunity to make unbridled, passionate love to her – which she told me she wanted more than anything else. And here was this derelict club brother who was a cheater and a louse and did not deserve her love, plus she was leaving him anyway, and I had known her long before they were even together... so, why should I not be with her? And I can tell you this situation really rolled in my mind over and over.

But I remembered back to the day when there was a president in the mother chapter who would send us to Los Angeles (the mother chapter was in San Diego) and promise us that he would get there later. He curiously never rode up with the pack. And, of course, when we got to Los Angeles we always managed to stay overnight, because it was a two hour ride up and we never just wanted to go, turn around, and come right back. Many times, that president would never even show up and we would go and come without his presence. No one ever thought to ask him why he was not riding with us or was missing in action so often. We actually started making a joke about the fact that he never showed up to ride with us to LA. But soon we found out why and the revelation was sickening. He was going over to one of the club brother's homes and sleeping with his wife when we were all on the road. When this news got out it nearly split the entire damned club. The club brother tried to shoot him, but he was stopped and soon the president left the club. I never forgot the look of pain in that brother's face. A President to whom he had looked up to like a brother or even a father-figure had destroyed his trust and violated his home. I promised myself then that would never be me if I ever became President. I promised myself that I could control my loins for the sake of the brotherhood. I never wanted a man who trusted me in a leadership position, to have an utterly broken heart because of my lack of discipline and inability to control my carnal desires. I chose then to run my future presidency, were I ever to have one, with honor and distinction. I wanted to practice the best tenets of brotherhood.

When the time came, and we found ourselves in the same town I had made up my mind that I would not be getting myself involved in a situation where a brother could ever be hurt by my actions. I decided to make myself a ghost and just hang around the brothers so, I did not answer her call when my phone rang. Just when I thought I had everything worked out there was a knock at my door. There she appeared looking more beautiful than I could have imagined with her eyes beaming and her magnetic smile lighting up the room. She stepped in the door and looked demurely up to me with her mesmerizing gaze. My lips were parched, and my mouth was dry. I wanted her more than anything in the world at that moment. I took her into my arms and hugged her tightly with all my might. She hugged me back and I could feel her body conforming around mine. I pushed her back at arms-length and said, "I want you more than anything goddess, but I would never be able to live with myself knowing that I had violated the sacred tenets of my brotherhood and slept with a brother's woman. Please understand that this is not a rebuke of you but rather a rebuke of my own salacious thoughts, temptations, and desires. You are perfect, I am the one who is foul. I am a National President and I know better. My heart beams knowing that we could be together and that you desire me as much as I desire you. For me that will have to be enough. And I thank you for making me feel like a conqueror. I will accept this hug from you and envision how we can be together next lifetime."

She looked at me and smiled. She said, "I accept your decision National President. I admire your integrity; you are every bit of the man I thought you were. I am glad my heart desired you, I can tell it was not wrong for doing so." With that she turned, stepped out of the door, and was gone. We never spoke again. I had done my duty and conducted myself as best I could in that situation. My integrity was intact. Now one would think that the Gods of things in this world would have smiled upon me, and I would be rewarded in some kind of a magical way for my piety. Alas, that was not to be the case.

A year or two later that president decided he no longer approved of me as a leader and turned against my leadership. He told lies about me and accused me of things I never did. He lied to his chapter about me and did everything in his power to turn his members against me and worked in concert with others to prematurely end my National Presidency. I was so disappointed and pissed off with this man for the way he turned against me. And the lies he told his members about me absolutely did not match the character I used to lead our nation. And, to think I could have had his woman – but I did not because of my loyalty to our brotherhood, and the fact that I did not made me shudder with anger! He did not deserve my loyalty!

But we all know, or should know, that kind of thinking is wrong. You see I learned from this experience that you do what is right because it is the right thing to do. Not because you expect some kind of reward, thanks, gratefulness, loyalty, or any other perk for doing the right damned thing. In fact, when you do the right thing there are many times when it will go unrewarded, unnoticed, or worse, punished. In the end I was proud of myself because no one could ever come back to me with an accusation of betraying the brotherhood. It is okay if he is a traitor because I can live with myself that I never was and will NEVER be!

My mother used to tell me, "Never expect a person to be grateful just because you did a good thing. People are not typically grateful for any reason. In fact, often they hate you for having the ability to be kind to them because they feel you have something over them that you never deserved to have over them in the first place. Do what is right because it is the right thing to do. If you look for a reward for doing right, you will often find yourself disappointed. If you do things simply because they are the right thing to do, then you will always be proud of yourself for the right reasons."

When that club brother finally departed our club and took his chapter with him, I wished him well. He never knew that I was a brother that never betrayed him even though he had eventually betrayed me. His loss not mine. I stood true to my MC, and to that brother, like I always have and always would. My loyalty can be neither bought nor sold, not even to experience the affection of a beautiful goddess. I am solid. Make sure that you remain a solid

President in all that you do. The reward is in the strength of conviction and there alone.

CHAPTER TWO
The President and the Club's Money

You probably know how I am going to start this chapter and I am sure you have heard it all before... the President shall NEVER handle club money! That should be the beginning and the end of it, but without explanation and context a good lesson often goes unheard, so let us get into the details so that you can take this chapter to heart and never violate its tenets.

Any president that handles club money will inevitably be accused of stealing the club's money. That is just how it goes. Members sit around and look for things to attack, especially when they are trying to target your presidency or get rid of you. Baseless accusations and allegations are always a great place to start. One of the easiest 'low hanging fruits' for your enemies to grasp at is the accusation of a president stealing the club's money. If you think about it, it really is hard to defend against; especially when you realize how much of your personal money becomes involved in the club and how quickly it becomes entangled in the club's finances, making it nearly impossible to separate.

If you have not been a president before, as soon as you become president you will quickly learn that you will spend an inordinate amount of your personal wealth advancing the condition of the MC. In one year alone, I spent over $20,000 just traveling from one Black Sabbath MC chapter to another for annuals! We were beginning to build our footprint and we only had about 20 chapters at that time, so I rode my motorcycle to every chapter's annual each year. Each time I rode I had to prepare my motorcycle for the trip. A set of tires plus installation was at least $700, changing the oil was $65.00, and then there was all the other maintenance required to properly maintain my bike for the journeys (fluids, brake pads, etc.). I could easily spend between $300.00 to $1500.00 per trip. And that was just on the bike! There was between $200.00 and $600.00 for gas, $60.00 to $300 per night for hotel rooms (with a 2 day stay minimum), and $150.00 to $300.00 during the weekend for food and drinks. Then there are the unforeseen over-the-road repairs like blown tires, repaired oil, and exhaust leaks, bent rims, and all kinds of other things that may have you calling a tow truck or having to spend an extra day on the road, taking more leave and vacation than you had previously planned – which means more money. So, if we average it out to $1,000 per trip (with a high of $4,000 and a low of about $60.00) times 20 chapters, you can see how I reached $20,000 (and that is on the low end) in personal expenses. As president, you will be required to attend all national club functions. You could easily conclude that since you are traveling for club business, the club should cover some (if not all) of your travel expenses? But such is often not the case. The expectation is that you always spend your own funds.

Moving on, let us say that in order to get the chapter's lights turned on at the clubhouse someone had to put down their credit card and a deposit that was not refundable until the end of the club's lease— which might be twenty years from now! And most often that person is ... you guessed it ... YOU, the President!

Now, let us say a package came in C.O.D. (cash on delivery), so you had to go down to the post office to get it because, after all, you are the president. Then rent on the clubhouse was a bit short because several members were laid off or brother Bubba is going through a divorce and his wife cut off the bank accounts. Who do you think would be expected to make up the shortfall? I bet you could have guessed. If not, I will tell you... YOU, the President!

What happens if the bar is short and you cannot open the clubhouse tonight for bike night until someone buys enough beer to get the bar up and running, so you send a prospect on a beer run with $100.00 of YOUR money — that you will get out of the cash register later. Someone did not get any change to put in the drawer so you hand a prospect fifty dollars (again, of your own money) so he can make change. You bought twelve loaves of bread for the fish fry tonight, plus you paid the internet bill and you paid for the website last Thursday, plus you just spent $1,500 on a mandatory run to another chapter's annual. Now, it comes down to the end of the night and you are counting out the register while the other brothers and prospects are cleaning up the club, when "Brother Umpty Frat", who is four months behind in dues and has not been on a club run in a year, happens to walk past while you are sticking $200.00 of the "club's" money into your pocket, witnessing your perceived "theft!" I do not need to tell you; you can just imagine the scandal! And when the brothers demand an accounting of all the monies, and you cannot recall all of the money you have spent in the last 24 hours because you were keeping a running tally in your head and not really trying to hold onto every damned receipt you touched... You can see how this sort of thing will go.

The problem is, right or wrong, a president is too involved in the success of the MC. At a personal level to also be handling the club's money, the president should not be:

- Counting down the drawers
- Collecting money at the door
- Handing money out to prospects
- Cashing in or out other drawers for the brothers
- Writing the checks for the bills
- Having access of any kind to the accounts

It is simply a conflict of interest for the president to have access to club funds. The MC will inevitably wind up owing the president money simply by the nature of his position but does not seem to understand the efficacy when he decides to take a little bit of it back. In the example above I wanted to illustrate that while squabbling with a few ill-informed idiots about the $200.00 you appeared to have "stolen" from the club that night, none of the club's members will ever even think about the $20,000 you spent that year in traveling on the club's behalf, representing them! They will not comprehend or care about the thousands of dollars you spent to keep the club's doors open. No. They will expect you to spring forth money from your loins like you were plucking gold from eternally giving trees. They will never want to accurately track your expenditures, but instead they will always want to track what they think you owe or what they think you are taking.

I have seen accusations as ridiculous as you can imagine. Way back when I was a prospect, a president lost his job in the mother chapter but because he bought a new truck and a new house in the same year, back biting club brothers accused him of stealing club money for these purchases for the next twenty years. The common thread was, "He didn't even have a damned job so how in the hell could he buy a new truck and a new house?" When I asked him about this accusation several years later, he told me, "I actually bought two houses, a truck, and a car for my wife. But the funny thing is that house they are talking about cost me two million dollars, so how in the hell do those idiots think the club had enough money for me to steal to accomplish that trick?" I never forgot that and later, when I became president, I suffered the same fate. So, that is why I am writing this for you. If you do not handle the club's money you will still have to deal with the accusations, but you can easily defend against them because you do not have any access to the money – so what in the hell are they talking about?

In general, you should have a system setup where the treasurer and the business manager or secretary handle the money. It should be a two-person or even a three-person system that requires a sign off on all checks. The club's credit cards should be signed out and signed back in and the account should be checked against receipts (online) when the cards are checked out and handed back in. This is to ensure that what was spent was authorized and justified. There are many more things that I can write about this, but that is for another book, plus I am sure you get the point. Use your bylaws to ensure that you get all of this handled to the point that you are never directly dealing with the club's money. It will save you heartache, I promise.

But there is always an exception to every rule. Right? What if you are in a small club or you are just building up your club, what are you to do? Sometimes you will have to have access to club money in a small club or other situations that you just cannot help. My advice is simple. KEEP COPIOUS NOTES! Keep all receipts and get the club's money out of your hands and to another officer as soon as humanly possible. I once had to account for money spent five years previous just to quell an accusation by a hateful idiot. I was glad I had the notes and the receipts to back it up.

There is nothing more important than your integrity as a club leader. Be smart enough to prevent anything from impugning your character. I know many of you will think, "I have got this handled and no one will question my authority, because they know I know better." You are the guy that will be saying, "Black Dragon told me so."

CHAPTER THREE
The Seduction of the Three "P's"

"Before you can be a good leader you must first be a good follower. That is what your brothers will be looking for, that is to see how well you follow the rules—first—before they will want to follow you. Members will imitate the leader. So, they will be looking to follow your lead to help them decide what their 'club-walk' would be. I have seen presidents attempt to change the bylaws just because a rule affects them in a negative way. So instead of following the bylaws and demonstrating to all that you are just as good at following the rules as you are at giving orders and expecting others to follow you. A lot of folks think that president's patch means they are all that and that it entitles them to privileges. I do not use my position to gain anything from my club. I am just a regular member. It is just that I happen to be the spokesmen right now. Tomorrow you might not be the president, so it is important not to lose yourself in that position. I always insist on treating myself like an ordinary member. This is a personal standard I demand of myself to ensure that I always stay the same. For example, I will fine myself if I don't make a mandatory ride, so there is never a question as to the standards required of all. We all have to pay fines for rule breaking president included. I have ensured that these standards are evident across the board. Again, so there is never a question. This keeps me the same member as president as I was before I became president, because if you change who you are after you win that position then you are not the person they voted for. And it is easy to lose your following when you become the president and then you change yourself. Those are the ones who do not last. Their reputations are damaged, and they won't survive.

You have also got to be a good listener to be an effective president. You must listen to what people are saying and then act upon that. If you are not doing any listening, then you are doing all the talking. If you are doing all the talking, how can you serve the members of the club?"

Dolla Bill 1%er
President
Outcast MC Nation Atlanta Chapter

The "Three P" Rule

The seduction of Power, Prestige, and Position

By Robert Schultz as taught to him by his grandfather, Grandpa Stehn. Who taught him as a young man to never be seduced by the darkness of the three P's.

Figure 3 Grandpa Stehn

Pictured above is Grandpa Stehn whom I felt like I knew personally because my best friend Robert Schultz taught me so many of his life stories about being a good, decent, and honest person, that I felt like he raised me too! I never knew how Bob became my best friend. We had nothing in common except that we had both served in the Navy. I met Bob when we worked as Senior Technical Writers at ARRIS Solutions in Suwanee, GA, and we were an unlikely pair. He is at least 15 years older than I am

Page | 21

and a white guy from a rural farm background with a work-ethic like a dedicated ox! Yet he cared about me, loved me, and took me under his wing. He was a former Naval line officer and as such taught me a great many things about leadership as I guided my club as National President. Many of his lessons started out with something Grandpa Stehn said. So, I asked Bob to write for the President's Bible, Stehn's philosophy on the "three P's." I hope you learn from this chapter as I have learned so much from Bob. I have truly flourished under his friendship and guidance. I shall be forever thankful to him for taking the time to care about me. Next you will read what he wrote. By the way, he is a damned good writer.

Throughout peoples' lifetimes they will be tempted by the "Three P's", namely Power, Prestige, and Position. Many will be seduced and eventually succumb to the "Three P's".

This is not always, nor inherently, a bad thing. Power, prestige, and position can be exercised morally and used to promote the common good. However, many times exactly the opposite happens.

The "Three P's" also come with the additional burden of the necessary time required to deal with those added responsibilities and the extra stresses associated with them. So, the first question you must answer is: "Do you really want this, and are you willing to pay the price?"

The more important question you must answer is: "If and when it happens, will you let it negatively affect your character, or your personal morals, or your business [MC] ethics?" Unfortunately, more and more these days, the answer seems to be "yes".

If you are not careful, obtaining power, prestige, and position in your personal or business [MC] life will corrupt you and erode your character including the morals and ethics you once held dear. As a person rises to higher and higher levels in the "Three P's" they may eventually start to believe they are "above" certain things and "above" other people. This attitude has the long-term effect of eroding one's character. The mindset that "I can do anything I want, to anyone I want, whenever I want" sets in and takes over their daily conduct and behavior.

A person must have a strong foundation upon which their character is based in order to resist being seduced and corrupted by the "Three P's". If you do not, you may find yourself becoming a different person, one who others in your life will neither like nor respect, and eventually not even recognize.

As written by historian and moralist Lord John Emerich Acton, in 1887: "Power corrupts. Absolute power corrupts absolutely." To that, I add "Power attracts the corruptible".

Therefore, be mindful. If you find yourself in a position of power, take care to not let it change the person you are.

_____End_____

Dark Seduction of the "Three P's"

The dark seduction of the "Three P's" will tempt every club brother who advances in rank. But nothing is worse than when the seduction happens at the top of the organization. Most of us have seen the devastating results a narcissistic president can have on the morale of the entire family and how badly he can destroy the unit if he goes unchecked. Whether or not you succumb to it will be a matter of your upbringing, your dependence on the guidance of a strong moral compass, and your willingness to check yourself the second you become aware of your inappropriate behavior, apologize, seek atonement, and then conduct yourself differently.

The seduction of the 'Three P's' is not always readily apparent in most of us. Sometimes it takes quite a while for the seduction to fully develop. Most of us start out as good people with good intentions so by the time we are fully involved we have become people that we barely even recognize ourselves. And I liken that transformation to a character in one of my favorite science fiction fantasy series of Gor, named Tarl Cabot of Ko-ro-ba.

Ko-ro-ba is a city on planet Gor. Planet Gor sits directly opposite planet Earth in the Milky Way galaxy of the sun Sol's solar system, though hidden from Earth's direct view by Sol. For that reason, planet Gor is also alternately known as Counter-Earth. This strange and exciting world was introduced to the public in the 1966 novel *"Tarnsmen of Gor "* written by John Lange who writes under the pen name John Norman. Gor is a fictional setting for a series of sword and planet novels. The series was inspired by science fantasy pulp fiction works by Edgar Rice Burroughs (such as *"Barsoom"* series). It also includes erotica and philosophy content.

But before you run out and buy the series, I have to put some disclaimers out there because even though I loved the book series, and I am using the main character to illustrate a point about the seduction of the "Three P's", there are some possible problems with the story line that some may find offensive.

So let me just put it out there that the Gor series repeatedly depicts men conquering and enslaving other men, as well as abducting, enslaving, physically abusing and sexually brutalizing women, who unbelievably grow to enjoy their submissive state.[3] According to the *Encyclopedia of Science Fiction*, Norman's "sexual philosophy" is "widely detested"[1] and as a consequence his beloved series was pulled by DAW publishing, which had published him from the 8th volume (Hunters of Gor) until the 25th volume (Magicians of Gor) after about 14 years, in the late 1980s citing low sales[4] " despite the fact that his books have inspired a cult like following and a "Gorean subculture."[2] Norman claimed the removal was because of "feminist influences" in a 1996 interview stating that after 22 reprints since the series' inception, new French and German contracts, a Czechoslovakian printing, Spanish and Italian sales that there was no evidence his books were no longer selling. He also claimed that he had been effectively blacklisted.[5] But after what seemed like an eternity, the "cancel culture" Gods could no longer black list his freedom of expression and his books once again found a publishing home with E-Reads with a new novel *"Witness of Gor"* (2001). The series is also back in full print again and according to E-Reads, "After the journey of the series from Blockbuster to Can't Give Them Away and back to Blockbuster they are among E-Reads biggest sellers."[6]

[1]Authors: Norman, John: SFE: Science Fiction Encyclopedia *www.sf-encyclopedia.com*. Retrieved 2020-7-11]

[2] Gracen, Julia *"Chaingangsalon" www.chaingangsalon.com*. Retrieved 2020-7-11

[3] *"Gor-Wikipedia" https://en.m.wikipedia.org/wiki/Gor*. Retrieved 2020-7-11

[4] Langford, David (1988) *"The Kink in Space"* SFX. Future Publishing (39) *https://ansible.uk/sfx/sfx039.html* Retrieved 2020-7-11

[5] *"No More Gor: A Conversation with John Norman"*, David Alexander Smith, The New York Review of Science Fiction, #92, April, 1996

[6] E-Reads "Are John Norman's Gors "Boy Books"? Richard Curtis *http://web.archive.org/web/20121031111019/http://ereads.com/2007/10/are-john-normans-gors-boy-books-2.html*

Now, with the overview out of the way, I shall continue.

In this series a college professor, Tarl Cabot, is kidnapped from Earth by the notorious Priest Kings, an insecticidal looking creature that rule/protect the planet Counter Earth, also known as Gor. Now the cool thing about planet Gor is that since its gravity is less than that of Earth, people like Tarl Cabot, who are kidnapped from Earth and taken there have superhuman strength and heroic-like capabilities. So, we see the flaming red haired college professor nerd, Tarl Cabot, turn into a superhuman, sword-wielding fighting machine virtually overnight!

There are some rules for living on Gor that are tightly administered by the Priest Kings. First, men and women were subjugated into slavery by any warrior with enough strength to make them his slaves. This, of course gave me great problems when reading the series, as a real descendent of slaves – but since Tarl was new to planet Gor he quickly established himself as a kind and gentle warrior who would not take slaves as men or women and would not force women into his bed reluctantly for any reason. I mean this guy was hella-cool! Being from Earth, where that sort of thing was not permitted, Tarl was more focused on figuring out how to protect the planet and entered many battles on behalf of the Priest Kings with his sword. This was the beauty of Tarl.

There were no guns or transportation allowed on Gor by the Priest Kings – this was to prevent humans transported there from taking over the planet and harming them. So, the Priest Kings had these (what would be called drones today, unheard of technology in 1966 right?) flying things that would rove the planet and report on anyone that created anything like a gun or any types of modern transportation. Thus, this limited everyone to riding around on the planet's animals and moving en masse in wagon trains, and the like. Consequently, the only method of advanced travel by air was limited to an elite few warriors, who were forced to form a "partnership" with a predatory, eagle-looking, 12 foot tall, thousand-pound, bird known as a Tarn. The Tarn bird could not be tamed (oh hell no that would be too easy) but rather it "felt (sensed)" your spirit and ability to "lead" it, and if it subsequently judged you "worthy" to mount it and become one with its soul (so-to-speak), it would follow your lead instead of eating you alive with a single gulp! This could, of course, happen at any time the Tarn felt that your inner strength and piety waivered, so riding a Tarn was always a precarious proposition that could instantly end in your demise. Yet, our hero Tarl Cabot became a talented tarnsmen pretty darned quickly and thus one of the toughest warriors on planet Gor! And so, the next 31 novels were underway.

Now, Tarl started off as one pretty straight-up dude in the beginning of the series. As I said earlier, he went about the business of establishing himself as a warrior fighting on the planet's behalf as an emissary of the Priest Kings. And at first whenever he conquered something, he immediately set all of the slaves free. Good guy. And the first several novels had Tarl refusing to take female slaves, setting male slaves free upon capture, and generally treating everyone respectable and good.

But as time went on and he spent more time on the planet he started to revel in his superhuman strength and began to grow tired of working for the Priest Kings. As one critic put it, "John Norman's 'Gor' series started with *"Tarnsman of Gor"* and four sequels, in which the might-thewed hero Tarl Cabot hacks his way through gory adventure on the subtly named planet Gor, all vaguely in the tradition of Edgar Rice Burroughs and John Carter of Mars. Later books in the series spices things up a bit, with special emphasis on Gor's slave industry. Tarl Cabot may be from fuddy-duddy old Earth, but he soon sees the advantages of owning gorgeous female slaves and being able to say, rather frequently, 'For that … you must be punished!'

As the Encyclopedia of Fantasy primly puts it, later volumes degenerate into extremely sexist, sadomasochistic pornography involving the ritual humiliation of women, and as a result. What happened was that the master Tarnsman Tarl Cabot of Ko-Bo-Ra becomes the merchant/slaver Bosk of Port Kar in the sixth series *"Raiders of Gor."* His role on Gor is redefined as he clearly changes and begins subjecting women into absolute slavery. The novels begin to focus more on the Gorean philosophy and less so on the hero that once was Tarl Cabot. Instead of freeing all of the slaves when he won at battle, he immediately shackled the males and placed the women into subservient roles as sex slaves to bow to his whims, while all of the time loving to be tamed by his male warrior machismo.

In a passage from *"Vagabonds of Gor"* (1987) is a description of a Gorean luggage system. Tarl Cabot hits town with his current slave and rents a locker to put her away for a while like "baggage" so he could explore the night life in the town. 'I had her climb into the small box in which she then lay down, on her side, her knees drawn up. We had left her in the hood, leash, and bracelets. [...] The box itself is of iron and very sturdy. It has various tiny holes in its front wall and in its lid, through which the occupant may breathe.' The paragraph has hundreds more words about the box, making sure to point out that passing chaps can peek through the holes at the naked flesh within.

As you can see that by the time Tarl Cabot, war hero, master Tarnsman, freer of slaves, and all-around good guy of Ko-bo-ra becomes the merchant/slaver Bosk of the Port of Kar, and with the change in the name he had completely transformed himself from a man of prudence, chivalry, and fair play into a man of little conscience or moral character. This was no longer the nerdy college professor kidnapped from Earth. No, he had become 'accustomed' to the privilege his fortune and fame had bought, along with the opulence of the ruling class. He even stepped up in the social and class structures departing the warrior class and donning the robes, titles, and accouterments of the merchant/slaver class, so much so that he changed his name as well. Bosk of the Port of Kar was completely unrecognizable to me, and I soon lost interest in the series. The former Tarl Cabot was completely gone as Bosk was unrecognizable. He tortured women, raped, and enslaved them and convinced himself the whole time that they absolutely loved it.

For me it was a disappointing reality and I stopped reading the series shortly after. The hero had let me down. When I thought about becoming a president of an MC, I never wanted the opulence and the expectance of "What Was Due Me as Leader" to go to my head, or worse, go to my heart and soul as treatment that was owed me for some reason, like it did Bosk of Port of Kar. I instinctively recognized, after reading that series, the ability of power to corrupt even the bravest hero. I made a mental note to always be Master Tarnsman Warrior Tarl Cabot of Ko-bo-ra and to try to never become merchant/slaver Bosk of Port of Kar.

I will never forget a young brother who was the most humble prospect you ever wanted to meet. His good cheer and willingness to aid a brother brightened the club and enlightened everyone around him. He could always be counted on to do a good job, he volunteered to do the dirty jobs no one else wanted to do and kept himself available for security duty and anything else the club needed. He was called "prospect-on-the-spot"! His chapter was new to our nation and as a consequence did not have enough experienced brothers to fill in the officer ranks. So, he quickly advanced and within a month or so of crossing over to his full patch, his chapter elected him to the position of road captain. Soon after, with his new position and responsibility he developed into a most unsufferable son-of-a-bitch with an arrogance like none the brothers had noticed before in him. Within two weeks of putting on his road captain patch his first official act was to suspend and fine a brother for a violation on a road trip citing that as Road Captain he was President while the MC was on the road. Ironically, the man he stripped had trained him to ride in the pack making it possible for him to get to the position of road captain in the first place. The transformation occurred so quickly and what I have noticed is that the seduction of the "Three P's" can be especially attractive when brothers rise in rank too quickly for whatever circumstances. It seems that premature advancement in rank combined with lack of experience and immaturity can give rise to a megalomaniac the likes of which no one would ever expect to see. Imagine such a great prospect as he eventually climbs the rank to become a president inflated with an ego that consumes him to the point of no turning back. Such is a guy you wish you never allowed into the brotherhood in the first place.

In another similar, but unrelated situation I witnessed a young man rise from prospect to Regional Sergeant-at-Arms in about one year. He wound up charging the club President and attempted to put him out of the entire MC Nation for hanging up the phone in his face during an argument. The irony in this story is that the same President taught him to ride cross-country and played nursemaid to him, babying him on a ride from Houston to Atlanta. It was amazing to see how his ego caused him to turn so quickly against a brother to the point of wanting to put him out of the club after the brother had done so much to show him the ropes of our lifestyle.

I point out these two stories to illustrate the beginnings of the narcissism that can occur with guys who had not even made it to the rank of president yet. Just imagine how awful it can be once a man becomes a maniacal nightmare as president of an MC and how it can destroy everything and everyone around him.

Dolla Bill 1%er told me that one of the things most important to him was that he never lose himself or become someone different than the exact men his brothers elected as President of the Outcast Motorcycle Club Nation Atlanta chapter. He said that it was important to remain the same person the men elected. There is so much to that philosophy that I decided to write an entire chapter about it.

The Power Paradox How We Gain and Lose Influence

Perhaps the worst casualty of succumbing to the seduction of the "Three P's" is ultimately losing the power and influence you have worked so hard to attain, especially when you know you are the best person for the job of leading the MC forward but your inability to handle the power ultimately caused you to lose it. Now the MC is left rudderless because you have been replaced by a less qualified leader who stalls the MC through unqualified leadership.

In his book *"The Power Paradox How We Gain and Lose Influence"* celebrated UC Berkeley psychologist Dr. Dacher Keltner teaches how to retain the power we attain by explaining the power paradox of gaining and losing influence. He believes that compassion and selflessness enable us to have the most influence over others and claims that even though power is ubiquitous, its use is totally misunderstood. Keltner states that power is taken for granted and corrupts. This is reinforced culturally by everything from Machiavelli to contemporary politics. But how do we get power? And how does it change our behavior? So often, in spite of our best intentions, we lose our hard-won power. He argues that enduring power comes from empathy and giving. Above all, power is given to us by other people. This is what we all too often forget, and it is the crux of the power paradox – by misunderstanding the behaviors that helped us to gain power in the first place we set ourselves up to fall from power. We abuse and lose our power, at work, in our family life, with our friends, because we have never understood it correctly— until now. Power is not the capacity to act in cruel and uncaring ways; it is the ability to do good for others, expressed in daily life, and in and of itself a good thing.

In twenty original "Power Principles", Dr. Keltner lays out exactly how to retain power; why power can be a demonstrably good thing; when we are likely to abuse power; and the terrible consequences of letting those around us languish in powerlessness.

How Great Leaders Don't Allow Power to Corrupt Them

"Control is not leadership; management is not leadership; leadership is leadership"—Dee Hock

An article written by Martyn Bassett Associates Inc. (*https://www.mbassett.com/blog/how-greater-leaders-dont-allow-to-corrupt-them*) suggests that a mixture of constant self-reflection, checking for changes in your behavior, instilling graciousness in your character, teaching and praising others, among other things will go a long way towards helping you to keep your feet grounded. Following along the ideas of Dr. Keltner the author went on to write:

- After finding yourself in a new leadership position, constantly check for changes in your behavior, particularly negative ones. It is easier to fix problematic conduct once one is able to determine what it entails.

- Instill graciousness into one's character, which involves the ethics of empathy, gratitude, and generosity. Empathy helps leaders understand the concerns of their team and establish a collective goal beneficial for all. On the other hand, gratitude involves thanking people for their hard work and dedication, displaying appreciation for jobs well done. Lastly, generosity entails sharing knowledge, opportunities, and credit where it is rightfully due. The combination of these morals and good practices will greatly benefit how well a group works together and what they will be able to achieve.

- "...[Lead] the way by not being selfish. The more you empower others... and embrace team and mentoring – I guarantee, you will manifest more opportunity than you can handle," says Gerard Adams, founder of Elite Daily.

- Overall, maintaining the virtuous qualities that granted you power is key in the longevity and effectiveness of your run as a leader. [This is exactly what Dolla Bill 1%er said.]

- Furthermore, leadership does not develop overnight. It is "a learned skill, not a genetic grant," says writer Michael J. Farlow. In order to rise through the ranks and be worthy of the "leader" title, it is important to establish and hone certain characteristics.

- "A first step is developing greater self-awareness. When you take on a senior role, you need to be attentive to the feelings that accompany your newfound power and to any changes in your behavior."

There is Actually a Fourth P You Should Add to the Three P's – Pussy

Since this is a book about bikers and for bikers in motorcycle clubs the language will be, in some cases, how we speak to one another. This subject is one of those cases. I have often said "I am a biker not a choir boy", so forgive me if I offend you but we will move on to the fourth P regardless, which we shall affectionately call "PUSSY". Now, if you are a female president of an MC reading this book, I suppose you may call it "DICK" if that is what applies to you; however, it could be "PUSSY" too and I acknowledge that.

Now getting down to basics, or as my ex-best friend T.C. Cox used to say, "Let's get down to how the cow ate the cabbage" (T.C. lost my friendship because he tried to double cross me for a woman. What a shit bird! If he would have asked me for the girl, I would have given her to him. Instead, he tried it the backstabbing way and got caught after she gave him up. You know how these jealous-hearted people can be, you cannot let them make you angry or take you out of character. You just have to keep it moving. But T.C. had some good sayings, which I still use to this day like, "I'm just trying to keep hope alive—that's all we have!" So, if you ever hear me say that you guessed it right it came from T.C. Cox. I do not know where that term came from or even what it means, like I had no idea cows even ate cabbage, but he used to say it all the time and I never thought I would actually get an opportunity to write it down, but here we are – so I have taken the indulgence). Anyway, one of the great things about being a rock star is having unfettered sexual opportunities to bed down the rock band's multitudes of stalking, groupie females. The motorcycle club nation has no fewer groupie females than any rock band you might imagine. In our world we are the rock stars, and we have a following of female adherents as beautiful as the female Amazon Warriors of the Thermodon River. And of course, being President provides unfettered access to even more women, in many instances, than that of all brothers within your chapter.

In my opinion this "Fourth P" may be the most dangerous "P" of them all that can push a president to commit atrocities against the club simply because the little head begins thinking for the big head and ruins everything good every time.

Since most brothers do not think about the MC as a business, but rather see it as their personal stomping grounds (even Presidents) I know that most of you will not take heed to this section. But I would be remiss in my duties if I did not at least address it. So, we will talk about this how it should be rather than how it mostly is on the MC set.

Bottom line, you should keep your penis out of the club. There are many women you can screw on the set, more than you can count, so as the Prez you should leave the girls in your club alone. I know, I know, some clubs have property of, yada, yada, I am not talking about that. We all know the rules of how that sort of thing operates. I am talking about a situation where you have a supervisor subordinate relationship over a woman in your club and you are using your position to pressure a sexual relationship, or you are involved with a subordinate and members of the club can see preferential treatment that occurs from that relationship, or a myriad of scenarios that play out from these sorts of relationships.

Let us understand first the definition of a "subordinate relationship":

In the business world, a direct subordinate reports to the supervisor and relies on the supervisor for direction, leadership, and feedback. It is the responsibility of the supervisor in this relationship to lead and help develop the skills of the subordinate. In the MC world, the President is the supervisor. That means that every member, auxiliary, support, prospect, property of, support club, and social club associated with the MC is a subordinate of the President. All of the women, in your downline, associated with the club are your subordinates and you are their supervisor.

One of the biggest misnomers in the MC world is that your club cannot be sued for inappropriate conduct, and most presidents have no idea that they can be sued personally for their misconduct. Believe me I have seen clubs, officers, and members sued and ruined over this dumb shit because they have not the sophistication required to understand that their actions might be criminally illegal, as well as causing a financial civil liability to the club and its brothers. Use some damned common sense and understand that just because you are succumbing to the darkness of the "Fourth P", everyone around you was not born yesterday! They know how to (and will) stop you criminally or civilly for being stupid.

There have been wars of entire nations which started over PUSSY! Do not underestimate the power of PUSSY to cause destruction within the MC nation. Actually, it is not the PUSSY itself that causes the problem but rather the president's inability to control his loins or think with the right head. Do not be that guy!

Having been a photographer for many decades I have had the opportunity to photograph and chase models all over the world. And I will tell you that photographers are rock stars, and we have our model groupies too that we can bed unfettered. But you have to be able to take a picture and produce a body of work or you are just a photographer wannabe. In the model world a lecherous man who is using a camera to try to get sex is known by models as a GWC or "Guy with Camera," and it is quite an insulting term. When models write reviews about photographers, they will often use that abbreviation (GWC) to let unwitting models know to stay the hell away from that would-be photographer because all he is after is cheap thrills and sexual gratification gleaned through the misuse of the access his camera provides.

Presidents who have no personality and try to use their position in the MC to get PUSSY are no better than GWCs. Perhaps we should call them a PWC, which is a new term I just made up and stands for "President with Club." It displays the weakest self-confidence and is a scheme quickly recognized by set-savvy girls and members alike. The worst case is when a president tries to coerce his club's women with pressure, offers of favors, expedited prospecting time, diminished assignments to work details, and all kinds of other nonsense.

Avoid Liability for MC Romances

Like romances everywhere, some MC romances go wrong. And, if the romance is between a president and a subordinate, things are very likely to go bad when they go wrong. So, what are the best practices an MC president should follow:

1. Apply a personal set of policies to which you adhere, no matter how sexually attractive she is, how expertly she twerks when she saunters by, or how hard she "begs" for it (in your best Tarl Cabot fantasy). Be the president and stay the hell away! There will be plenty of time to make up for missed opportunities when you become a regular member again. Now you are the leader so you must act like it. Instead of getting more and more PUSSY perhaps you should be concentrating on running the MC and getting less.

Authors note: Gee, I wonder how many enemies I just made?

2. Make it clear if and when you are enticed by that "gotta have that chick" that intimate relationships between Prez and club members is inappropriate and prohibited. This can be called "a line-drawing exercise." While you are at it, setting this example and standing by it can and will set the policy for your junior officers as well! Viola! You have saved the club from a lawsuit, and you did not even know it.

3. But no matter your policies, nothing can completely protect against the realities of human relationships. So, you have to continually self-reflect, practice, practice, practice, and repeatedly train your junior officers, members, and associates about issues related to sexual misconduct and harassment in the MC. I know this is hard because there is a whole lot of ass grabbing, strippers, hoes, groupies, boom boom rooms, stripper poles, wet t-shirt contests, orgies, and every damned thing else happening in the MC. So how do you walk that fine line? You are Prez! Figure it the hell out! Your job is to protect the club. What we did Saturday might not work Monday, Tuesday, and Wednesday. So, make the fellas step up and recognize that it is not about "I", the club is about "WE". Insist that they make the big boy decisions when it is most important to protect the future of the brotherhood, and that no matter what you are always on the big boy sheet of paper for the MC!

4. Do not condone inappropriate behavior with silence. Do not try to silence others when they see your inappropriate behavior as a risk to the club. Be willing to step down if your

relationship is more important than the future of the MC. Do not be selfish, immature, or stupid.

5. In a situation where you have an employee working for the club you can ill afford to have the club sued or personal civil suits levied against you and your officers. If you have a girl working the bar and she is being paid a salary, she WORKS FOR THE CLUB and she is an EMPLOYEE! Stay out of her damned pants, skirts, Daisy Dukes, thongs, whatever you want to call them. This is a recipe for disaster. STAY AWAY!

What are the legal risks?

Here are some Supreme Court rulings that could potentially come into play should your MC wind up getting sued for sexual harassment shenanigans:

- The *Ellerth* and *Faragher* rulings in 1998 established that employers can be liable for sexual harassment if a supervisor was involved, even if no tangible negative employment action was taken against the subordinate.

- The *Burlington Northern v. White* 2006 decision extended the definition of an adverse employment step, while the *Crawford v.[county governments] of Tennessee* 2009 ruling broadened the class of people who can charge retaliation; both cases involved sexual harassment.

There are many ideas I urge you to consider that I have presented in this chapter. It is my desire that you will study it often, so much so that I have dedicated more than five thousand words to address these concerns. I want you to take from this chapter that leadership is an honor and a privilege not some sort of right that is owed to you. Asking you to consider putting your ego aside and working only towards achieving what is in the best interest of the MC at all times should not be too much to ask, should it? Avoid at all costs the temptations of the three "Ps" and oh yeah, do not forget the fourth "P" either! Good luck!

CHAPTER FOUR
The Obstacles to Change and the Strength of the Status Quo

In the pursuit to change certain aspects of your MC to what is believed to be a "better" way, a better structure, a better environment, better protocols, do not assume anything will magically happen just because you are now the President. It can happen, just not because one day you decided it would. All clubs eventually face restructuring, but most if not all patched brothers will resist change vehemently because what has been ingrained becomes almost impossible to replace. If you want change do not underestimate the obstacles to change and the strength of the status quo.

When I was a prospect, eventually a member and finally a junior officer coming up the ranks, I remember saying to myself, "Man if I ever become "P" I will change [this or that] I swear!" I finally got my chance when I became President of the Atlanta chapter and was eventually appointed as the first enforcer of the Mighty Black Sabbath Motorcycle Club Nation.

I had always liked the Flaming Knights MC Nation's colors when they first came to San Diego, California back in the early 1990s. Their colors depicted one huge blazing orange knight covered in flames, but it was not the colors or design I appreciated so much, what was so cool, what I loved about the one-patch was the fact that it was one huge patch. It was 16 inches wide and 18 to 20 inches long. This one-piece patch covered the brother's entire back. At the time, our back patch was a one-piece patch that was far less than half that size, about a ten-inch diameter circle. It looked like a target right on our backs and I hated how small it was. But eventually I became the Atlanta "P" as well as the National Enforcer! I knew there had to be a way I could configure a new patch and make everyone love it because it would be far better than the original! Right? Right!

The idea began to take shape one night as I was driving behind Ol' Skool, an Atlanta brother I was following to his house to hang out. Ol' Skool was riding on a 1977 Honda 750 that he had cobbled together with bailing wire and spit, with a little customization if you can imagine. Ironically, during one stroke of genius he decided to move the back taillight/brake light to the right side of the bike above the rear passenger's foot peg. He figured this would make the bike look cool, but it only made the bike nearly impossible to see at night, especially if you were coming up from behind it on the left side. I discovered this after almost running into the back of him about four times. From my truck, I could not see his light any time he applied his brakes and I repeatedly found myself slamming on the brakes, barely missing him. To top that off, Ol' Skool had dreadlocks that went halfway down his back and completely covered his Black Sabbath MC patch so you could not even see the white patch on his back. He even had on black gloves so that when he held his hands up to give arm signals, his black gloves on his black arms, in a black cut, with black hair covering his back patch and no visible taillight, made him virtually invisible. As a president I became irate that my club brother would remove the signal indicators from his bike, move the brake light to an un-seeable location and wear all black in the middle of the night, I could barely keep from pulling him over and cursing him out. Instead, my mind started rapidly running through different scenarios of ways I could put together something that would keep my brothers safe at night despite themselves!

I thought back to my days In the United States Submarine Navy. The Navy has all kinds of best practices processes developed to keep sailors from harming themselves when performing maintenance or using machinery. These guidelines cover everything from forcing sailors to adhere to step-by-step operations procedures to donning certain types of clothing to performing specific hazardous jobs like firefighting. These methods are necessary because sailors often find ingenious ways to cheat interlocks, are absent-minded when putting a part back on a machine after a maintenance procedure, or intentionally bypassing safety systems to shortcut workflow. The Navy works overtime to create processes to prevent these disastrous mistakes from happening. The Navy lovingly calls this collection of processes, "sailor-proofing" or making things "sailor-proof." So, watching my brother operating his motorcycle with total disregard for his visibility and safety sent my mind reeling to figure out how I could "club-brother-proof" my MC from brothers who wanted to ride invisibly cool on "blacked-out" motorcycles in the middle of the night, while inviting death to visit their doorsteps. That is when the huge Flaming Knights MC patch came to mind! It dawned on me that if I could make the Black Sabbath MC patch as big as a brother's back—at least 16 inches wide by 20 inches tall – and make the white in the patch out of a reflective material, much like the material you find on traffic safety vests, I would create a system that would allow a brother to be seen at night, even if he had dreadlocks down his back to his butt, wore all black clothes including black gloves and had no visible taillights! This patch would glow in the dark and work not only as a club patch but as a safety parameter club-brother-proofing against the stupid.

After great expense I had come up with the new, enlarged colors complete with reflective background that met every safety requirement I had imagined. After all, I was the National Enforcer and "P" of Atlanta, the Mighty Black Sabbath MC Nation had to accept this perfect idea! After all, not only were these colors as big as the old Flaming Knights' patches, they were safety colors as well! Who would not love this?

I introduced them to my chapter, and they were an instant hit. We voted them in, and the Atlanta chapter had the coolest looking colors in the nation. I wish I could say that the nation's OGs had the same reaction, but when word got out across the nation, I was immediately targeted to be put out bad! My great idea was a big flop and the OGs wanted blood. They saw my idea as an insult and resisted it wholly. Many things went back and forth, and I was basically about to be put out of the club when an OG named Sugar Man saw the new colors. He fell instantly in love with them and wore them to the annual President's meeting. Sugar Man had such a standing in the club that when he wore them no one would dare challenge him. Just like that, the new colors were accepted, and no one uttered a word against the almighty Sugar Man. The colors were adopted and are worn by the Nation to this day. But this did not happen because of my planning, had it been up to my plan it never would have succeeded.

The path to change in any organization is often littered with good ideas that never get to realize the light of day. The MC is no different. Successfully creating a meaningful change in the club is seldom going to be easy, but through hard work, planning, intuitive delivery, and some good-old-fashioned luck, you can make it happen. There have been many research studies that provide data on what works and—sometimes more importantly—what does not work when implementing change in organizations. We are going to apply some of that data to what it might take to change things in the MC. If you have seen it before you will understand as I have dissected it here to match what happens in MCs. To see the original article (*https://blog.prosci.com/avoid-these-change-management-obstacles*).

Obstacles to Changing Behaviors and Policies in an MC

Below are six major obstacles to changing behaviors and policies in an MC. I have taken the framework for this section from the 2018 edition of *Best Practices in Change Management* and adjusted them slightly to better understand these common change management obstacles from an MC perspective:

1. Lack of support from the executive board, often the OGs, and in some instances the national body resulting in a lack of sponsorship from any.

2. Lack of understanding of how to manage change, buy-in, or to secure resources.

3. Resistance to and therefore a lack of support for a specific solution or situation.

4. Change-resistant club culture fearing loss of traditions or norms (this is how we have always done it!).

5. Fear of loss of power or club stature because of change.

6. Pursuing too much change too soon (change saturation) and lack of prioritization

Though a president may be trying to initiate change to bring the MC to the "modern" era, as it were, he may find himself in a stranglehold by an uncooperative executive board, possibly the OGs, founders, or in national MCs, from the overreaching national board sticking their nose into local chapter business. In this way a president's crusade for change can die simply from a lack of support or active executive board (local, OG or national) buy-in. This fairly significant impediment can have a heavy impact on one's work towards managing change in the MC. Support by the board, the OGs and the nationals can instantly change the direction of your projects because if they support you the entire club will support you. If they do not, your intended change may be doomed. Leadership turnover can also kill your change management resulting in a loss of support for your efforts by "new" members of the executive board.

In the same way that effective support can mobilize and activate the organization, poor support can inhibit and delay progress. If a president tries to employ change, he himself does not show enthusiasm towards, the executive board, the nationals, OGs, and club brothers may interpret his lack of enthusiasm as an indication of how unimportant the initiative is. A president's lack of enthusiasm becomes the executive board's lack of support, and the initiative dies before it has a chance to succeed. It is crucial for the president to be fully onboard for any change he expends his political capital towards. He should also seek to attain and display the appropriate level of support from the club's thought leaders, executive board, and contributors to maintain their level of enthusiasm throughout the life of the project.

1. Lack of support from the executive board, often the OGs, and in some instances the national body resulting in a lack of sponsorship from any.

   Failing to win the support of the most important voices in the chapter or in the club at a national level can stop even the most comprehensive change dead in its tracks. Never underestimate the importance of politics in the MC because if you do you can be swallowed whole by it. Be a smart politician when you must play that game. Become adept at winning the allegiances you will need to get your projects done.

2. Lack of understanding of how to manage change, buy-in, or appropriate resources.

Without a good explanation of every aspect of how the proposed plan will manifest the desired outcome for the MC at every level of the process, the MC may not have a good understanding of how to manage the change, resulting in a lack of club member buy-in, a lack of investment or a lack of desire to direct necessary resources to manage the change. Without proper buy-in at each stage of the project, there is a risk resources (money, manpower, time, prioritization) once allotted to your project will be siphoned away when facing budgeting constraints or competing projects.

For example, the MC elected that all members needed to have training on motorcycle safety to make them safer pack riders, but as president, you did not thoroughly explain that your research revealed that the club would be 200% less likely to have an accident once this training was completed. Without this clear understanding of how the intended change would actually help the family once completed, there is likely to be resistance in spending the budget and devoting the man-hours necessary to complete the project. Suddenly, a member is killed on his bike without having burial insurance, resulting in the club voting that all members should have burial insurance purchased by the club. Unfortunately, the brotherhood cannot afford both projects, so one must go. Without clear communication from the onset of the project, it will be difficult to demonstrate the significance to train members to prevent an accident rather than pay for burial insurance after an accident. Without this clear understanding among club members your plan could lose priority and budgeting, particularly when it was never very popular in the first place due to lack of good communication.

3. Resistance to and therefore a lack of support for a specific solution or situation.

Resistance to a specific solution or situation can create a lack of support no matter how good the change may be for the brotherhood. Often the resistance comes from splinters within the family refusing to understand the need for a change or because they cannot see how it may benefit them. Resistance can be especially fierce within groups directly impacted by the change. These impacted groups may not understand the MCs reasons for wanting change or may just dig their heels in and refuse any reasonable attempt at a conversation because they do not want to open their minds that change could be good.

For example, when I enhanced the Mighty Black Sabbath Motorcycle Club Nation's colors the OGs decided the introduction signaled the beginning of the end of their rein of power and influence within the structure of the brotherhood. Even in-depth explanations of the safety features the patches contained would not sway their views. They wanted the old way because it was secure to them and represented a way of life in which they felt comfortable.

They felt that if they bought into the new patch they would be buying into the new school while selling themselves out as the old school. But when Sugar Man, a highly respected OG, demonstrated that he was not threatened by the new look, and embraced it, the rest of the OGs no longer felt threatened and came along for the ride (most of them anyway). The change was accepted, and the patch was a hit. The brothers named it "Turtle Shell" and it has carried on our 50-year history for the past thirteen years.

Creating buy-in for change via the support of respected thought leaders or influential/heroic figures is a key step to any successful change of club policy or club culture. This method starts by providing the why of the change up front including both the benefits to the club as well as the "what's in it for me" (WIIFM) benefits for groups and individual brothers within the MC.

4. Change resistant club culture fearing loss of traditions or norms ("this is how we have always done it").

Previously failed attempts at change can highly prejudice the brotherhood against ever trying said initiative again. Internal politics and personal agendas can also negatively influence a change-resistant MC.

For instance, if a previous president changed a finance bylaw that allowed him access to the club's bank account, where this had not been the rule before, and he wound up stealing the MCs money, it would not be a stretch to imagine the club never wanting to revisit changing such a bylaw for similar reasons in the future. Even if it can be proven that this is the most efficient way for the MC to run by a new president asking for a similar bylaw change. The untrusting club may just be too jaundiced to accept the new plan for change.

Also, the culture of the MC may foster resistance to change just because "it has always been done a certain way" and brothers may feel comfortable with the power of the status quo of doing it that way. Just because you can demonstrate a better or more efficient way to accomplish a task often just hearing that "we have always done it that way," can be enough to block a campaign you want to push.

For example, if the club has had its annual party in the winter for the past 21 years, but you have figured out that moving the party to the summer will make 5 times more money, be easier to host, and more folks will come because it is warmer outside. All those good reasons can be negated because the fellas cannot imagine doing things any other way than the way they have done them, and they just cannot buy into the fact that moving the party could make more money—no matter what you prove to them with the numbers.

Sometimes it is better to bide your time and try to implement certain changes later, like perhaps when a sufficient number of new members are acquired, and the new members are not so emotionally invested in keeping the old annual date for the purposes of nostalgia alone. Knowing when to approach an attempt to implement change is as important as the result of the change itself. Be willing to ask yourself hard and honest questions about whether the current environment will be friendly or oppositional to your change and if your change has a chance for successful implementation at this time.

5. Fear of loss of power or club stature because of change.

There are many folks who will fear change because they believe it will cost them power, club stature, or privilege.

For instance, a 10-term Sergeant-at-Arms may resist a bylaw change that would place a new requirement of term limits on his office because of the obvious loss of power he would experience if such a thing were to be voted in by the brotherhood.

Always be cognizant of what your proposed changes will mean to the power, stature, position, privileges, and prestige of brothers and officers effected by them. Knowing this in advance can help you to understand from whence your opposition may come. Be prepared to astutely answer the "what's in it for me" and the "why would I give that up" questions as well. Understand that you may have to play politics and compromise, giving a little to get a little perhaps accepting not getting ALL that you want to get MOST of what you want.

6. Pursuing too much change (change saturation) and lack of prioritization.

In his enthusiasm to better the MC, an overzealous new president can come to power and try to bring in too many sweeping changes at once and end up causing more harm than good. Attempting to implement too many changes simultaneously can fatigue the club resulting in change saturation. In addition, the sheer volume of an extensive number of change projects can cripple the ability of the brothers to prioritize the proposed changes. This lack of prioritization and oversaturation negatively impacts the MC leaving little time to devote to the change effort and no direction from the club leaders as to which efforts to prioritize.

It is easier on the club to rework one area of the bylaws at a time, ratify and incorporate them into the culture than it would be to forsake the current bylaws wholesale and try to start brand new.

Recognizing that members have a limit on the number of changes they can successfully process through is a key part to employing successful strategies in change management. Even when over saturation cannot be helped, being aware of it can help you lead the MC family through change, prioritize changes, and successfully implement them in the chapter(s).

Assess the Obstacles to Any Change You Want to Implement

When trying to implement change within the MC use this checklist below to help you access the biggest obstacles you may face:

I want to create change _____

Will you:

> - Face ineffective sponsorship from executive board, senior leaders, founders, OGs, or the national body?
> - Lack sufficient resources and buy-in for the change to occur?
> - Expect resistance due to egos, fear, embeddedness, territorialism, tribalism, tradition-hawks, or political agendas?
> - Experience a change-resistant culture because of lack of budget or manpower?
> - Face opposition because you are trying to bring on too much change simultaneously, to the point of change saturation?

Focusing attention on proactively overcoming these obstacles can help mitigate common risks and ultimately help you achieve better outcomes for change in your Motorcycle Club nation.

There is a lot more to learn about how to implement change in your MC and how to manage that change than this chapter can provide. The purpose of this chapter is to introduce you to the science of change management and inform you that there are professional organizations that write papers and conduct studies about change management that can teach you methods and best practices towards achieving effective change in your MC.

One methodology I would recommend is the Prosci Change Management methodology (*https://www.procsi.com/resources/articles/change-management-methodology*). Prosci's change management methodology is developed based on research with over 3,400 participants over the last twenty years. It comes from real project leaders and teams reflecting on what worked, what did not, and what they would do differently on their next project.

◊◊◊

CHAPTER FIVE
Hierarchy and Communication

To be a phenomenally successful president and ensure effective communication and club movement among your brothers, you will need to know how hierarchical structures of rank and communication work within an MC. You will also need to know how to employ these strategies outside the MC to keep the MC moving forward with minimal conflict from other MCs, law enforcement, business vendors, and government agencies. Of course, knowing is only half of the battle; you must also master the art of engaging these skills and utilize them consistently as treasured tools within your leadership tool chest.

The basic idea is to exceed at effectively communicating with each level in the hierarchical structure of the organization with which your MC interacts according to MC protocol, governmental protocol, and/or business protocol. As president of your MC, you will be expected to learn the chain of command of each of these organizations and become an expert at communicating at every level.

How Hierarchy and Communication Works Internally (Inside the MC)

An MC is comprised of an internal structure that has many levels of responsibility and reward. From Hang-arounds to the National President, each new position attained within the MC generally comes from applying the principles of hard work, persistence, expertise, and sacrifice. When a person has worked hard, to obtain another level of success within the MC, they duly expect to exercise the responsibility, recognition, acknowledgement, and reward they worked so hard to attain. It is vital you understand how valued these levels of accomplishment are to the brothers who have achieved them. By understanding the significance of this fundamental value, it will not be hard to realize how angry and devalued you could make a brother feel if you fail to recognize him at the level of hierarchy he has earned. Such a mistake can cause you great difficulty when trying to accomplish the agenda of the MC by wasting time working against brothers you have offended instead of working with them. If they think you are arrogant and out-of-touch when dealing with peers and subordinates, you will lose their respect and create enemies where you once had brothers. When angry brothers feel devalued the consequences can cause club relationships to become quite terse. People who feel underrated can become jealous, angry, and consequently start looking for ways to topple your presidency. Much of this can be avoided simply by treating people the way they are supposed to be treated according to their rank, title, and position. Including brothers at the appropriate steps and levels of club communications empowers them and gives them value. This is one of the greatest ways to begin practicing these principles of leadership.

Example 1: Internal Club Hierarchy and Communication

I had an open-door policy within my MC, which permitted any member to come talk to me about anything at any time. When a request was denied by the Sergeant-at-Arms, one member, aware of my policy, went behind the sergeant's back to request an audience with me (like a child pitting mommy against daddy). I heard out his complaint, and seeing an easy resolution, I allowed him his request. The next day, the sergeant came running to me screaming his head off. You see, he had already handled this problem and his fix was the opposite of mine. He told the brother, NO! Now the sergeant felt devalued, unappreciated, and more importantly that my inappropriate intervention had prevented him from performing his job. He instantly became convinced that I could no longer be trusted because I had undermined his position. Our relationship deteriorated that day. Soon we openly argued about everything, and the chapter's morale suffered as a result. I could trace it all back to that one lapse in communication protocol on both of our parts.

In the military, a commanding officer can have an "open-door" policy, but there is still an expectation and a duty to communicate across personnel on all levels. Therefore, a sailor can talk with the commanding officer about something he does not want to share with anyone else in the chain of command, but he still has a duty to notify the chain of command that he wants to talk to the commanding officer. He must submit a request for an appointment to see the commanding officer. That request will be approved by the entire chain of command from his leading petty officer, his department chief, his division officer, his master chief of the command, to his executive officer. Even though the only person on the crew to know what the conversation is about is the commanding officer and the sailor, the entire chain of command will know that the meeting is going to take place. No one is surprised, taken off guard, blindsided, or uninformed.

This level of communication is just as important in the MC. It ensures that everyone is in the communication loop at the appropriate level. For instance, in the previous example, had the communication hierarchy been maintained, the sergeant would have notified the higher-ranking officers (the VP and myself, the President) that he had an issue with the member, had solved the issue and perhaps outlined what the issue was about (although not if it was something personal between the sergeant and the brother), his resolution, and the affect (if any) to the MC. Conversely yet equally, my responsibility to the hierarchy of communication should have been to ask the brother if he had first contacted the Sergeant-at-Arms, then the VP, about his desire to meet with me and/or the issue. If the member had conveyed to me that he had not communicated on all levels, I could have saved myself and the chapter a lot of grief and morale issues by postponing the meeting until the proper procedures had been followed and handled correctly. I should have instructed him to notify them of his request to speak to me and notified the VP and the sergeant about the meeting request and/or results of the meeting — before a final decision had been made. Had I done that I would have already known of the sergeant's resolution and could have taken the time to consult with him before I overturned him. I should have had a final report (written or verbal) for all parties involved that either resolved the situation or presented further options to seek a resolution. This is a construct of highly effective communication.

Internal Club Hierarchy and Communication (Special Request Chit)

When I was in the Navy, we used a formal slip of paper to track such communications requests. Every sailor was required to use it to request everything from leave to permission not to shave. It was called a Special Request Chit or simply a Request Chit. The Request Chit was a basic slip of paper, that in my day, was filled out by hand, but perhaps these days it is filled in on a computer. I looked one up and it looks vastly different than the ones 30 years ago, when I was in the Navy, but it seems to serve the same purpose, so I included a picture of it below. On this chit you can request everything from leave to special pay. There is also a customized block to request other things, like a meeting with the commanding officer. This type of structure of effective communications is essential within any organization like an MC. There is a check box and signature for every officer in the chain of command. This type of communication ensures the entire chain of command is informed about most actions that take place within the organization.

SPECIAL REQUEST/AUTHORIZATION

PRIVACY ACT STATEMENT
THE AUTHORITY TO REQUEST THIS INFORMATION IS CONTAINED IN 5 USC 301.
THE PRINCIPLE PURPOSE OF THE INFORMATION IS TO ENABLE YOU TO MAKE KNOWN YOUR DESIRE FOR ITEMS LISTED OR FOR SOME OTHER SPECIAL CONSIDERATION OR AUTHORIZATION. THE INFORMATION WILL BE USED TO ASSIST OFFICIALS AND EMPLOYEES OF THE DEPARTMENT OF THE NAVY IN DETERMINING YOUR ELIGIBILITY FOR AND APPROVING OR DISAPPROVING THE SPECIAL CONSIDERATION OR AUTHORIZATION BEING REQUESTED. COMPLETION OF THE FORM IS MANDATORY, FAILURE TO PROVIDE REQUIRED INFORMATION MAY RESULT IN DELAY IN RESPONSE TO OR DISAPPROVAL OF YOUR REQUEST.

1. NAME:	2. RATE:

3. SHIP OR STATION:	4. DATE OF REQUEST: (YYYYMMDD)

5. DEPARTMENT/DIVISION:	6. DUTY SECTION/GROUP:

7. NATURE OF REQUEST: ☐ LEAVE   ☐ SPECIAL LIBERTY   ☐ SPECIAL PAY   ☐ COMMUTED RATIONS   ☐ OTHER (BELOW)

8. NO. OF DAYS REQUESTED:	FROM (DATE AND TIME):	TO (DATE AND TIME):

9. DISTANCE (MILES):   MODE OF TRAVEL: ☐ CAR   ☐ AIR   ☐ TRAIN   ☐ BUS

10. LEAVE ADDRESS:	11. TELEPHONE NUMBER:

12. REASON FOR REQUEST:

13. SIGNATURE OF APPLICANT: (Use CAC for digital signature)

14. I am eligible and obligate myself to perform all duties of person making application.	SIGNATURE OF STANDBY:	DUTY STATION:

	RANK/RATE/TITLE:	SIGNATURE:	DATE:
15. RECOMMENDED APPROVAL ☐ YES ☐ NO			
16. RECOMMENDED APPROVAL ☐ YES ☐ NO			
17. RECOMMENDED APPROVAL ☐ YES ☐ NO			
18. RECOMMENDED APPROVAL ☐ YES ☐ NO			
19. RECOMMENDED APPROVAL ☐ YES ☐ NO			
20. RECOMMENDED APPROVAL ☐ YES ☐ NO			

21. ☐ APPROVED ☐ DISAPPROVED	SIGNATURE:

22. REASON FOR DISAPPROVAL:

NAVPERS 1336/3 (Rev. 10-2011)   FOR OFFICIAL USE ONLY - PRIVACY SENSITIVE

Example 2: External Club to Club Hierarchy and Communication on the Set

I once experienced problems between myself and the MC's new National President. I went to an annual party to essentially challenge his authority. My mind was singularly focused on dealing with the issues between us and in doing so, was prepared to deal with the bevy of "yes men" that were sure to surround me and take off my patch. To this I mean things were terse! The second I entered the room I was swamped by admirers, which was normal since I launched the "Black Dragon Biker TV" YouTube channel, the "Black Dragon" Facebook page, and "Black Dragon Biker TV" Instagram channel, the "Dragon's Layer Motorcycle Chaos" podcast, four nationally published books, and an online news magazine "BikerLiberty.com". Anyone watching would have thought I relished in the celebrity, but I have to tell you, I do not think it will ever be something to which I will ever truly grow accustomed, but how I truly feel in my heart does not affect what people feel in theirs.

After I signed autographs and took selfies, I found myself on the hunt again for the new National. That is when I walked past a 1%er club that had not come up to me during my entrance. Instead, they were waiting for me to come to them and address them according to MC hierarchical protocol. But because my mind was completely on something else, I stormed right past them as though they did not exist. Now, from their perspective, they saw my actions as, "Here this arrogant ass thinks he is all that because some folks think he is a celebrity. And we would have given him his celebrity status after he came over here and acknowledged us our hierarchy on the set, but instead he has chosen to front us off! Now we will embarrass him and teach him a lesson in MC protocol that he has obviously forgotten!" But what they were thinking is nowhere near what was on my mind. But this is a clear example of how a small failure of proper communication can cause a problem big enough to get someone hurt and involve your whole MC Nation in some BS you never wanted nor intended to initiate. Naturally, their next step was to surround me, but I was not about to be in the mood for that nonsense. In my mind, one of them may well have taken the brunt of the punishment that was meant for someone else, namely the new National. I had come prepared for an altercation and it would not have mattered who got some. At that point, I was like a loaded spring under tension ready to release. Fortunately, the situation was saved by an alert sergeant. After all, had I left three or four of their brothers lying in an eternal dirt nap you can see how quickly the entire MC nation would have been at war and only God knows what resolution there would have been. Luckily, the astute Sergeant-at-Arms got between us and when they asked him what my problem was, he told them it was internal club issues, and he would handle it. And just as quickly as it had started, it was over.

A president (current or previous) must always stay focused while on the set. You do not have the luxury of a mental lapse. You represent the entire MC in your every action. You cannot ever afford to let your communications skills slip or fail to recognize the importance of playing your role and maintaining your club's lane where appropriate. The set can be a dangerous place for presidents who make that mistake. They jeopardize the safety of everyone. They are expected to know better. Make sure you know the protocol of hierarchy and communication.

Example 3: External Club to Club Hierarchy and Communication in the Clubhouse

There was a situation on the MC set where a full patch brother from a 1%er MC was visiting the clubhouse of a 99%er MC. The 1%er MC club brother was feeling a bit cocky and drinking heavily so he was not on his best behavior. He spotted a young woman he wanted to pursue, so he figured he would make his presence known. A full patch brother of the 99%er club he was visiting quickly intervened informing the 1%er brother that the woman he was attempting to pursue was his daughter. He continued to inform the 1%er that his daughter was not interested in a romantic interlude with him that evening and that his attempts should cease immediately. He told the outlaw that he would much appreciate it if he moved along and got back to minding his business. The 1%er was more of the opinion that the 99%er's daughter could speak for herself and he would continue his pursuits until such time as he discovered for himself whether, or not, the young woman wanted to receive his attention. So, the warning did not sit well with the outlaw, who felt the need to exude his dominance, and continued to disrespectfully pursue his drunken agenda—as he felt untouchable in his colors and thought no one would dare take things to the next level. Consequently, after about three or four more warnings the 99%er patch, fed up with the disrespect of his family, went to putting hands and feet on that 1%er. It was a fair one-on-one fight in which the 99%er was victorious in winning the day. The 1%er was thrown out of the clubhouse, unceremoniously I might add, and he with his pride shaken, his pugilist skills defeated, was on his way.

News of this brawl spread quickly on the set and the streets began to talk. The 99%er president made the mistake of thinking, "Because it was a fair fight, and it was one on one, everything was alright." He did not understand that a communication protocol was initially missed, and now an urgent meeting must occur, or trouble was headed his club's way, it would be coming unannounced, when it was least expected, and someone could likely be killed. He did not recognize that it was his responsibility to get things squashed because the situation was not going to resolve itself. Because he did not comprehend the hierarchal nature of set communications between clubs, he was unaware of the junior club's duty to reach out to the senior club first. And he also did not understand the danger his club was in. His fear of dealing head on with the 1%er club caused him to procrastinate about initiating a meeting. The optics were terrible as he appeared to ignore trying to do anything about fixing his club's situation. Countless presidents called and tried to counsel him, but he acted as though the trouble would magically disappear. In his mind, if he had not heard from them everything was alright and there was nothing to worry about. He was repeatedly warned about MC protocol that called for the junior club to call the dominant club and try to get an emergency meeting to push the point of peace and try to find out what could be done to rectify the situation, but his fear paralyzed him and the obvious happened. Two months later the dominant club showed up guns blazing leaving a couple of the 99%ers wounded with several gun shots each. Of course, the 99%er president sought an emergency meeting, but the dominant club was very nasty about their terms for peace since the president had not come to them before the policing action. The dominant club president kept asking him why he did not reach out before things took a turn for the absolute worse, but because of his fear he had no answers. The 1%er president was aware that other presidents around the set had tried to counsel the 99%er president about how to handle the situation, but he would not listen, so his hand was firm and merciless against him. As a result, the club lost its stature and support from its patrons because folks knew they were no longer good with the dominant. In less than a year the 99%er club lost their clubhouse because the set and their patrons stop showing up to bike nights fearing another shooting in which they might be caught up in the crossfire. It was not long before the president was forced to leave the club after they turned on him, blaming him for their losses. Although there may not have been anything that could have been done to stop what occurred if some strategies of communication protocol had been employed perhaps the entire situation could have been avoided. In hindsight, here are a few examples of how to think during a similar situation, which could have helped things turn out differently:

Educate Club Member's on Communication Protocol

As a president you must train your men, in advance, to prepare themselves to handle all kinds of situations with skill and diplomacy. Understanding hierarchy and communication is important to accomplishing those tasks.

Club members should follow a communication protocol within the MC. Pride gets a lot of brothers in more trouble than they ever wanted. Make sure to teach your brothers about having too much pride, especially at the wrong times.

1. When the 99%er brother first noticed the untoward behavior of the 1%er towards his daughter he could have immediately notified his Sergeant-at-Arms. This would have involved an officer in the situation from the start. Even 1%ers recognize and respect the authority of a club Sergeant-at-Arms.
   - In understanding how nasty things can get on the set, he could have instantly sent his daughter to the car. Thereby muting the situation before it could even get started.
2. Once notified, the Sergeant should send notice to the VP and Prez that a potential situation was occurring as he rounded up a few brothers to go stand between the 1%er and the girl.
   - By moving in a wall of silence, the presence of the club would have exuded itself with no words needing to be spoken.
3. The sergeant should then make a call to the 1%er's sergeant, whose number he should have on speed dial.
   - There is nothing like watching what happens when someone gets a text message from their Sergeant-at-Arms written in all caps "STAND DOWN DAMNIT!" Such a text message can make the toughest brother deflate his chest and start acting like he has some sense.
   - The 1%er sergeant may have also sent some brothers immediately over to get their brother, as no club wants issues that stem from another brother's inability to handle his liquor or check his attitude when dealing with other clubs on the set.
4. If things continue to go down the wrong path and a confrontation ensued, the president should immediately reach out to the 1%er president for an emergency meeting on neutral ground to figure out what could be done to remedy the situation. As long as the two clubs are talking the chances of an armed conflict are greatly diminished.
   - If the proper communication protocol had been followed from the onset, the 1%er club would have been able to clearly see that the 99%er club tried to follow every level

of communication hierarchy available to them in an attempt to avoid trouble forcing them to potentially look at their brother and the motives behind his erratic behavior.

Example 4: External Club to Local Law Enforcement Hierarchy and Communication

We had a situation wherein one of our chapters had an opportunity to rent an abandoned neighborhood bar. It soon became the MC clubhouse in that town. Everyone is familiar with the terrible reputation MCs have, so the landlord was not particularly interested in having the MC in his bar; however, with the economy in an unhealthy state, he was happy to get anyone who could pay the rent consistently. Begrudgingly, he let us rent his beautiful, fully established bar for our clubhouse. This bar was wonderfully furnished and because it was in a small town, the rent was cheap. It had a kitchen, serving area, restaurant, full wet bar, walk-in freezer, commercial ranges—everything you could possibly want. So, as you might imagine we really wanted to be there. Our problems originated within the neighborhood itself, particularly, the police department and local police chief.

As soon as the community became aware of our presence, the barrage of complaints to the police began each time we went to the clubhouse. The chief assigned units to sit outside the clubhouse each weekend and on bike nights. The units' job was to pullover every bike and car that entered or left the parking lot and pass out as many tickets as they could write. The police department became so menacing with their harassment, they would even write tickets for bikes parked in front of the club on the grass. These tickets were written for using the sidewalk as a thoroughfare. It was clear the cops were going to hassle the club until they drove us out of the neighborhood.

When the chapter president called me, I gave him specific instructions for opening the channels of communication on the appropriate levels necessary to effect the change his chapter needed:

1. Arrange a meeting between the club's executive board and the police chief and executive officers to discuss the club's purpose, history, and willingness to cooperate with any reasonable guidelines to get the club on better footing with the police department. This is also a good opportunity to deliver a respectful warning that harassment would not be tolerated.
   - The chapter had come to build a relationship but could easily bring forth negative attention of the department to the press if the MC's attempts at diplomacy went unheeded.
2. Simultaneously, to show that we were serious about stopping the harassment, I had the president submit a letter of intent to the mayor and the city council that explained our intention to meet with the police chief to openly discuss the intimidation and harassment techniques being used against us and what we could do to stop them.
   - A copy of this letter was also sent to the police chief and the neighborhood watch association that continually lodged complaints against us, as well as to the local press.
3. After his meetings with the police chief, I had the president send follow-up letters with summaries to all interested parties.
4. The club's executive board attended the next neighborhood meeting to announce a club open house day to allow the neighborhood to get a tour, enjoy some barbeque, take the kids for rides on the bikes, and answer any questions.
5. We made sure to publish press releases to all local media outlets to publicize our upcoming charity runs and feeding the homeless endeavors.
6. He met with every MC president in the city to make sure they told their members what we were facing and what kind of behavior would be accepted in the new clubhouse and what would not be tolerated (like burning rubber leaving the clubhouse, racing in the neighborhood, etc.).

7. A copy of all press releases was sent to the police chief, mayor, and neighborhood council each and every time the club held a charity event.

The club's profiling problems disappeared within four months. The Black Sabbath Motorcycle Club has become well versed in running these types of positive campaigns. Twenty years ago, in the San Diego mother chapter, a man's throat was slit inside the clubhouse. When the San Diego City Attorney decided she would shut us down, I designed the same playbook to get the city off our backs. The skillful employment of principles of hierarchy and communication has proven successful again and again.

CHAPTER SIX
Leadership Mini Book

The heaviest penalty for declining to rule is to be ruled by someone inferior to yourself.
Plato

Leadership Principles – The Mini Book (Abridged Version)

Everything I have written in this book can be summarized in the few pages contained within this chapter. Consider this the abridged version of "President's Bible Chronicle I "Principles of Leadership."" That is to say, many of you will be able to read this "mini" book and completely understand the extent of what is being discussed without needing to read another page—especially those of you with a military or other leadership backgrounds.

I have written over 100,000 words in the "full" book to better explain these principles and provide some of my experiences leading men as the president and eventually national president of my MC nation. Read this mini book first so you can have the whole lesson in mind as you go further throughout these pages with your investigation. Enjoy!

Sincerely,

Black Dragon
Lifer
National President - Retired
Mighty Black Sabbath Motorcycle Club Nation
A Breed Apart
Since 1974 and Still Strong.........///
Black Sabbath Forever Forever Black Sabbath (BSFFBS)

Leadership

As President of a motorcycle club, you will be consistently challenged to make a difference in the lives of the men who are your brothers, in daily contribution towards improving the quality of their MC culture and safety—within the clubhouse environment, on the road, on the set, and in their personal affairs. Most will look to you for leadership in all aspects of their lives.

There is no book that can prepare you for all you might see as president and this book does not attempt to do that, but it will help you to prepare you to be both inspired and crushed by all that you will experience while helping you discover the skills you will need to succeed through it all. I will discuss some leadership principles to guide you when you face things not even I can foresee—and I have been involved with my club for over thirty years—to forewarn you and tell you what to avoid. But if you have strong leadership principles you need not worry. You can make it through anything if you simply have the courage to lead. This is not a promise that you will not make any mistakes, but you will know how to handle those mistakes and make good on them when they occur.

Perhaps one of the first things to mention is that you are the SERVANT of the MC, not the BOSS of it. In fact, you are the lowliest person within the MC because full patch brothers in good standing are the highest level of membership the MC has to offer. As president you become the humble servant of these full patch brothers and all other club affiliates. Your job is to find out what the voting body desires and utilize your office to make it happen. As the servant of the brotherhood your duty is to be the best you can be so that the family can be the best it can be. And you cannot be your best without putting together a course of study that allows for improvement over time, either through experience, research, or both. The best way to do this is to examine yourself and constantly seek improvement!

Know Yourself and Seek Self Improvement

The principle of leadership should be developed via the use of leadership traits. By evaluating yourself, using the leadership traits you will learn in this book, you will be able to determine your strengths and weaknesses. You can then improve these weaknesses (and strengths) until you are satisfied you have mastered your areas of deficiency. You can improve yourself by employing these techniques:

1. Make an honest evaluation of yourself to determine your strong and weak personal qualities
2. Seek the honest opinions of your brothers or superiors
3. Learn by studying the causes for the success and failures of others in the MC
4. Develop a genuine interest in what is best for the MC and in people, the WE of the MC
5. Master the art of effective writing and speech to perfect your ability to communicate
6. Have a definite plan to achieve the goals of the brotherhood

Be Technically and Tactically Proficient

A president who knows their job thoroughly, possessing a wide field of knowledge, is of more benefit to his MC than a know-it-all who has not trained or prepared himself. Before you can lead, you must be able to do the job. Actually, you should be able to perform every officer job in the MC. The best presidents are the ones who have performed every job all the way up the ladder until he became president. This is a leader you cannot get anything over his head by attempting to dazzle him with BS. He has been there and done everything you are talking about. He knows what you are going through before you actually even experience it. He has tactical and technical competence learned from books and on-the-job training. To develop technical and tactical proficiency, you should:

1. Know what is expected of you, then expend time and energy on becoming proficient at those areas. If the requirement is to ride 30,000 miles per year, you should ride 60,000. You want to be president, right? Then get used to doing things like a president—always bigger, always more!

2. Form an attitude early on of seeking to learn more than is necessary. The more you know the more you can do. The more you can do the more you can lead others at doing. Presidents do more because they know more, they have experienced more, and they are competent at successfully completing more than most under their command!

3. Observe and study the actions of capable presidents. You want to be president then prepare yourself to be president! If you are already president, be a better president by learning every day. We all know a president, whether in our club or another club, that we admire, respect, and sit in awe of his accomplishments. Network with that president. Learn what worked right and make it work in your club.

   Many protocols I instituted in the Mighty Black Sabbath Motorcycle Club Nation I learned from presidents who ran other MCs. Our National High Council of Presidents was borrowed from the Zulus MC Nation—the former National President "Wolverine" taught me himself. I met with "Big Dogg", former National President of the Front Runners MC. I had discussions with nationals and presidents from 1%er nations, traditional clubs, mom and pop clubs, motorcycle ministries, COCs, and NCOM. Each time, I had my pencil and paper out taking notes. I wanted to know how the successful guys did things so that I could mirror what they did.

4. Spend time with the people who are recognized as technically and tactically proficient at their area of expertise. If you know a guy who has ridden across the United States so many times that he has had to replace the engines on his motorcycles because he keeps burning them out and you want to learn how to ride like that—go

spend time with him.

"Highway" of the Buffalo Soldiers MC Nation West Coast is one of those people. So is "Reef" of the Mighty Chosen Few MC Nation. I have spent years talking to these men on the phone about riding and how they do it and I've even had the pleasure of riding with "Highway" since about 1997. "Big Cell" from Fast Harleys Only calls it "Getting Yonder, " in fact there is an entire magazine created behind his quote. These men are technically proficient. You can learn from men like these.

5. Prepare yourself for the job of the president before you get there. If you have eyed the position of president as something you want in your bailiwick then start preparing yourself for the job years before you actually run for it. Take on positions of increased responsibility and let the club see what you are all about.
6. Seek feedback from superiors, peers, and subordinates. Ask them how you are doing as president. Stand by and listen to their responses but resist the urge to take it personally. It builds character and will help you improve.

Know Your People and Look Out for Their Welfare

This is one of the most important leadership principles. A president must make a conscientious effort to observe his brothers and how they react to different situations. A brother who is nervous and lacks self-confidence should never be put in a situation where an important decision must be made. This knowledge will enable you, as the president, to determine when close supervision is required. To put this principle in to practice you should:

1. **Put your brotherhood's welfare before your own.** There were generals in history that refused to eat any food other than what their men ate. If you are looking out for your men first, you will always know the pulse of the heartbeat of the club, its morale, and the level of endurance the men have.

2. **Be approachable.** "Dolla Bill", 1%er president of the Mighty Outcast MC Nation Atlanta chapter said, "I am only a full patch brother in my nation, nothing special. I am just the guy they chose

to represent them as president for the time being. I am still the same person I was when I put that president's patch on." Stay approachable to the members and extended family of your club. That way you never get "out of touch" with reality when it comes to the brotherhood.

3. **Encourage individual development.** Teach your men to soar. Do not keep it to yourself. If they fly, the MC flies. A high tide lifts all ships in the harbor so help your brothers by setting a high tide within the MC. Do not be jealous of a superstar brother. He just might take your place one day and that should be a good thing. You do not need to extinguish his light for your light to shine. Someone helped you to be great, so pass it on!

4. **Know your club's mental attitude**. Keep in touch with their thoughts. A club on the MC set refused to have any national meetings, though chapters continually asked for a sit-down. The national president was not interested in hearing their thoughts. Another VP would argue during phone meetings and refuse to answer questions about policies or decisions on the main chat or phone line with his presidents. Instead, he said, "Call me personally if you want to talk about that." When he got them on the phone alone, he would berate them and suppress their issue.

    Needless to say, these two idiots only got one term. They were voted out with a landslide. Simply put, they fell too deeply into the idea of "Do as I say because I am the leader." Grown men will vote with their feet and leave your club if they must—or they will ensure you never serve a day past your first term. Some will do whatever it takes to have you removed early. No matter how much you hate to hear complaining, it pays to keep in touch with the thoughts of your members. That is, after all, your job!

5. **Ensure fair and equal distribution of rewards.** Reward fairly! Do not play favorites. This can be difficult but is essential if you want a successful presidency. Treat everyone fairly according to the bylaws and treat all of your members equally. It is just that simple. Well

simple to say, perhaps not so simple in practice. It is up to you whether or not you are up to such a lofty task.

6. **Provide sufficient recreational time and insist on participation.** An MC on the circuit had a clubhouse they were using to run an after-hours joint. The club was making thousands and thousands of dollars each night, but they only had about 12 brothers to run the clubhouse. The president expected these men to work their regular jobs at 40 hours per week and then another forty to sixty hours running the clubhouse at night. Needless to say, he burned those brothers out and eventually the whole chapter patched over to another club. They went to where they were treated like brothers and not some working dog to enrich his pockets. Oh, did I forget to tell you that he never gave any of them one dime and the money magically disappeared out of the club's accounts?

The point is that you cannot ever forget what brought you together as a club, and for most of us it was the love of riding the steel side-by-side with our brothers. When you stop having recreation time and enjoying the riding life, the MC starts to wilt and eventually dies. Do not be an MC chained to a clubhouse trying to make money. Shut that clubhouse down from time to time and go ride those motorcycles. This is a lifestyle that is supposed to be fun!

Keep Your Brothers Informed

Club brothers by nature are inquisitive. To promote efficiency and boost morale, a president should keep his brothers informed of happenings in the club, providing explanations as to why things are to be done. Secrecy should never be part of a democratic MC. Informing your brothers makes them feel that they are a part of the brotherhood and not just a cog in a wheel. Informed brothers perform better! The key is to be sure the brothers have enough information to do their job intelligently and to inspire their initiative, enthusiasm, loyalty, and conviction. Techniques to apply this principle include:

1. Whenever possible, explain why tasks must be done and the plan to accomplish a task.

2. Be alert to detect the spread of rumors. Stop rumors by replacing them with the truth.
3. Build morale by publicizing information concerning the successes of your club.
4. Keep your MC informed about current bylaws and regulations affecting their promotion, privileges, and other benefits.

Set the Example

A president who demonstrates professional competence, courage and integrity sets high personal standards for himself before he can rightfully demand it from others. Your appearance, attitude, physical fitness, and personal example are all on display for your brotherhood. Remember, your club reflects your image! Techniques for setting the example are:

1. Show your brothers that you are willing to do the same things you ask them to do. Presidents still pick up the parking lot, clean the bathrooms, work behind the bar, and carry the trash out. At least grown-up (mature) ones anyway.
2. Maintain an optimistic outlook. The whole 'the sky is falling' routine gets old. So does the 'Woe is me' attitude. In the face of adversity keep your chin up! The brothers and extended family are watching you and they never stop watching. Never let them see you believing that the MC will fail, because if you do then it will fail.
3. Conduct yourself so that your personal habits are not open to criticism. No president is perfect, but that does not mean you should let the club see you with your ass hanging out. If you have bad habits, do them away from the MC, out of the MC's colors, and away from any place that would put a negative light on the MC. The president must always be above reproach. So, NO, it is NOT okay for you to be drunk, high, out of control, or out of sorts in front of the club. Go get counseling, go to rehab, do what you have to do because if the president falls the entire MC falls.
4. Avoid showing favoritism to any subordinate. What more needs to be said about this?

5. Delegate authority and avoid over supervision. Develop leadership among your brothers. If you cannot trust your brothers, they will never trust you.
6. Leadership is taught by example. So be the damned example you would want to see in a president!

Ensure That the Task Is Understood, Supervised, and Accomplished

A president must give clear and concise orders that cannot be misunderstood; then by close supervision, ensure that these orders are properly executed. Before you can expect your men to perform, they must know what is expected of them. Remember: your given orders are derived by the vote of the full patch brothers in good standing. You are not a dictator. Your orders are designed to give the voting body what it has voted for, not to accomplish your own agenda. Keep in mind your dedication to the bylaws first and foremost when giving orders. If you do not cherish the bylaws as president, then who will? The most important part of this principle is the accomplishment of the will of the full patch brothers in good standing. In order to develop this principle, you should:

1. Issue every order to accomplish the will of the MC and not your own agenda.
2. Use the established chain of command.
3. Encourage officers and brothers to ask questions concerning any point in your orders or directives they do not understand.
4. Question officers and brothers to determine if there is any doubt or misunderstanding in regard to the task to be accomplished.
5. Supervise the execution of your orders.
6. Exercise care and thought in supervision. Over supervision hurts initiative and creates resentment, while under supervision will not get the job done.

Train Your Brothers as A Team

"Teamwork makes the dream work!" Teamwork is the key to successful operations. Teamwork is essential from the smallest chapter to the entire mighty motorcycle club nation. As president, you must insist on teamwork from your brothers. Train, play, and operate as a family. Ensure each brother knows his position and responsibilities within the framework of the extended family. To develop the techniques of this principle, you should:

1. Stay sharp by continuously studying and training.
2. Encourage full club participation in recreational and club events.
3. Do not publicly blame an individual for the MC's failure or one individual for the entire MC's success.
4. Ensure that training is meaningful and that the purpose is clear to all members. Continuously teach MC protocol and the bylaws by reviewing a little bit about the bylaws and MC protocol in every meeting. Your members cannot know these things if no one trains them, but you will be surprised how fast they learn if someone does.
5. Train your MC how to ride in formation based on realistic conditions. Always emphasize safety first!
6. Ensure your officers know their jobs so that they can teach others. Insist that every person understands the functions of the offices and positions in the MC as well as the function of the chapter as part of the mighty MC nation.

Make Sound and Timely Decisions

The president must be able to rapidly evaluate a situation and make a sound decision based on that estimation. Hesitation or reluctance leads brothers to lose confidence in your abilities as president. Loss of confidence creates confusion and hesitation within the MC. Techniques to develop this principle include:

1. Develop a logical and orderly thought process by practicing different scenarios.
2. When time and situations permit, plan for every possible event that can be reasonably foreseen.
3. Consider the advice and suggestions of your officers and brothers before making decisions.

4. Consider the effects of your decisions on all members of your chapter(s) and nation. Never move without thinking or out of anger or emotion.

Develop a Sense of Responsibility Among Your Members

Another way to show your brothers you are interested in their welfare is to give them the opportunity for professional development. Assigning tasks and delegating authority promotes mutual confidence and respect between a president, his officers, and men. It also encourages subordinates to exercise initiative and to give wholehearted cooperation to the accomplishment of club tasks. When you properly delegate authority, you demonstrate faith in your brothers and increase their experience in exerting their authority, increasing their desire for greater responsibilities. To develop this principle you should:

1. Operate through the chain of command.
2. Provide clear, well thought out directions.
3. Give junior officers frequent opportunities to perform duties normally performed by senior brothers.
4. Be quick to recognize your brothers' accomplishments when they demonstrate initiative and resourcefulness.
5. Correct errors in judgment and initiative in a way to encourage the individual to try harder.
6. Give advice and assistance freely when requested by your brothers.
7. Resist the urge to micromanage.
8. Be prompt and fair in backing officers and brothers.
9. Accept responsibility willingly and insist that your officers live by the same standard.

Employ Your MC Within its Capabilities

A president must have a thorough knowledge of the tactical and technical capabilities of the MC. The term "stay in your lane" comes to mind. A president must know the capabilities of each brother in the club and is responsible for keeping the brotherhood "in its lane" even when some over-zealous brothers attempt to coerce the brotherhood into taking chances they have little likelihood of completing. Successful completion of a war-like task relies on your club's preparation and experience. If you plan to lead your men into conflict without proper training or mindset, failure is very likely to occur. Failure on this level can destroy the entire MC, so never let your feelings overrule your head. A loss will lower your club's standing on the set, decrease morale, and possibly cost brothers their lives or freedom. Be sure your club is truly prepared for and has the ability to actually accomplish something of this nature or find another way! Techniques for development of this principle are to:

1. Avoid allowing idiots to goad your brothers into conflicts beyond their capabilities.
2. Be sure that club expectations for ending conflicts always remain reasonable.
3. If the time comes for you to go to war, involve only those brothers capable of handling that kind of club business and can keep their mouths shut.
4. When it comes down to engaging in conflict, execute without mercy because there will be no turning back. Failure is not an option.

Seek Responsibilities and Take Responsibility Before you become President

Until you become Prez seek opportunities for professional development that will qualify you to hold the job when you get it. Actively seek challenging assignments within the MC to build your credibility and strengthen your portfolio. Use initiative and sound judgment when seeking higher authority. When given a task you must own it and take responsibility for your actions, no matter how things turn out. Regardless of the actions of your subordinates, the responsibility for decisions and their application falls on you. If you ask to be put in charge, know that any success AND failure will be attributed to you. This is also true when you become president! Techniques in developing this principle are to:

1. Learn the duties of your immediate senior officer and be prepared to accept the responsibilities of these duties.
2. Seek a variety of leadership positions to build your experience.
3. Take every opportunity that offers increased responsibility.
4. Perform every task, no matter whether it is top secret or seemingly trivial, to the best of your ability.
5. Stand up for what you think is right. Have courage in your convictions.
6. Carefully evaluate a subordinate's failure before acting against that subordinate.
7. In the absence of orders, take the initiative to perform tasks you believe your senior brother would direct you to perform, if present.

REFERENCE

MCRP 6-11B, Marine Corps Values: Appendix A, B

REV: July 2008

◊◊◊

CHAPTER SEVEN
The 14 Principles of
Motorcycle Club Leadership

Leadership Traits of the MC President

The Marine Corps has defined fourteen leadership traits that I want to convey to you in this manual. I will be adjusting my explanations slightly to make them more recognizable for MCs, but the purpose and execution of those traits will keep the same "esprit de corps" ("the spirit of the body").

I think that was one of the most important things STSC SS Nelson and GMG1 Maybee taught me in boot camp – leave things better when you leave than when you found them. That concept resounded throughout my Naval career to every command I was ever in thereafter.

The goal of this section is to familiarize you with these leadership traits and give you some examples of how they may be employed in your MC nation. It is my expectation that you will study these traits and once learned, you will work hard on your personal development to obtain the expertise of employing better leadership skills, with the hope that you will make your brotherhood better when you leave it than it was when you found it.

JJ-DIDTIEBUCKLE : 14 Leadership Traits of the MC President

The Naval service often uses acronyms to get sailors to remember concepts. An acronym is an abbreviation formed from the initial letters of other words and pronounced as one word or group of words, (e.g., ASCII, NASA). [1]

The fourteen leadership traits can easily be remembered by using the acronym "**JJ-DIDTIEBUCKLE**":

- **J**ustice
- **J**udgment
- **D**ependability
- **I**nitiative
- **D**ecisiveness
- **T**act
- **I**ntegrity
- **E**nthusiasm
- **B**earing
- **U**nselfishness
- **C**ourage
- **K**nowledge
- **L**oyalty
- **E**ndurance

[1] Dictionary.com

◊◊◊

CHAPTER EIGHT
The Leadership Principles
of Justice

Justice

Definition - Giving reward or punishment according to the merits of the case in question. The ability to administer a system of rewards and punishments impartially and consistently.

Significance –Displaying fairness and impartiality is critical to gain the trust and respect of your club brothers and maintains discipline and cohesion within the MC, particularly in the exercise of responsibility.

The importance of justice and fairness have been long argued across civilizations throughout the entire world since the beginning of man. Religious texts tell us that the Gods in the Heavens often argued these concepts among one another, demonic angels, and human beings. In Western civilization, wherein discussions of ethics and morality are concerned, perhaps no greater thought has been aligned to them than the idea of justice which can be found in Greek philosopher Plato's "From the Republic" or Harvard philosopher John Rawls' "A Theory of Justice." Scholars, educators, and philosophers have long held that justice is a crucial part of morality which is useless without justice being central to its core.

Many MC presidents fail to understand the stabilizing effect that fairness has on the club. When members know that everyone will be treated the same and justice will be delivered evenly there is nothing they will not do to support the brotherhood. But when there is an underlying feeling of favoritism of any sort, the extended family will split into fragments and cliques will form eventually causing the entire organization to implode. It is important to understand these principles so that you can mete out justice appropriately and ethically as a vital component for the future of the MC.

The Markkula Center for Applied Ethics at Santa Clara University published the article *"Justice and Fairness"*[1] on their website, in the Spring 1990 and a revised version in August 2018; wherein many principles of justice were cited to which I have modified slightly for application in this book.

Principles of Justice

The article identified the most fundamental principle of justice as defined by Aristotle more than two thousand years ago is that "equals should be treated equally and un-equals unequally."

This principle is also sometimes expressed as: "Individuals should be treated the same, unless they differ in ways that are relevant to the situation in which they are involved." For example, If Prospect A and Prospect B do the same work for the club, transferred from hang-around at the same time, and there are no relevant differences between them, then justly both Prospects should crossover to a full patch at the same time. If Prospect A gets to crossover before Prospect B because of their hair color or family influence, then we have an injustice—a form of discrimination—because these differences are not relevant to what is thought of as the proper considerations for crossing over from a prospect to a full patch brother in a traditional MC.

There are many differences that can be deemed as justifiable criteria for treating people differently within our system. For instance, we think it is fair for the President of the MC to treat his own son with more attention and care in his private affairs than he would the children of other club brothers; we think it is fair when brothers are sent to the front of the chow line and served by the properties before prospects, females, hang-arounds and supporters get to eat; "we think it is just when the government gives benefits to the needy than it does not provide to more affluent citizens;" [1] we think it is just when a club brother who has done wrong is given punishments that are not meted out to others who have done nothing wrong; and "we think it is fair for those who exert more efforts or who make a greater contribution to a project to receive more benefits from the project than others. These criteria—need, contribution, and effort—we acknowledge as justifying differential treatment, then, are numerous."[1] So, we find some discrimination in the club acceptable and others unacceptable. As President you will have to draw the line.

Different Kinds of Justice

The Markkula article defined the differences in justice as:

1. **Distributive Justice:** The extent to which society's institutions ensure that benefits and burdens are distributed among society's members in ways that are fair and just. When the institutions of a society distribute benefits or burdens in unjust ways, there is a strong presumption that those institutions should be changed.

    In the MC, we know from experience that feelings like this cause club splits, cliques and coupes within the club. The feeling that things are not just can destroy the MC family nucleus.

2. **Retributive or Corrective Justice:** The extent to which punishments are fair and just.

    In the MC, generally, punishments are held to be just to the extent that they take into account relevant criteria such as the seriousness of the crime and the intent of the offense committed against the bylaws, and discount irrelevant criteria such as a member's status as an officer, or how much time they have in the club as a member.

3. **Compensatory Justice:** The extent to which people are fairly compensated for their injuries by those who have injured them; just compensation is proportional to the loss inflicted on a person. Sometimes we see this in third world countries where a person may have to pay a family whose family member they killed via DUI.

    In the MC we see these kinds of compensations between MCs who will compensate one another when injustices are committed, and between members within the same club as well.

Stability and peace in your MC will be the evidence you should be looking for to prove that you are ensuring justice is being employed throughout your MC society. As the ethicist John Rawls pointed out, "the stability of a society depends upon the extent to which the members of that society feel that they are being treated justly." Your MC ultimately depends upon the feelings of its members – that they are subject to equal treatment. Rawls holds that the members of a community who depend upon each other will retain their social unity only to the extent that their institutions are just. The Markkula article also tells us that philosopher Immanuel Kant pointed out, "human beings are all equal in this respect: they all have the same dignity, and in virtue of this dignity they deserve to be treated as equals. Whenever individuals are treated unequally on the basis of characteristics that are arbitrary and irrelevant, their fundamental human dignity is violated."

Taking these concepts into consideration you can see that justice is a central part of the ethics by which you should operate your MC. Consider how you will apply the principles of justice towards the moral and ethical resolve of the MC. It is important to meet situations head-on and apply standards based upon the merits, qualifications, and efforts each member possesses and contributes. Presidents should learn to resist the urge to surround themselves with "yes" men or create fiefdoms of privileged brothers who have special liberty from the justice that is applied to others. Though this may appear to be a form of job security on its face you can see that in the end it will be a floating boomerang waiting to catch you from behind when you least expect it. In the end a president who understands that we are all equally qualified to enjoy the benefits, workload, and opportunities of the MC depending upon our appropriate positions and contributions; and that politics, favoritism, and personal agendas have no place in determining the look or feel of justice in the MC, will institute a system a fairness to which all brothers can be proud.

But how do you improve justice in your MC, especially if you feel like things were not just when you took over as the MC President? In fact, the feeling that things are not fair in the MC is the catalyst behind many takeovers, club splits, and changes in leadership at the top.

In her article "The Just Organization: Creating and Maintaining Justice in Work Environments" written for the Washington and Lee Law Review in the fall of 1993 (Volume 50 | Issue 4 | Article 8 | 09/01/1993 | Rev. 1489)[2], Karen Newman wrote a twenty-seven-page commentary about justice in work organizations. She gave a detailed definition and overview of justice in the organizational context, then linked justice with the moral quality of the work climate, arguing that each leads to and reinforces the other, then she delivered a report with empirical research on the effects of justice in simulated organizations. Finally, she concluded with a discussion of how organizations can become more just, and why justice made good business sense.

It is not hard to draw the conclusion that any MC organization, corporation, or business could benefit from her research and her article could be a good place to start when researching reasons and methods to increase the level, quality, and perception of justice in your MC.

Newman writes:

> "One of the most enduring themes in life in America is justice. Indeed, our national founding documents are based on justice. Our pledge of allegiance even ends with the words "and justice for all." One might just as well call Dr. Martin Luther King's "I Have a Dream" speech his "freedom and justice" speech.

> Yet the concept of justice, though so thoroughly a part of our national heritage, receives little attention in the workplace."

And even less attention in many of our MCs. Which, as President, is a tragic fact you can change. But do not expect it to be easy to change an MC culture steeped in unfair practices where some brothers are treated like they are better than the bylaws, while other brothers are not because once a privileged class is created it will be difficult to persuade those brothers to give up their superiority and allow themselves to be treated like everyone else. Expect and plan for virulent pushback.

Even though justice is an exceptional concept that people want to feel exists within their organizations, Newman suggests that successful employment of or importance of the practice of "justice is not well understood in many organizations." But she argues, and I agree, that organizations should seek to grasp it, understand it, and make sure fairness is a large part of the culture because "research suggests justice clearly has an important effect on organizations."

If you can imagine that so much in the MC depends on brothers' attitudes, work ethic, loyalty, and selfless actions, if you knew that all of that could be negatively affected by there being a lack of fairness would you not move quickly to improve the fairness within your MC immediately?

Newman also noted something that many would never consider and that is:

> "Perceived justice is more important for understanding human behavior than "objective" justice. Even if one could measure objective justice of an outcome or a procedure, the reactions of people to the outcome or procedure is as much a function of their values and beliefs as a function of the actual events. Thus, to understand the relationship between justice and human behavior,

one must examine justice in the realm of subjective perceptions."

Think about it. Even though you may be running a fair MC if there is even a remote perception of unfairness – that someone or some group gets treated better than others – the negative results to the brotherhood will be the same as if that perception were true—even if that was the furthest thing from the truth.

In the Navy we used to have a saying that addressed that very concept; "Perception is reality!" Often people believe in what they think and feel more so than they believe in true facts. Therefore, our sailors were required to, "avoid even the appearance of impropriety," because once an opinion is formed it can take a life all its own. This kind of thinking we have seen in recent global events when in 2020 the world experienced the SARS2 COVID_19 worldwide pandemic also known as Coronavirus. Despite what medical science proved, people believed what they wanted to believe based on their own perceptions, politics, conspiracy theories, in countries around the world. This kind of poisonous thinking can infect the MC also, so it is important to control perceptions as much as any other factor regarding justice in the MC.

Another definition to justice that Newman adds is that of procedural justice. "Procedural justice has to do with the process by which a decision is made, rather than the decision itself." With that, some thought should be given towards the perception of club brothers as to how the club arrives at a decision for one brother compared to another—in that the procedure itself is fair and just, and will be administered evenly amongst the organization, and if then the perception of the club members equates to fairness. For instance, if one brother is given a six-month probation after receiving a committee hearing from his peers who heard his case and voted for his sentence—there is the perception of the club that the procedure for carrying out justice was meted correctly. However, if another brother, who commits the same exact infraction of the bylaws, is given the exact same sentence, but instead of getting a committee hearing he is punished by the word of the president alone who says, "Take his colors and give him a six-month suspension, we do not need a hearing we know he is guilty," then brothers, especially the punished brother, might see the procedure as unjust. And they will be correct in that assumption. Why does one brother get the opportunity to have a hearing, explain his case, bring his witnesses, and argue the virtues of his evidence while the other brother does not? Even though a guilty verdict would result in the same sentence the procedure to get there was unfair, or the perception of the process followed is viewed as unfair by some members—which takes us back to the axiom: "Perception is Reality!"

Newman explains how our MC club members will make judgements about procedural fairness by drawing upon the work of Blair H. Sheppard and associates who offer a simple categorization scheme for analyzing procedural justice.

> "They argue that two types of judgements are made in determining procedural justice: a judgement about "balance" and a judgement about "correctness." Balance judgements require a comparison between the focal actions and other actions occurring in similar circumstances. Correctness judgements do not rely upon comparisons among actions, but rather on the intrinsic quality of the action and the process by which it was achieved.
>
> Balance is most easily thought of as a type of equity judgement—whether a process is fair, given what one deserves."

Thus, a brother's judgement about procedural fairness could be based upon his observation that two brothers facing discipline for similar offenses experience the same process (not outcome) in determining their guilt or innocence.

> "Correctness" has to do with whether the process was right, both in terms of the way in which rules were applied in the particular case and with respect to moral judgements concerning what is the right process. Correctness judgements involve the moral climate of the organization as well as the moral values of the person involved."

Newman cites Professor Gerald S. Leventhal's six criteria for judging objective procedural correctness:

> "Consistent application of procedures across individuals, safeguards against bias in the process, use of accurate information, correctable decisions, adequate opportunity to participate for all relevant parties, and conformity to prevailing ethical standards.

> The first two of Leventhal's criteria are specific elements of a more general criterion, *equality of access* to the process. The third and fourth contribute to *accuracy* by ensuring the use of appropriate information and correction procedures. The fifth is participation or *voice*. The sixth is adherence to *ethical* standards. Subsequent research has shown all of these criteria of fairness to be important in determinations of procedural justice, but the last two, voice and ethicality, are particularly important.

The last factor to include in a definition of procedural justice is its referent. Justice according to what criterion? Justice for whom? Justice at what level of aggregation?"

Table 1 shows two criteria used for judging justice, balance (the comparison criterion) and correctness. The referent level for justice determination may be at the performance level, refer to the system, or relate to individual dignity.

JUSTICE GOAL	BALANCE	CORRECTNESS
PERFORMANCE	Checks & balances to minimize bias	Neutrality, accuracy, & thoroughness
SOCIAL STRUCTURE	Balance of power to minimize domination	Consistency, trustworthiness, & integrity
DIGNITY, RESPECT	Opportunity for voice	Recognition of membership in the social system

Table 1 Justice Judgement

To improve the opportunities for fairness and justice to be a strong part of your MC culture there are some things you can take from Newman's studies to add to your environment.

1. Justice and rewards are not easily defined nor are they the same in every culture. In western civilization fairness, democracy, and having a voice are the pillars of society. But in other cultures, there are specific justices and rewards for specific classes of people. Motorcycle clubs must exist in the same way. Justice and rewards in your MC might not look like justice and rewards in a different MC; therefore, your MC's culture must reflect what is best for your brotherhood. But creating an environment where the outcomes and processes are the same for all members is perhaps paramount in establishing a system that works for everyone.

2. Perception of justice is just as important, if not more so, than the reality of justice. Establish your justice systems such that they are

transparent for all to see. Activities done under the cloak of darkness draw a cynical eye from all concerned. Avoid even the perception of impropriety at every level of your justice system. Where privacy is a concern, it must be protected but ensure balance is maintained between transparency and privacy so rumors will not prevail.

3. Ensure that checks and balances exist within your justice and rewards system to minimize bias and elitism. An appeal system is a good start.

4. Ensure neutrality and accuracy in proceedings and disciplinary hearings. Having one dictator act as judge, jury, and executioner is not neutrality. Allowing an adjudicating participant to simultaneously be one of the parties in the complaint is not neutrality. Disciplinary boards should be comprised of disinterested full patch brothers in good standing who have nothing to do with the complaint.

5. Ensure that there is consistency, trustworthiness, and integrity in the procedures, policies, and processes used to adjudicate disciplinary boards, voting, promotions, awards, and other programs to avoid even the appearance of impropriety. Remember, "Perception is reality."

6. Ensure a balance of power within the MC social construct and during disciplinary proceedings. In this way no personal agendas can be used to unfairly persecute any member.

7. Allow all members to have a voice in proceedings pertinent to them or club processes. For example, in a disciplinary board a defendant should be afforded the opportunity to mount a defense, including presenting witnesses, questioning accusers, and arguing the virtues of his evidence. In decisions made by the MC, full patch brothers in good standing should be afforded a vote at the table so their opinions can be known. In this way everyone gets a voice and is

therefore recognized with dignity and respect.

8. Build systems of recognition of membership in the club's social construct. Address members by their fair titles according to the accomplishments and privileges they have earned. In this way everyone is recognized within the brotherhood and has the opportunity to advance their roles, responsibilities, positions, titles, perks, honors, and privileges.

9. Remember to praise in public and criticize in private. This practice will enable you to maintain the respect of your men and officers even if you have had to punish their unacceptable behavior. It is a subtle quality of leadership that often takes some time to acquire.

These steps can help you build a feeling of fairness and justice within your organization from the bottom up to the top down.

Example - Fair apportionment of tasks by a Sergeant-at-Arms during a clubhouse spring cleaning. The men respect fairness and feel good about giving their all because they know they are not being called upon to do more than their fair share. As President you are responsible for ensuring that everyone is being treated fairly according to the bylaws. You ensure the Sergeant-at-Arms protects the high and mighty, all the way down to the new hang-around. You must keep sharp eyes in this regard because sometimes bullies will attempt to hide their spiteful conduct in plain sight. Imagine the Sergeant assigning the worst tasks to a Prospect he does not like or does not want to let into the club. Or perhaps he feels like he is punishing the Prospect's poor behavior by unfairly assigning him tasks. When does the fine line between punishment and bullying get breeched? As President you will often be responsible to decide. Make sure that if you find authority being abused you exercise justice fairly to correct the situation, leaving no one above the justice of the bylaws, no matter how important, or unimportant, they are – even if they are one of your most trusted officers, and most especially when administering justice to yourself.

[1] *www.scu.edu/ethics/ethics-resources/ethical-decision-making/justice-and-fairness/*

[2] *https://scholarlycommons.law.wlu.edu/wlulr/vol50/iss4/8*

◊◊◊

CHAPTER NINE
The Leadership Principle of Judgement

"Life is tough but it's tougher when you're stupid."

Sgt Striker
Iwo Jima

"The Stupid Shall be punished"

US Navy Submarine Captain Raaz 1993
Commanding Officer
Submarine Training Facility (SUBTRAFAC) San Diego

Judgment

Definition – The ability to weigh facts and possible courses of action in order to make sound decisions.

Significance – Sound judgment allows a president to make appropriate decisions in the guidance and training of his brothers and the employment of his MC. A president who exercises good judgment weighs pros and cons accordingly when making appropriate decisions.

My boot camp company commander STSC/SS Nelson used to often say, "Bunch! You can teach a man almost anything except sound judgment. That is an innate trait. Either you have it or you don't. And if you plan to go far in this man's Navy you damned well better have sound judgment!"

When I left boot camp and went to Submarine School New London/Groton, Connecticut I finally found out what he meant. Some of my school buds and I decided we would skip over to Hyannis Cape Cod for a little rest and relaxation on a 48-hour pass to chase the Cape Cod women and hope to score big! At that time, you had to have a specially signed piece of paper that allowed you to leave the base, go have fun, and come back. It was called a "liberty chit." I cannot ever remember being asked to see it by anyone, but if you were ever asked to produce it and you did not have it you would automatically be punished for being AWOL (absent without leave). Our liberty chits expressly gave us 48-hours of "liberty" from Friday evening until Monday morning and specifically required us to be back on base by 08:00 hours to muster in for duty and classroom activities. Well, needless to say we just did not make it back on time. Hyannis was about two hours and nine minutes from the front gate of Submarine School Base Groton, Ct. and since we got lost because we did not have a map, of course, we were woefully late. You see we had been chasing women up to the very last second, not leaving any time for emergencies or mechanical failure, or getting lost, to get back on time. Instead of taking two hours and nine minutes to get back it took us four hours and thirty minutes.

Now, if you do not know anything about the Navy, I can tell you that there are two mistakes you never want to make no matter what. The Navy will always look at you with skeptical eyes and punish you mercilessly almost quicker than anything else you can imagine if you make either one or both of these mistakes:

1. Show up late to muster (roll call).
2. Miss ship's movement.

Showing up late to muster meant your career could be seriously in jeopardy as the chances were that you would be busted and reduced in rank and paygrade! It could also mean that you were going to be kicked out of the submarine force instantly and sent to the worst place that submarine school would threaten fearful prospective submarine sailors they would be sent if they experienced failure. And that was an AO (auxiliary oiler) in the IO (Indian Ocean) which was rumored to be a place that was "Hell on Earth!" We never really knew if that threat were true or not but when submarine school promised us, we would go to an "AO in the IO" and there we would surely meet our demise, we believed them!

There we found ourselves standing tall outside of Command Master Chief Coons' office getting ready to meet our fate! Command Master Chief Coons was so ancient he had barnacles for testicles! At that time, he had like 45 years in the Navy which was virtually unheard of. I think he may have even been MCPON of the Navy at one time. It was rumored he had been in so long that all three of his sons were Master Chiefs too! My four shipmates and I popped tall before the ancient Master Chief. We had never actually been on a ship together, but shipmate was a term you called brothers with whom you served at any duty station including submarine school. Three out of the five of us were all but crying real tears – that is why I am not naming names (smile) – and one of my shipmates was just sick with the biggest end-of-the-world goofy look you ever wanted to see. But not me. I was not about to cry. "Let us just get on the transport and get to that AO in the IO and get it over with," I thought. "We will go there and die and that would be that no need for all of this pomp and circumstance about it—Hell our submarine careers are over," as far as I knew, "so why the hell waste all of this time with Master Chief Coons? No need to take his crap on top of all of this other bad stuff we were facing."

Once we were in his office and standing at attention before his desk, Master Chief Coons demanded each one of us tell the story, and since I was the one driving, it all came down on me.

"Bunch got lost Master Chief, we were asleep, what could we do about it? It was all in Bunch's hands!"

So, Master Chief Coons looks at me and says, "Is that right Bunch? It's all your fault?"

"Well Master Chief Coons I was driving, and I got lost, and yes, they were asleep, so yeah Master Chief it was all on me. I say kick them loose and I will go to that AO in the IO and figure out what I will do with my career from there since I will not be no submarine sailor no more. No need to bust us all just because one idiot couldn't figure out his way back home. When do I ship out Master Chief?"

"Bunch SHUT UP!" He screamed. "I'll ask the Goddamned questions not you! Do you understand me Seaman?"

"Yes sir, I mean Yes Master Chief." (Oh yeah, I nearly forgot to mention you never call a Master Chief "sir." That was like calling him a son-of-a-bitch. I was really batting a hundred right then.)

"So, geniuses what have you masterminds learned from this little experience that you would not do again if presented with the same set of circumstances?"

Seaman Genius One: "I have learned to never let Bunch drive again Master Chief next time I will take the wheel!"

Seaman Genius Two: "I have learned that I will never go to sleep again so that I will always know where I am. That way I will not be trusting Bunch again and wake up an hour late for muster in a town an hour away!"

Seaman Genius Three: "I have learned that I never should have left with Bunch in the first place Master Chief Coons! I will not be hanging around him anymore if we make it out of this with our careers."

Seaman Genius Four: "Aw Master Chief Coons it was not Bunch's fault. Hell, any one of us could have gotten lost. Next time I would probably leave a little bit earlier. I will go on that AO in the IO with Bunch, no need to send him by himself. He will probably wind up getting in trouble over there too and getting himself sent to Diego Garcia (another Hell on Earth place they threatened us with) or something. He is gonna need me to look after him Master Chief sir. I, I, mean Master Chief Coons sir!"

By this time, the Master Chief is about to squeeze his cigar until it exploded. "And young genius Seaman Bunch the obvious ringleader of this charade, what in the Hell, pray tell, have YOU learned, and what would you do differently?"

"Well, Master Chief Coons I cannot say I have learned anything, Hell anyone could get lost!"

"You have not learned anything?"

"Well, no Master Chief Coons but there are some things I would do differently so as not to wind up in another situation like this ever again in my career."

"Oh yeah, well you better tell me what that is right now because I am really getting pretty damned pissed off right now Bunch!"

"Well, first of all next time I would have a map and the whole route detailed out with a yellow highlighter going and coming. Next, I would make sure to allot enough time to get back planning for any unforeseen incidents like getting lost. But you know Master Chief what the main thing I would do differently next time is?"

"Yeah, what is that Bunch?"

"I would make sure that all of the guys bust their nuts and get their rocks off before midnight so we can get back on time next time; we were laying around with them pretty ass gals way too damned long Master Chief! I cannot tell you how much damned time we wasted chasing poontang in the first place! It took hours! Hell, that is what the whole trip was all about but rest assured Master Chief we scored big! You would be proud to know your submarine sailors all got laid—mission accomplished, it just took too long! I have gotta get us some better lines cause for the longest time we were striking out like a mothafuka Master Chief! And that is truly what took us so long to get back on time, honestly speaking!"

"BUNCH GET THE HELL OUT OF MY OFFICE DAMNIT AND TAKE THESE GODDAMNED MORONS WITH YOU AND DON'T YOU EVER BRING YOUR ASS BACK HERE DO YOU UNDERSTAND ME? GOD BETTER HAVE YOUR SOUL IF YOU EVER SHOW BACK UP IN MY OFFICE AGAIN SEAMAN!"

We darted out of his office feeling quite relieved that our submarine careers were still intact. I left thinking that the only reason we got out of there with our skins was because the Master Chief now had confidence in my future judgment to get myself and the fellas back to the base on time. The ironic thing is that I was not the senior man in that group, in fact a couple of them were senior to me but I was still somehow singled out as the leader. That experience taught me that if folks were going to consider me the leader, I had to use good judgment to make sound decisions in the future because Master

Chief Coons did not yell at one other guy that was senior to me. He yelled at me only. He expected me to be the one that got everyone back home and I knew in the future, in his mind, I would be that sailor. I made up my mind that I would be ready for the task.

I would have to start thinking very differently about how I was going to handle things with my shipmates and how I was going to have to be the responsible one, even when they were not. I had to become more serious, and I also had to plan for every possibility when we were out together chasing girls and taking road trips. I had to develop a sixth sense for trouble and be able to see into the future weighing two options against possible outcomes and choosing the best one based on my experience, the rules that were applicable to my shipmates and myself, and trends as they developed in front of my eyes. You see, the Master Chief was not messing around and another visit to his office would be a last visit to his office—we were on a kind of probation, not written, not formal, but just as serious as if it were a court sentence handed down. Master Chief Coons was watching, and I knew it, even if no one else did. And I knew his eyes were mainly upon me. I was going to have to develop good judgment fast to avoid landing us back in Coons' office—and since I had no background in exercising good judgment, I had to develop my skills in discernment and using good judgment immediately! That is when I discovered that STSC SS Nelson was wrong. Good judgment was not necessarily an innate skill that you possessed or did not. I realized that it was a character upon which you could improve. And thus, I did! We never wound up back in his office ever again and the bros counted on my every word as they made me the de facto leader of our group. We graduated submarine school with honors.

When you have sound judgment you can think through various scenarios with the discernment to figure out how things might turn out if you choose one path over another. Call it looking into the future with a crystal ball. Presidents who cannot successfully speculate (guess) about the future and get it right, will be short sighted and unable to make decisions beyond those that are made during the moment. You will be bound to make poor decisions that will negatively affect the club's longevity and its forward progress. No one can see the future with absolute certainty, so you must develop good anticipation skills to make the right guess most of the time. Without the innate ability to see into that crystal ball and foretell the consequences of one's actions, your club will suffer from your short sightedness and you will be an ineffectual president.

So, how can you develop the leadership skill of practicing good judgment?

In the 2018 article "Six Ways to Improve Personal Judgement" (*https://meliuscareers.com/blog/six-ways-to-improve-personal-judgement*), the leadership development team at Melius said judgment is "One of our ten essential skills for the next decade!" They argue that the ability to make decisions using imperfect data, creating the least bad solution, is one of the many areas where human brain power is more elastic than computers. The article goes on to explore how to improve your judgment in situations where leaders are expected to make decisions. It outlines six steps for leaders to use to improve their judgment in situations where choosing between different alternatives is essential.

1. **Be aware of personal bias.** Recognize where your unconscious preferences and motivations influence how you make decisions.
2. **Consider opposite points of view.** Good judgment is about making the best decisions rather than ensuring your viewpoint wins out.
3. **Accept your mistakes.** Good presidents are self-aware, able to take the responsibility for mistakes and to take negative feedback when required.
4. **Learn from experience.** Bank what works and avoid repeating what did not.

5. **Avoid flip-flopping.** Use instinct where necessary to decide and start to act.
6. **Automate**. Repeat and routine to free your mind for more important decisions.

In his article in the *Harvard Business Review "The Elements of Good Judgement"* (February 2020), Sir Andrew Likierman essentially tells us that in a meeting of brothers at the table facing a serious issue, once the facts have been assembled and the argument for and against the options are spelled out, but no clear evidence supports a particular decision, the brothers around the table will then turn to the Prez to look for THE answer.

They know there is no clear path and the way to head is murky. They know none of them have a clue as to which decision should be made, and they know that the Prez is sitting in the dark just as much as anyone else. So, in looking towards him (you) for a decision they are not necessarily looking for him (you) to have the right answer, what they are most looking for is the Prez (you) to exercise good judgment—*"an interpretation of the evidence that points to the right choice."* They are looking for him to make the least bad decision based on the facts!

Do not be confused in this. The club expects you to make those kinds of decisions as you are trusted, expected, required to know what to do when no one else has any clue simply because you are Prez! The MC will call upon you to employ all the wisdom, experience, and judgment of the "man-in-charge," to make the best call when no other brothers are capable. When they cannot figure it out, they will call upon you. The question is: are you honing your judgment skills so that you can make the right judgment calls?

Likierman defines judgment as:

> "The ability to combine personal qualities with relevant knowledge and experience to form opinions and make decisions—[it] is 'the core of exemplary leadership' according to Noel Tichy and Warren Bennis (the authors of *Judgment: "How Winning*

Leaders Make Great Calls"). It is what enables a sound choice in the absence of clear-cut relevant data or an obvious path. To some degree we are all capable of forming views and interpreting evidence. What we need, of course, is *good* judgment."

Likierman continues by saying:

> "A lot of ink has been spilled in the effort to understand what good judgment consists of. Some experts define it as an acquired instinct or 'gut feeling' that somehow combines deep experience with analytic skills at an unconscious level to produce an insight or recognize a pattern that others overlook. At a high level, this definition makes intuitive sense; but it is hard to move from understanding what judgment is to knowing how to acquire or even to recognize it."

In an effort to better understand the elements of improving one's ability to make good judgment calls Likierman interviewed CEOs, senior law partners, generals, doctors, scientists, priests, diplomats, and others to understand their observations of their own people's exercise of judgment so that he could identify the skills and behaviors that collectively create conditions for fresh insights that enable decision makers to discern patterns that others miss. He discovered several practices leaders could use to adopt skills they could cultivate and relationships they could build to inform the judgments they make. He called them the six basic components of good judgment. I have adapted his ideas slightly for how they would apply to presidents who lead motorcycle clubs.

Six Basic Components to Good Judgment

1. Learning
2. Trust
3. Experience
4. Detachment
5. Options
6. Delivery

1. **Learning:** Listen Attentively, Read Critically
Good judgment requires that you turn knowledge into understanding. This may sound obvious, but as is usually the case, the devil is in the detail—and in this case in your approach to learning.

Many presidents rush to bad judgments because they unconsciously filter the information they receive or are not sufficiently critical of what they hear or read. The truth is, unfortunately, that few of us really absorb the information we receive. We filter out what we do not expect or want to hear, and this tendency does not necessarily improve with age. (Research shows, for example, that children notice things that adults do not.) As a result, leaders simply miss a great deal of available information—a weakness to which top performers are especially vulnerable because overconfidence often comes with success. Presidents who wish to hone their judgment skills will have to become good at taking in information and avoid filtering it based upon preconceived notions. Leaders with good judgment tend to be good listeners and readers.

Likierman warns us of "information overload" impeding our ability to make good decisions, particularly with written material. A national president of a major MC receives volumes of email, phone calls, text messages, and IMs from all over the country every day. Confronted with such a deluge of information, it is tempting to skim and to remember only the material that confirms our beliefs. That is why smart leaders demand quality rather than quantity in what gets to them.

Overload is not the only challenge when it comes to reading. A more subtle risk is taking the written word at face value. When we listen to people speak, we look (consciously or unconsciously) for nonverbal clues about the quality of what we are hearing. While reading, we lack that context. And in an era when the term "fake news" is common, decision makers need to pay extra attention to the quality of the information they see and hear, especially material filtered by colleagues or obtained through search engines and social media exchanges. Are you really as careful in assessing and filtering as you should be, knowing how variable the quality is? If you believe that you never unconsciously screen out information, consider whether you choose a newspaper that agrees with what you already think.

People with good judgment are skeptical of information that does not make sense. None of us might be alive today if it were not for a Soviet lieutenant colonel by the name of Stanislav Petrov. It only recently came to light that after the fall of communism, one day in 1983, as the duty officer of the USSR missile tracking center, Petrov was advised that Soviet satellites had detected a U.S. missile attack on the Soviet Union. He decided that the 100% probability reading was implausibly high and did not report the information upward, as were his instructions. Instead, he reported a system malfunction. "I had all the data [to suggest a missile attack was ongoing]," he told the BBC's Russian service in 2013. "If I had sent my report up the chain of command, nobody would have said a word against it." It turned out that the satellites had mistaken sunlight reflected from clouds for missile engines.

To improve:

Active listening, including picking up on what is not said and interpreting body language, is a valuable skill to be honed, and plenty of advice exists. Beware of your own filters, defenses or aggressions that may discourage alternative arguments. If you get bored or impatient when listening to data, ask questions and check conclusions. If you are overwhelmed by written briefing material, focus on the parts that discuss questions and issues rather than those that summarize the presentations you will hear at the meeting. Look for gaps or discrepancies in what is being said or written. Think carefully about where the underlying data is coming from and the likely interests of the people supplying it. If you can, get input and data from people on more than one side of an argument—especially people you do not usually agree with. Finally, make sure the yardsticks and proxies for data you rely on are sound. Look for discrepancies in the metrics and try to understand them.

2. **Trust**: Seek Diversity, Not Validation
   Though it has been said, "It is lonely at the top," the presidency should not be attempted as a solitary endeavor. Presidents can draw on the skills and experiences of others as well as their own when they approach a decision. Who these advisers are and how much trust the president places in them is critical to the quality of that president's judgment.

   Unfortunately, many MC presidents give audience to brothers who simply echo and validate them. They seem to feel like it gives them some sort of job security. I have seen disgraced presidents run their MCs into the ground or get them shutdown altogether by law enforcement or diamond clubs simply because they regarded anyone who raised a concern or an objection to their decisions as a cynic and a naysayer, thereby disregarding their crucial warnings until it was too late to save the club . In these MCs we see that brothers who stood by their opinions were marginalized, suspended, or worse, put out bad—while echo chamber sycophants are promoted, uplifted, and given voice. The problem with this is an echo chamber of yes men who simply repeat what the president wants to hear is that they are incapable of offering sound advice from which the Prez can make an appropriate and informed decision. I am often reminded of the president whose member got into a fight with a diamond club member and he failed to get a sit-down initiated before it was too late. As a result, his clubhouse was shot up and some of his brothers were wounded. I wonder about his lack of judgment and how the decisions were made. How could his brothers believe that their problem would just go away? And many of them did not. When they voiced their concerns, they were scoffed at and put down. He thought their critiques of how the situation was being handled was an attack on his leadership. Instead, their warnings were quite correct. The rest was history. The club suffered at the hands of the president's inability to trust diverse opinions enough to plan for an outcome just in case they were valid.

Likierman tells us:

> "The historian Doris Kearns Goodwin, in her book *Team of Rivals,* noted that Abraham Lincoln assembled a cabinet of experts he respected but who did not always agree with one another. McKinsey has long included the *obligation* (not a *suggestion*) to dissent as a central part of the way it does business. Amazon's Leadership Principles specify that leaders should 'seek diverse perspectives and work to disconfirm their beliefs.'"

If CEOs and presidents of major corporations can look for dissent of their opinions and diverse perspectives as a catalyst for fostering good judgment, then as the president of your brotherhood you should do the same. Just because everyone is telling you what you want to hear, or even what they think you want to hear does not mean what you are hearing is good for the MC. Devise a formula for vetting your ideas, goals, and ambitions through your trusted full patch brothers. It will be a formula for the continued success of your brotherhood.

To improve:

Cultivate sources of trusted advice — brothers who will tell you what you need to know rather than what you want to hear. When you are recruiting people on whose advice you will rely, do not take outcomes as a proxy for their good judgment. Make judgment an explicit factor in appraisals and promotion decisions. Do not be put off by assessments that a candidate is "different." Someone who disagrees with you could provide the challenge you need.

3. **Experience**: Make it Relevant but Not Narrow
Beyond the data and evidence pertinent to a decision, good leaders bring their experience to bear when making judgment calls. Experience gives context and helps us identify potential solutions and anticipate challenges. Previous encounters similar to a current challenge allow the leader to scope out areas in which to focus their energy and resources. But—and it is a big but—if the experience is narrowly based, familiarity can be dangerous.

For instance, if I am considering opening new chapters on the East coast of the United States, I may question the judgment of my presidents who have only had experiences expanding chapters on the West coast. It may be time to seek the advice of clubs on the East coast that would not mind consulting with us on the matter. It could save us a good deal of grief and wasted time to contact folks with boots-on-the-ground experience in the area. In fact, when opening one of our chapters we did exactly that. An esteemed MC in Colorado worked hand-in-hand with us and the local dominants to ensure our acceptance into the political system. This is not something our people could have done efficiently without their guidance. We had plenty of experience opening chapters on the West coast where we were from and had thirty plus years of relationships with local MCs. But as we were moving Eastward, we discovered many of our ideas about the MC protocol in other areas were often diametrically opposed to the truth of the situation on the ground because our scope of experience was so narrow it was not completely relevant to the politics and protocols we needed to know and understand to expand into this new area. In making the decision to ally with an experienced MC in the area, we exercised good judgment that worked out well for the nation.

In addition, Likierman pointed out:

> leaders with deep experience in a particular domain may fall into a rut, making judgments out of habit, complacency, or overconfidence. It usually takes an external crisis to expose this failure, for which the lack of lifeboats for the Titanic is the enduring symbol and the 2008 financial crisis the moment of truth for many apparently unassailable titans. The equivalent today are those leaders who have underestimated the speed with which environmental issues would move center stage and require a tangible response.

Many times, you will hear presidents scream, "This is how it has always been done!" This rhetoric as an excuse to make a decision out of habit rather than recognizing moving trends and doing the research it takes to make a decision using good judgment. Falling into this kind of a rut could spell disaster for the brotherhood if one is not careful. If you have become a Prez who no longer moves around on the set as much as your younger brothers, who are out there on the ground seeing the movers and shakers who are up and coming, then you are out of touch whether you want to admit it or not. Do not let over familiarity and habit make you a complacent or lazy president.

Being out of touch can negatively affect your good judgment because you no longer have relevant facts about the matter upon which you are about to make a decision.

To improve:

First, assess how well you draw on your own experience to make decisions. Start by going through your important judgment calls to identify what went well and what went badly, including whether you drew on the right experience and whether the analogies you made were appropriate. Record both the wrong and the right. This is tough, and it's tempting to rewrite history, which is why it can be helpful to share your conclusions with the executive board, previous presidents, founders or OGs, who might take a different view of the same experience.

4. **Detachment**: Identify, and Then Challenge, Biases

    As you process information and draw on the diversity of your own and other people's knowledge, it is critical that you understand and address your own biases. Although passion about objectives and values is a wonderful leadership quality that can inspire followers to greater efforts, it can also affect how you process information, learn from experience, and select advisers. The ability to detach, both intellectually and emotionally, is a vital component of good judgment. It is a difficult skill to master. As research in behavioral economics, psychology, and decision sciences has shown in recent years, cognitive biases such as anchoring, confirmation, and risk aversion or excessive risk appetite are pervasive influences in the choices people make.

One of the interesting examples of this was how clubhouses I observed in an area kept getting shut down for liquor law violations despite seeing one club after another falling into the same trap. You cannot continue to do business in the old way if the rules of conduct are changing before your very eyes. There was a time when clubs could easily play the "accepting donations" game in lieu of getting liquor licenses but as cities are getting stretched by ever decreasing budget shortfalls, they are looking for new sources of revenue. They are cracking down on businesses that operate outside of the tax scheme and in some cities motorcycle clubs fall directly into their target profile. As a result, undercover liquor cops are busting MCs for outdated clubhouse practices. And yet, presidents, incapable of detaching themselves from biases and familiarity, continue to lead their clubs down the same dead-end paths. In another example, if law enforcement decided to change the law such that any MC that takes a patch from someone as part of a "patch policing action", causing the guilty MC to go to jail for twenty years—how could it be smart to continue to snatch patches for any reason? A president insisting "This is how we have always done it," in these circumstances would not seem to be exercising good judgment where the longevity of the club or the liberty of its members was concerned. When he announced at the next church, "Today we will be patch policing club X and taking all of their patches or else," club brothers with good sense would have to look at him and ask him if he had not lost his damned mind!

Avoid anchoring your decisions to outdated ideas of how things have always been done. Other things to consider are "risk aversion", being afraid to take risks and do something new, or "excessive risk appetite", taking too many risks or too big of a risk—again without being prudent enough to make a decision based upon sound judgment. These are cognitive biases that you must be aware of as the "Prez" so that you can avoid having them negatively affect your judgment.

It is precisely for their ability to resist cognitive biases and preserve detachment in decision-making that we often see CFOs and lawyers rise to the CEO position, especially when an organization is in a period of crisis and people's jobs are under threat. This quality was widely praised after the International Monetary Fund chose Christine Lagarde as its director following the dramatic exit in 2011 of her predecessor, Dominique Strauss-Kahn, in the wake of a lurid scandal. Although Lagarde was not an economist—unusual for an IMF chief—she had demonstrated her abilities as France's finance minister despite little political experience. And, undoubtedly, having been a partner in a major international law firm equipped her to approach negotiation with detachment—a critical capability at a time when the global financial system was under severe stress.

Success Is Not a Reliable Proxy for Judgment

Likierman warned us not to rely on success alone to determine the quality of someone's judgement. He said:

> It is tempting to assume that past successes are a sign of good judgment, and in some cases they may be. The multigenerational success of some German midsize companies and the sheer longevity of Warren Buffett's investment performance are frequently cited examples. But success can have other parents. Luck, the characteristic that Napoleon famously required of his generals, is often the unacknowledged architect of success. Those in sports can vouch for the importance of luck as well as skill. Grant Simmer, successively navigator and designer in four America's Cup yachting victories, has acknowledged the help of luck in the form of mistakes made by his competitors.

Sometimes, what looks like sustained success may conceal trickery. Before the Enron scandal broke, in 2001, CEO Jeff Skilling was hailed as a highly successful leader. Toshiba's well-regarded boss, Hisao Tanaka, resigned in disgrace in 2015 after a $1.2 billion profit overstatement covering seven years was unearthed. Bernie Madoff founded his investment firm in 1960 and for 48 years was seen as both successful and a man of the highest integrity.

Some of the biggest and oldest MCs we have ever known could point to their longstanding successes as a sign of having good judgment on their part. Yet when we see court case after court case where some of these presidents and their men are getting handed decades if not hundreds of years in jail sentences is it at all logical to assume that just because they have been around a long time or have risen to the level of being the largest or most powerful that they are exercising good judgment towards ensuring the long-term survival of their mighty MC nations? Remember, you are on top of the world until you no longer are.

When I was in the United States Navy, we required sailors to exude "Sustained Superior Performance" which was an idea of thinking that looked more at what you are doing right now to keep the Navy in the fight, than what you did yesterday. The requirement that you maintain "Sustained Superior Performance" forces Sailors to continuously rely on good judgment and sound reasoning to move forward and to never get bogged down in the ego-inflated thinking of superiority based upon past successes. We also used to say that "You are only as great as your last 'awe-shit' or your last 'atta-boy!'" This simply meant that you are only great as long as you are great and not one moment longer. You had to work hard to stay on top.

When you are trying to assess whether a brother has good judgment, do not just look at his achievements. Instead try to assess the brother according to the six elements described in

Likierman's article. Does he ask you questions or is he just making a pitch? How did he get where he is and to whom does he listen? What kind of training has he done? Does he like to challenge his own assumptions?

More motorcycle clubs could use this kind of thinking in electing officers in general, not just presidents. As I have said many times before the "I think," "I want," "I like," "I feel" attitude towards elections hampers club officers more often than any other obstacle that faces the brotherhood. It handcuffs the MC to working with officers who are popular but not necessarily qualified.

To improve:

> Understand, clarify, and accept different viewpoints. Encourage people to engage in role-reversal simulations, which forces them to consider agendas other than their own and can provide a safe space for dissent. If employees are encouraged to play the role of a competitor, for example, they can experiment with an idea that they might be reluctant to suggest to the boss.

I have actually practiced having brothers take on the role of officers in an enemy MC (devil's advocates if you will) as I considered how we would handle a sit-down during a contentious interaction. The brothers presented their viewpoints and hit me with everything positive and negative they could think of that the opposing MC might attempt to impose. We actually engaged a few other brothers, and the conversation became so terse that it was almost exactly like dealing with the other side. We developed scenarios for everything we thought might not go our way. The result was that we so prepared for the interaction that we were blown away at how expertly we managed it. We got everything we wanted and gave up nothing we wanted to keep. How often does that happen?

Finally, people with good judgment make sure they have processes in place that keep them aware of biases. Major decisions should require that biases be on the table before a discussion and, when necessary, that a devil's advocate participate. Acknowledge that mistakes will occur—and doubt the judgment of anyone who assumes they will not.

5. **Options:** Question the Solution Set Offered

   When making a decision, a leader is often expected to choose between at least two options that have been formulated and presented by their advocates. But smart leaders don't accept that these are the only available choices. During the 2008–2009 financial crisis, President Obama pressed Treasury Secretary Timothy Geithner to explain why he was not considering nationalizing the banks. Geithner recalls, "We had one of those really tough conversations. Are you confident this is going to work? Can you reassure me? Why are you confident? What are our choices? I told him that my judgment at the time was that we had no option but to play out the thing we had set in motion."

   Obama was doing what all good leaders should do when told "We have no other option" or "We have two options, and one is really bad" or "We have three options but only one is acceptable." Other options almost always exist, such as doing nothing, delaying a decision until more information is available, or conducting a time-limited trial or a pilot implementation.

Tim Breedon, formerly the CEO of the UK financial services company Legal & General, described it to Likierman as "not being boxed in by the way things are presented."

I am going to let you in on a small secret. You do not have to be a world leader to face the same kinds of crisis world leaders face. The only real differences will be the size, scope, number of people affected, and the amount of money it will cost. Like them you have citizens, an economy, soldiers, territory, and you face voters too! So, on a much smaller scale, you will experience incredibly similar crisis. Therefore, it is not out of the realm of reality that you should require yourself to ask the same kinds of questions they might ask!

> "We have no other options, why not?" "What else can we do?" "Have we considered all options?" "What if we do this thing that no one says we can do, what will be the consequence?" "So-what if it has never been done before, what would it take to do it—and what are the ramifications if we do?" Think inside what may be considered appropriate but also be bold enough to question what was previously thought to be implausible, or better yet, impossible.

Like, "Why can we not ally with that club just because we have always been enemies before? What would happen if we did? Who is to say we cannot?"

When You Have to Move Fast

Likierman warned us that sometimes situations cause us to have to move fast. In those times we really need to have our judgement skills in order. He said:

> In most cases, good judgment requires reflection before action. A pause for reflection may well make you less likely to be swept along by anger or fear and more likely to ask for additional evidence, consider reframing the question, formulate new options, or reevaluate whether a project is feasible. For example, when you receive a provocative or hostile email [or social media post], counting to 10 (or even 1,000) will help you build emotional detachment and save you from writing something you might later regret.

> Of course, sometimes you need to act fast. Starbucks CEO Kevin Johnson provides a case in point. One day in 2018 an

employee in Philadelphia called the police, asking for the arrest of two black men who were sitting at a table but had not ordered. As social media users started to call for a boycott, "his response was personal, swift and concrete: he fired the employee who had called the police, agreed on a settlement with the two men and closed all 8,000 US stores for an afternoon of anti-bias training," according to the Financial Times. The speed of Johnson's response almost certainly prevented a disaster from turning into a catastrophe for Starbucks.

Compare that response to the response from United Airline after passenger, David Dao, was dragged off a Chicago-to-Louisville flight in 2017. Instead of addressing the widespread outrage in reaction to the video of Dao's ordeal, which had gone viral, Oscar Munoz, the CEO of United, sent a supportive letter to staff members. Good for morale, perhaps, but not as a first response, and Munoz was criticized in the press as klutzy and heartless.

If you are in a bad situation in your MC, ask yourself three quick questions before responding:

1. Do I tend to act impulsively and then regret it?
2. Do I have insufficient relevant experience?
3. Are the stakes high?

If your answer to any of these is yes, think hard rather than react with your gut.

I recall when a motorcycle club was being challenged in a town by a 1%er club that had it in for them. The president told his club they would not be accepting any intimidation that night and the response should be immediate and hostile should they be confronted. When his men were face-to-face with the hostile MC one of them swung a knife and nearly severed an officer's arm of the 1%er club. The next day, the word was out that any club member seen out in the street would be shot off their bikes and blood would flow mercilessly should their patches ever be seen in that city. Overnight the club disappeared never to be seen again.

In another instance, a MC President ran into a bar and shot up members of a rival club because his men were outnumbered and were being pulverized in a fight inside. Sadly, his members knew this particular bar was frequented by the rival club and decided they would go there anyway just to ripple still waters. In the melee the MC President killed the President of the rival club and severely injured several others. Never in his wildest imagination did he realize that night would change his life forever, and that he would spend the rest of his natural life behind bars rotting in a prison as a result of his poor judgment. Would it not have been more prudent to order his men to steer clear and not to go into the rival club's bar to avoid even the possibility of a conflict?

After all, were there not 1,500+ more bars and clubs throughout the city they could have gone to? Instead, men's lives had to be destroyed and the hearts of their families broken for nothing. So many clubs have seen brothers killed, freedom lost, and families destroyed over the needless addiction to swing the biggest balls through the air rather than avoiding it all by using good judgment. And all too often presidents are to blame because many seem too unwilling to insist that their brothers take a different path.

But you are the Prez. You can make the difference if you are strong enough to exert your good judgment on puerile situations.

In another case a president ordered the killing of a president of a rival club, who was executed in broad daylight on a highway in front of dozens of people, only to see his men, along with himself, turn on each other in court and go to prison for decades (how many times could we tell this story). Remember winning the battle is not necessarily winning the war. Making a pointless stand will never suffice to sitting down at the table and coming to a solution, even if some elements of that solution will not be to your club's liking—sometimes a compromise is better than the alternative.

In hindsight, many bad judgment calls were inevitable simply because important options—and the risk of unintended consequences—were never even considered. This happens for a variety of reasons, including risk aversion on the part of people supplying potential answers. This is why thoroughly exploring all viable solutions is key to a leader's exercise of judgment.

It's not the president's job to come up with all the options. But he can ensure that the executive board and trusted full patch brothers deliver the full range of possibilities, counteracting fears and biases that cause the team to self-destruct. When all the options can be debated, the judgment is more likely to be right.

To improve:

> Press for clarification on poorly presented information and challenge your people if you think important facts are missing. Question their weighting of the variables on which their arguments depend. If timing appears to be a key consideration, determine that it is legitimate. Factor in the risks associated with novel solutions—stress and overconfidence—and look for opportunities to mitigate them through piloting. Follow King Solomon (a popular nominee in answer to my question "Who do you think has/had good judgment?") and dig out people's stakes in the final decision. A telltale sign is being oversold on a particular

outcome. What are the personal consequences to them (and to you) if their solution works or fails? Consult those you trust. If there isn't anyone, or enough time, try to imagine what someone you trust would do. Get clear about rules and ethical issues because they will help you filter your choices. Finally, don't be afraid to consider radical options. Discussing them could make you and others aware of some that are less radical but well worth considering and may encourage other people to speak up.

6. **Delivery:** Factor in the Feasibility of Execution

You can make all the right strategic choices but still end up losing out if you don't exercise judgment in how and by whom those choices will be executed. In 1880, the French diplomat and entrepreneur Ferdinand de Lesseps persuaded investors to support digging a canal in Panama to link the Atlantic and Pacific Oceans. Because de Lesseps had just completed the Suez Canal investors and politicians—failing to understand that building a canal through sand does not qualify you to build one through jungle—did not give his plan the scrutiny it deserved. His approach proved disastrously unsuitable, and it was left to the U.S. government to complete the canal by taking a very different approach.

When reviewing projects, smart leaders think carefully about the risks of implementation and press for clarification from a project's advocates. This is as important for small decisions as it is for big ones.

A leader with good judgment anticipates risks after a course has been determined and knows by whom those risks are best managed. That may not be the person who came up with the idea—particularly if the proposer is wedded to a particular vision, as was the case with de Lesseps. More generally, flair, creativity, and imagination aren't always accompanied by a capability to deliver, which is why small tech firms often struggle to capitalize on their inspiration and are bought out by less-inventive but better-organized giants.

We see this with the explosion of so-called "popup clubs" across the United States and around the world in the past decade. Though big clubs are insanely angry about it—as coalitions and boards are trying to do everything in their power to limit them. Popup clubs seem to be here to stay. There was once a time when it was nearly impossible to break a new club into a closed area, but now we are seeing them spring up in locations many thought they could not. This is because they are small and efficient. They are recruiting in ways the big clubs would never consider nor even accept. It is not taking one, two, three, or even five years to get patches in their clubs. Many are patching in members in less than ninety days. They are using the internet and social media to recruit and communicate (something major clubs would never even consider) along with the vibrancy of youth to multiply. They are not stuck to brand loyalty of only riding American made v-twins and they are accepting members who love to ride looking past stereotypes. Some are not even committed to continuing the race divide that exists between clubs. Instead, they are proudly starting mixed-race and even coed clubs. And have you noticed how many clubs are springing up out of nowhere these days sporting diamonds on their chests and state rockers as part of their three-piece patches? The only thing keeping them from overwhelming the set is that many still do not have the capability to deliver over the long term as they have not been in the game long enough to know how to defend themselves. They are often swallowed up by the big clubs, who are less inventive, but more capable of ensuring that their will power is exerted over the startups. The older clubs are better organized giants. But for how long will that remain the case?

To improve:

> In assessing a proposal, make sure that the experience of the people recommending the investment closely matches its context. If they point to their prior work, ask them to explain why that work is relevant to the current situation. Get the advocates to question their assumptions by engaging in "premortem" discussions, in which participants try to surface what might cause a proposal to fail.

Conclusion

Likierman concluded by saying,

> Leaders need many qualities but underlying them all is good judgment. Those with ambition but no judgment run out of money. Those with charisma but no judgment lead their followers in the wrong direction. Those with passion but no judgment hurl themselves down the wrong paths. Those with drive but no judgment get up very early to do the wrong things. Sheer luck and factors beyond your control may determine your eventual success, but good judgment will stack the cards in your favor.

I have come a long way since those early days in the Navy when great leaders like Master Chief Coons and STSCS/SS Nelson helped me to begin my development as a leader. I learned early to develop my skills in exercising good judgment. I have not always been successful, but I would like to think my club experienced more wins than losses when I was at the helm. If you are just now thinking about honing those skills it is not too late. I am reminded of a saying from the former commander of Submarine Training School Facility San Diego, California (SUBTRAFACSD) Captain Raaz, "We all deserver the right to get smarter later. Now that being said, the stupid shall be punished!" Good luck!

Example - A President properly apportions his club's priorities when dealing with a crisis where they may have to come face-to-face with a hostile MC Nation with whom they are having a disagreement. In this case making a mistake in the handling of the situation could lead to disastrous consequences. He brings his officers together, asks for their inputs and plans for various scenarios, considers his options, and prepares for the meeting that has been requested. He reflects upon the trend between the two clubs and plans a strategy for the meeting. He predicts several outcomes and accordingly plans the club's response. This is a president who is thoughtful and reserved. He plans his club's actions with experience and with the counsel of his officers. He does not react out of anger, fear, intimidation, or without research. He uses good judgement to move his brothers forward ready to handle anything that comes his way with an appropriate and effective response.

CHAPTER TEN
The Leadership Principle
of Dependability

Dependability

Definition – The certainty of proper performance of duty.

Significance – The quality that permits a president to assign a task to an officer with the understanding that it will be accomplished with minimum supervision. Also, the quality that permits the president to ensure that the MC will depend upon him to lead with minimum supervision to the best of his abilities.

Too many Presidents wake up with a God complex that consequently convinces them no one but themselves can do anything properly. They attempt to do it all, severely limiting the growth and morale of the brothers under them, producing officers and members who are incapable of moving the MC forward without their overbearing supervision. Some presidents take solace in that situation feeling that they have accomplished job security. This is not true! It simply means the MC will suffer from poorly trained officers if and when you are removed from office, which will be long before you planned to move on, without properly training anyone. You must beware that incapable men are seldom afraid of attempting to take over an organization even if they have no skills to properly lead – especially after they have been watching you and you have made leadership look so easy. Remember: Everyone is replaceable including a highly competent president! You can be deposed at any time and if you have not properly trained your brothers to lead when you are no longer present the chapter will suffer from the poor leadership you left behind, tearing apart what you worked so hard to build.

You must build a brotherhood of dependable men and officers if you expect it to be able to survive past you, instead of you, despite you, or together with you. It is about the success of the MC, not your success. You cannot do it all and you are wrong to try or think you can. You must learn to delegate responsibilities among your capable officers and brothers that you have trained. You must learn the power of delegation. It comes after you are able to depend upon your officers and men just as much as they are able to depend upon you! It frees your time, spirit, and mind from mundane activities that can be handled easily by others while you dedicate your resources towards greater goals that need to be accomplished. Goals that your position is appropriately designed to pursue but you will not find the time if you do not figure out how to delegate authority properly.

Yet, some presidents never learned the chain of command or the bylaws when they were juniors in the club and somehow, they have outlasted everyone and become incompetent leaders. Consequently these "information-light" presidents know so little about the jobs of the officers below them they are not competent enough to present them with tasks commensurate to their abilities to accomplish them, or even assign them duties as listed in their bylaws. How could they if they do not know the bylaws themselves? They are incapable of delegating responsibility because they cannot trust anyone. They find themselves trapped by their own inadequacies, trying to do everything themselves. If you find yourself in that position and you do not have what it takes to train and inspire your men, you must now learn what it takes. Doing everything yourself, even if you could, will only work to handicap the officers and men of the MC brotherhood.

Note: Some clubs do not have written bylaws that a President can consult, as impossible as that may be to believe. If that is your club this is a problem that needs immediate attention.

You may be a Prez with so little confidence in your knowledge of your MC protocol and lackluster leadership skills you fear any confrontation that may come from demanding a junior officer perform his job. Therefore, in a misguided attempt to avoid conflict, you wind up being indecisive and incapable of leading your men in any direction. Once again, the club suffers because it devolves into chaos over time.

Finally, there is the vindictive Prez who is a divider and not a unifier. He looks for every opportunity to turn members against one another to deflect the MC's attention from his own inadequacies. He cannot delegate authority because he trusts no one and the brothers do not trust him. He cannot depend on the brothers because he is too busy trying to divide and conquer them—turning them against one another. Often the brotherhood goes on for a long time before they figure out that it is the "P" who should go and not everyone else that has fallen casualty to his incompetence.

The certainty of the proper performance of duty means that the Prez knows how the chain of command works within his MC. He knows the function and responsibility of every job in the club as well as, if not better, than his officers, full patch brothers, prospects, properties, hang arounds, social clubs, associates, and friends of the club. He is competent and confident in his knowledge of the MC's protocols, traditions, customs, and the family's social construct. He is certain in the requirements of the bylaws and the local customs and traditions of the MC set that locally influence the club's actions. With the knowledge and confidence of command he can appropriately oversee the operations of the brotherhood. He can train, educate, and inspire his club brothers to act succinctly within their responsibilities to accomplish assigned tasks and projects with minimal supervision.

So how do you build dependability in your brothers and present them with training and opportunities to lead? First start with ensuring that you have tuned up your own dependability skills. In the article *"Increasing Your Dependability: The Key to Trust and Confidence,"* by Susan Keller for the Keller Institute ([1]*Kellerinstitute.com/blog/increasing-your-dependabilty-key-trust-*

and-confidence), Susan talked about some practical steps any person may use to become more dependable.

Three Practical Ways to Become More Dependable

1. **Seek Greater Responsibilities**

   "Take the initiative in seeking responsibility, Volunteer to help and to ask others what you can take off their plate. Then deliver! Those that do not seek greater responsibility are typically seen as lazy and unmotivated. But do not take on more than you can actually handle. That will ultimately bite you as you become seen as unable to deliver results."[1]

She talks about being able to deliver results and how that lends toward the club being able to depend upon you. So, you should be thinking about improving on delivering what you have promised the club you would deliver. And what exactly, you may ask, did you promise to deliver? Go look at the job description the club has written for your position. The club has not written a job description? Okay, then go look at the bylaws. What do the bylaws spell out as your core responsibilities? The first thing any president promises is to fulfill the job description—competently and to the best of your abilities. What if your bylaws do not spell out your job description? Well, then write one! That is right – write your job description!

Call church with the officers and any brothers that want to participate, sit down, and write it out. At the end you will have your job description—your promise laid out before you for all to see. Make sure to include your updated bylaws. Hell, while you are at it, write the job descriptions for all officers. Next, sit down with the brothers and find out the issues of the club. This is how a president seeks out greater responsibility. Too many incompetent presidents just take over the title and are happy sitting around with a crown on their heads. Uselessly they strut around, like the king who wore no clothes, doting on themselves while staring at their reflections in the mirror. They are good for nothing and the MC will not advance even one step during their rein, in fact it is more likely to take several steps backward. But a superior president gets busy getting busy the moment he takes office. He is like the tinkerer always looking for projects upon which to thrust himself. He seeks greater responsibility even though he has taken ultimate responsibility for the club as Prez, it is still not enough! He finds out what the brotherhood wants to fix, change, make better or needs, and then sets about putting together a plan to handle those challenges. In this way you will build your credibility in being dependable within your brotherhood. Being thought of as dependable is a reputation many MC presidents would kill to have. Once you have established your own dependability you can require it of your brothers.

2. **Live up to your Word**

   This cannot be overstated. A president's word is basically all he has. If you cannot keep your word, then you are valueless and not dependable. Remember in the step above we talked about keeping your first promise to fulfill the expectations of your job description. In this step we are talking about keeping your word generally in anything and everything that you promise above and beyond the job description of the bylaws. This is a basic building step in shoring up your dependability.

   > Keller states, "Deliver on your promises whenever possible. That requires being wise before you make them. Do not set deadlines you cannot make. Do not promise results you cannot deliver. Undersell and over-deliver." [1]

One problem presidents have is that many of them want to please everyone. It is just not possible – you simply cannot please everyone. Unfortunately, in trying to do so many presidents get into the undesirable habit of telling people what they want to hear instead of the truth of how things really are. Do not make the habit of stalling people with flattery and over-inflated promises of things they want to hear. You may be afraid of confrontation or have a problem saying "No." If you want to be thought of as dependable people will have to know that you will speak the truth even if it hurts their feelings or if the truth is ugly.

3. **Be Gritty**

> "You have to be willing to do both the dirty work and to take on a new challenge. Many a leader has undermined himself because they reflected an attitude of 'what was good for the goose was not good for the gander.' They tell their team by their actions, 'I am above doing that.' Their team will take on the same attitude." [1]

When I was establishing myself as a leader in the submarine world and later as the leader of an MC, I found that the men respected a leader who knew the job as well, if not better than they did. They trusted a Leading Petty Officer (LPO) who could do the job because he had done it himself, and what he was asking them to do was well within his wheelhouse. When the men described a problem to me, I could give them relevant solutions because I knew everything about what I was asking them to do. When the brotherhood believes in you, they will take on your attitude and follow your lead.

When asking yourself, "Exactly how dependable am I" take into consideration something Keller said when she drilled down into the concept of dependability:

"If we borrow from systems engineering, dependability is the measure of a system's availability, reliability, and its maintainability, maintenance support performance, and, in some cases, other characteristics such as durability, safety and security. Replace the word system with your name. Then ask again, 'how dependable you are?'"[1]

As Prez you cannot discount the importance of presenting the same personality no matter what is going on. This concept is called consistency. A leader that is all over the place because he cannot control his emotions is dangerous to the MC. You must not make decisions out of anger, fear, loathing, contempt, excitement, or revenge. You must act based on facts and not feelings. Take the time you are afforded to think through the situation so that you can present consistency your members will grow to rely upon.

I often talk about the "I think", "I like", "I want", "I feel," aspect of the modern MC. Presidents who react on how they "think", "like", "want", or "feel" about situations. They often find themselves having to revisit decisions and right the wrongs they have perpetrated against members once the truth is discovered that they lacked the patience to determine initially through appropriate investigation and due diligence of following process. Often these presidents bite on the first story they hear and react with emotion rather than prudence which always gets them into this kind of trouble. They have not yet learned that once you become president no one can be trusted without verification. Unfortunately, few brothers approach the President with the complete truth because they are trying to get you to decide something to their favor for their agenda. Therefore, you cannot just believe everything you hear on the face of it (prima facia), regardless from whence it comes. Often even your closest and most trusted brothers will mislead you or not tell you the entire truth just to win their way in a situation, especially once they have figured you out and know how you will react and know they can "play" you. I myself have had this happen to me many times over the years. Do not despair as it is human nature to try to win at all costs. It takes a special brother not to fall prey to such emotions. It is okay, fore warned is fore armed. You have to protect your reputation by ensuring that you are making decisions based on facts. There was a phrase frequently used by former President Ronald Reagan, taught to him by Suzanne Massie to describe this kind of fact checking: "Trust but verify"

Suzanne Massie, an American scholar, met with President Ronald Reagan many times between 1984 and 1987. In one of her meetings, she taught the President the Russian proverb "Doveryai, no proveryai" ("Доверяй, но проверяй") which means "Trust, but verify".

If you continually have to reverse your decisions because you did not do your due diligence in finding out the facts before you made them, your men will not find you very dependable. You will appear "wishy-washy", unreliable, undependable, and untrustworthy. Always trust but verify.

Keller's first axiom: **"Better Consistency = Better Dependability."**

Get your emotions in control and lead through a level lens. If you are ruling via the bylaws, it is far easier to be consistent than when you are winging it as you go.

Also, it pays to be predictable as a leader. I have heard people say, "He is an asshole but at least his fair and therefore I can accept him." So, what does that actually mean? It means this leader is predictable. Members can respect that he is not so easy to get along with but no matter what the situation he will be fair because he is predictable, and you know that he will treat each situation in a calm and rational manner. You already know what he is going to do before he does it. This has a calming effect on clubs. This is a dependability that members look for and expect, giving them something to count on.

Keller's second axiom: **"Confidence Grows as Predictability Increases."**

She told a story about a friend of hers who grew up with a fear of not knowing "which dad would come home from work. The dad who was cheerful and wanted to throw the football in the front yard, or the dad who had a hard day at work and exploded on everyone when he walked in the front door. In her mind, her dad was not dependable and the environment, as a result, was chaotic. It affected everyone in the home and the mother grew tense anticipating the husband's mood and passed this anxiousness right on to her children as she attempted to have the house perfect for his arrival."

Are you the sociopath no one can be around when you are pissed off resulting in tension in the club when you arrive because no one knows which president to expect when you walk in the door? If you are then you are not very dependable, are you? At least not in how the brothers will see you. The interesting thing about an MC is that alpha males will only tolerate this kind of behavior for a time. I have known presidents to be stabbed in the back or their brains blown out in meetings as a result of prolonged instances of being an unpredictable jerk. Think about it!

Keller's third axiom: **"Increased Dependability Leads to Increased Responsibility."**

If all you want to be is a "paper president", to hold the title, chase the women, bask in incompetence, and walk around with your chest poked out, then you probably will not take the effort to become more dependable. After all, if you are a dependable Prez you will probably seldom sleep, your phone will ring round the clock, folks will seek out your guidance in their marriages, relationships, jobs, personal affairs, how to handle their ex-wives, how to recover from addictions, and everything else you can imagine. You will find it a familiar theme throughout this book that as you increase each skill in leadership more responsibility will be thrust upon you. Your position in the MC will not be kind to your personal life, recreation time, or privacy. You will be invited in to have an opinion or offer advice at every level in your member's lives. This is the burden of wearing the crown in the MC world. Club membership is kind of like a cult for some people and the opinion of a dependable president is highly sought.

After you have established your own dependability, you will want to build the dependability among your officers and men. The best way is to get it moving quickly so you can establish your direction early. As Keller puts it:

> "If you allow people not to be dependable, other members will notice. Their stress will increase as will their dislike of you, the president, because they see you doing nothing about an obvious problem. On the other hand, if you deal with those who are undependable fairly and quickly, you will create a culture of trust and confidence within the MC."
> [1]

Six Ways to Increase Dependability in Others

Keller offers six ways to increase the dependability of the officers and brothers in your club.

1. **Be Clear and Concise about What is Expected of your Staff**
    No one can read your mind. You should not expect your officers and brothers to try. If you are not clear when giving orders and directions, you cannot depend upon the results you will get in

return. Building dependability among your brothers is directly proportional to the conciseness of your communication. Start your term as President by cleaning up your communication. Be brief, don't overtalk. When you give instructions have them repeated back to you so that you know that what you communicated was understood. In the Submarine Navy we called it "Repeat backs!"

For example, if the captain was commanding the navigation of the submarine, he might need to have the helmsman turn the boat from one course to another. He would engage the helmsman in a communication protocol that ensured the helmsman heard his commands, responded to them correctly, and initiated them properly. This litany of communication is standard for giving and carrying out orders aboard submarines. In the case of this example, the captain wants the boat to turn right from a compass heading of 090 degrees and steady upon a course of 180 degrees. He would say to the helmsman (the crewmember steering the submarine), "Helm, right ten degrees rudder make your course 180 degrees." The helmsman is expected to turn the ships rudder right ten degrees until he steadies upon the new course. But first he would "repeat back" the order to verify it with the captain before complying; therefore, the helmsman would respond, "Right ten degrees rudder make my course 180 degrees, aye sir!" Now that the order has been acknowledged via "repeat back", the captain knows that his order is understood as he gave it. His response gives permission for the helmsman to initiate the order, "Very well Helm." Then the helmsman turns his rudder and steers to the new course. After his rudder is right ten degrees the Helm would say, "Sir my Rudder is right ten degrees." The captain now knows his order is being carried out. He acknowledges, "Very well Helm." After the submarine steadied upon course

180 degrees the helmsman would announce that the order has been carried out as instructed, "Sir steady course 180 degrees." And the captain would respond, "Very well Helm you are steady course 180 degrees."

There is absolute dependability in the line of communication that happened between the captain and the helmsman. There could be no mistaking the captain's commands nor the helmsmen's carrying out of those orders. Now, of course you probably will never use this granularity of communication with exchanges between you and your club brothers but when I was a Chapter President and eventually the National President, I always thought about the conciseness of my communications in this way and ensured I was being "overstood" as my Pensacola, Florida President Ole' Skool would often say. "Overstanding" delivers dependability in communication. But there are other things to strive for like how does the MC communicate what it deems as dependability from its members?

As Keller puts it, "You must convey to your employees exactly how the company defines the word "dependable."

In the MC world, I would call an example of that as establishing a baseline for the minimum requirements of participation to be considered a full patch brother in good standing, a prospect pursuing membership, a probate pursuing a full patch, or a hang-around pursuing a prospectship. Surprisingly, many full patch brothers have no idea what the MC defines as dependable—as many have never even read the MC's bylaws. If they have no understanding of the rules of the club, how can they know how to be dependable?

For instance, a clear definition could be, "In order to be a member in good standing you must make two meetings a month, pay your dues on time, go on two club runs per month, and log 5,000 miles per month on your motorcycle." It would then be known that the club considers a dependable member one who does, at minimum, those established requirements. And there are many other things in the bylaws with which one might be compelled to comply with in order to be seen as dependable, including "making meetings on time", "not lying to the brothers", "never messing with a brother's woman", "never stealing from the club", "returning receipts for all monies spent on club business", and on and on. So, as Keller indicated, clear communications help to establish dependability in your club. Make sure you have a handle on that aspect of your leadership.

2. **Evaluate Reliability**

When you take the helm as president you should think of yourself as the leader of a business and be business-minded with your approach. To make your club perform at its maximum efficiency you must take action to improve the people, processes, and culture. This means you will need to have a grasp on the state of the brotherhood so that you know what to improve upon. One thing biker club presidents fail to do is conduct evaluations on their officers and guide them toward improvement or fire them if they cannot improve—you know, like a business.

Taking a business approach at evaluating your supporting team is one of the most basic things a leader can and should do. Often presidents think they are stuck with their officers because everyone is voted in, but there are many ways to get rid of derelicts. One way is to hold a derelict strictly to the bylaws. If he is an officer that regularly misses meetings and the bylaws state no officer shall miss more than two meetings, when he misses his third compel him to comply with the bylaws. If he does not comply you can then take the action to fine, suspend or even force him to step down from his role as an officer in the club. All this is done by the vote, of course, but as Prez you can push the issue. Have your officers establish a plan for improvement and hold them to it. You should see these officers as your staff. They are part of your administration. If they fail, you have failed. Do not allow that.

3. **Weed Out the Bad Apples**
Face it, every MC has a few "bad apples" that reside within. Most of the time we just try to ignore them while their poison ferments and putrefies within the brotherhood. We seem to think that if we put our heads in the sand these venomous vipers will simply cease to exist—"out of sight and out of mind". But the fact is they do not go away, they do not die, they multiply spreading their viral load from member to member until you look up and your infected club is divided – or worse good people start to leave refusing to be connected in any way with the likes of the poisonous ones.

In fact, one of the biggest problems I had as National President was firing people I knew were bad. I often procrastinated until the last possible moment before letting them go. And I got to see those same monsters come together to turn on me and try to wrestle control of the club. Even as I knew they were no good, I did not possess the hutzpah to fire them. One bad apple can have a spoiling effect on all members of the club, so weed out the bad apples in your MC. Pull them from the stem and toss them in the rubbish heap. You will be glad you did!

4. **Conduct Personal Interviews with Problem Staff**
"Once you have got a handle on who may be part of the problem confront the individuals privately." [1]

To evaluate your officers simply compare their actions to their job descriptions and how they carry out their duties according to the bylaws. If they do not have job descriptions, write them.

"Request a meeting away from the other members, find out why their history of incidents continue to happen. Sometimes, they were not properly trained, were unaware of the club's policy or were simply insubordinate. Ask questions to find out what they think the problem is." [1]

Explain how you plan to conduct your administration and what part you plan for them to play in it. Tell them what is important to you and your goals for moving the MC forward during your tenure. Find out where they want to go in the future and ask for their ideas and contributions. Get buy-in for your goals, if possible, so you can expect that they will be working with you instead of against you. Let them know that this is the time to wipe the slate clean and begin again from zero, but this will be the only opportunity for that.

5. **Establish a Suitable Solution**
Problem brothers will have varied reasons for their continued incidents. "For example, a valued [brother] who is consistently late due to personal issues beyond [his] control may require an adjustment to [his] schedule to improve [his] dependability," Keller said. "An inexperienced and ambitious [brother], but slow learner, may be worth the investment to retrain whereas irresponsible and continuously insubordinate [brothers]" should be disciplined and censured as they are a waste of time, money, and club effort.

6. **Update your Bylaws to Include Repercussions for Unfavorable Behavior**
I suggest that new presidents push for an update to the bylaws shortly after they get into office. If you have followed these suggestions and gone through your club, evaluated the officers and members, and presented your own dependability you will have the credibility to get it done. This is how you push the agenda of your administration using the church table, the gavel, and the vote. All is fair and done correctly according to the rule of law.

Example: A newly elected president gets to business right away after winning his election. He meets with his members to establish the club's priorities toward accomplishing a new set of goals upon which they all agree. He meets with his officers to establish is expectations for them in executing their duties and meets individually with problem officers he has observed as not performing their jobs before he became Prez. He gets to the bottom of their issues and works out a plan for improvement. He meets with problem members and establishes what is required of them under his presidency. He quickly establishes programs and assigns projects to move forward the club's agenda. He establishes communications protocols he expects to be followed by each member of the club to ensure dependable understandings of how business will be conducted. He moves to have the bylaws updated to reflect all the club has agreed upon.

◊◊◊

CHAPTER ELEVEN
The Leadership Principle
of Initiative

Initiative

Definition – Acting in the absence of orders, direction, or inspiration. Forming orders from chaos.

Significance – Since a President works without supervision, emphasis is placed on being a self-starter. Initiative is a founding principle of MC leadership.

Welcome to being President! Unless you belong to a national club you will not be receiving official orders again for the length of your term in office. Now you will be the one who generates the direction in which the club shall go. That is right, you are now the one giving the orders! You will create the inspiration others will follow. You are the shepherd and the keeper of the MC much like a military leader – particularly since traditional MC brotherhoods were started as paramilitary type organizations.

But being the head of a motorcycle club is not exactly the same as being the leader of a military command. In the military a commander receives his direction from his superiors, then issues lawful orders upon which the men are bound by duty and the uniformed code of military justice to follow, even if following them requires the ultimate sacrifice. However, in the MC brotherhood the President's direction comes from below, not above. Directions often come from the votes of the full patch brothers in good standing. The president then issues the orders necessary to accomplish the will of the club. It is the duty of the brothers, according to the bylaws, to follow the orders of their president and see that what they have voted for happens.

The bylaws determine if those orders require the ultimate sacrifice, or perhaps that is not the type of club you lead. But in our kind of brotherhood this special relationship makes the position of "Prez" both the highest and the lowest position in the MC. It is your responsibility to deliver to the MC what it votes for its direction, rather than what you figure you want the direction to be as Prez. Think of your capacity of service in office as being the "SERVANT of the WILL of the MC." Now, you may be thinking, "If I am following the will of the club how am I actually controlling its direction?" This is where the art of seduction, the skill of finesse, and the power of suggestion comes into play. The effective "Prez" will be able to gently guide the brotherhood through INSPIRATION! As an inspirer you can challenge the family to head in the way that you feel will be best, this is how many of the greatest directives are created. So, we place an emphasis on a president being a self-starter.

Initiative is a founding principle of Navy and Marine Corps Warfighting philosophy just as it is in MC culture philosophy. Initiative is the quality that refuses to allow a president to fall asleep at night until after he has figured out a dozen ways to solve his brotherhood's problems the next day. Initiative is what drives a president to outride every single brother in his chapter ten times over just to set the example of what a riding MC looks like. Initiative is what drives a president to order his Sergeant-at-Arms to check the clubhouse for lapses in security just because of a hunch or an uneasy feeling—and it turns out that he saves the MC from imminent attack in so doing. Initiative is what drives a president to take his RC to the status of MC, or his traditional MC to the status of OMC, or to expand his brotherhood nationwide transforming his club from a local mom and pop RC to a mighty motorcycle club nation. Initiative is the drive that comes from the inside of one's soul and being then pushes and pushes until that innate drive creates something positive and good. Those possessed with initiative simply cannot rest until they have accomplished great things. If you have no initiative, you can find it! Initiative can be achieved through practice, meditation, and mental determination. Do not allow your MC to be in the same place it was when you leave the presidency, as when you found it.

So, what are the steps to develop initiative? In an article written on Mindtools.com by the Mind Tools Content team (*Taking Initiative -*

Career Development From MindTools.com) they quote French writer Victor Hugo who said, "Initiative is doing the right thing without being told to." When building your skills in initiative one of the first things you need to consider is what is the right thing to do and then determine that no matter what it takes you will get there at the end of the day.

The article noted that researchers Michael Frese and Doris Fay define initiative as "Work behavior characterized by its self-starting nature, its proactive approach, and by being persistent in overcoming difficulties that arise in pursuit of a goal."

When you begin building your skills in initiative you assign yourself a mindset that determines that once you have identified a goal or a problem that needs to be solved, then you will be a self-starter in defining the steps needed to accomplish your task, acquire the specialized skills and knowledge necessary to bring it to conclusion, then endure all of the obstacles and challenges that will clutter your path, until you see it through to completion. All of this without anyone telling you, teaching you, or defining for you what needs to be done to make it happen.

As the President of an MC if you do not show initiative in leading you can believe your brothers will not show initiative in being members. Your officers will be lackluster, your recruiting will drop, your retention will drop, the club's morale will drop, and you will find yourself fighting a losing battle to keep the brotherhood alive. The bottom line is as I have said earlier—the brotherhood will draw its initiative from your leadership.

The Mind Tools Content Team defined six steps to developing your initiative that I will explain in a way that makes them relevant for MCs.

1. **Develop a Plan:** Developing a plan around what you want to accomplish is paramount to making it happen. Having a plan also helps you to identify the capabilities of your brotherhood. A phrase used often in the Navy Submarine service was, "If you fail to plan,

you have planned to fail!" This is true in almost anything you do. Although some folks can make remarkable things happen with spur of the moment thinking, this is an exception to the rule. "Planning is everything."

The article states: "Research has shown that people who have a long-term plan are more likely to take initiative. Professionals who know what they want and where they want to go are far more likely to show initiative at work, especially when the action or decision will help them further their career goals."

This is also true for leading your brotherhood. No need in planning to get a clubhouse if your brothers are too lazy to even pay dues on time. In developing that plan, one of your first steps would be to find a way to make the brothers become more responsible before even moving on to step two.

2. **Build Self-Confidence:** One of the toughest things about taking the initiative to do something is that because no one is telling you what to do, or how to do it, you are going to have to be self-confident in your ability to get it done. You will have to believe in you. You are defining the criterion for success and quite frankly if you are not self-confident you may find yourself too self-critical, or too frightened to get the job done.

    The content team says, "It can take courage and a strong sense of self to show initiative, especially if you fear that people may disagree with your actions or suggestions." One of the ways they say you can build self-confidence is to set small goals to achieve some quick wins initially. Also "push yourself to do positive things that you would otherwise be scared to do—this will not only help you build your self-confidence, but it will help you build the courage to accomplish bigger, scarier tasks later on."

    Before I had the confidence to serve as National President, I was successful at being National Enforcer first. The smaller failures and victories I experienced on that level prepared me for the big leagues I was eventually to encounter (which is why I am against two-year national officers. You need some "time on the pond" as we used to say in the Navy before you know what is going on). But there were many other accomplishments I had in my life that also prepared me for the eventuality of that level of responsibility in the brotherhood.

3. **Spot Opportunities and Potential Improvements:** You must also understand tact and politics and how to win friends and influence people. As the boss of the MC, it is your responsibility to sway and lead your brothers rather than bulldoze them with aggression.

   The content team states: "People who show initiative often do so by spotting and acting on opportunities that their colleagues or leaders have not noticed. They are curious about their organization and how it works, and they keep their minds open to new ideas and possibilities."

   Although this may be true, it can also create enemies as those in superior positions can take your initiative as plans to overthrow them. Unfortunately, this is one of the problems that comes, especially if you are going to spot areas of improvement that maybe your National President missed. When looking to influence people do not forget the value of including what it takes to get their buy in. That keeps you from having to go it alone—even if you are the boss.

4. **Sense-Check Your Ideas:** Dreamers are special people who suggest to us ideas that many of us never imagined possible, let alone believed that they could be achieved. Unfortunately, a lot of dreamers dreams actually cannot be achieved so you must always balance your dreams with a good dose of reality. Sometimes you may want to accomplish a dream that is possible, but it just is not possible for your MC... YET!

   For instance, if you have an RC that you want to build into an MC— that dream may not be possible just yet. Therefore, you would need to take the initiative to get the RC ready to make the transition later. Make sure your club can accomplish the goals you have convinced them to strive for before you exhaust manpower, resources, and finances.

5. **Develop Rational Persistence:** To quote Robert the Bruce, king of Scotland, "If at first you don't succeed try, try again", but this axiom can only go so far. There is a difference between being dog-eared and unrealistic. If you have made a good plan and sense checked your ideas, you should be on a good path.

    The content team says, "Persistence is the art of moving forward even when you encounter inertia or difficulty. People who show initiative often encounter difficulties and setbacks along the way, so resilience and rational persistence (where you listen to, consider, and appropriately modify your direction depending upon other people's input) are essential if you want to achieve what you have set out to do."

    They suggest that managing change effectively can make the difference between success and failure and my chapter in this book on the resistance to change may help.

6. **Find Balance:** I cannot stress this to you enough. The MC is about "WE" more than it will ever be about "I"

    The content team says, "While it is important to take initiative, it is just as important to be wise in the way that you use it. In some situations, it can be inappropriate to take initiative, and people who generate too much extra work for other people can upset others."

You have seen the MC Prez who wants to send his chapter to every party on the set to "support the set.", but he gets in the parties for free. His MC brothers have to pay for each of the seven annuals he wanted to go to that night. We have all seen those war movies wherein the squad leader keeps volunteering his men to go from one death defying mission to the next and it seems to me kind of crazy when he says to the Colonel, "My men are up to the task sir, we will take that ridge," yet he has not consulted with even one member of his squad—after they just got back from taking four other ridges and suffered 66% casualties. Think about it before you become that guy. You may be some sort of super-human in love with pain but are your brothers?

The Initiative to Start a Mighty MC Nation

When I became the first Enforcer of the Mighty Black Sabbath Motorcycle Club Nation, I was given a task by the Father, founder, and first National President Paul 'Pep' Perry. He told me that he wanted me to figure out a way to expand our culture across the United States of America, from coast to coast with chapters in between. He wanted me to show the world a club known for professionalism in riding and strength in brotherhood. He wanted me to be able to offer our family to men and women everywhere and to make our brotherhood a recognizable name as big as any MC out there. Finally, he told me that he knew I could come up with a way to get it done and that he would leave me to it and to report back to him after I had it done. There was no training, no preparation, no direction—in fact, he was asking me to do something he could not do himself, so he could not have told me how to do it even if that was his desire. There would be no assistance. I would have to come up with the initiative on my own to head out of San Diego and put our club in areas we had never been. The story of how I put that plan together and how the brothers carried it out as epic and one I will probably tell in Chronicle II of the President's Bible series. But first I must tell you how the United States Submarine Navy trained me, made me tough, and through trial by fire, taught me how to build the self-confidence in the 1980s that I would use in 2008 to begin to build a mighty MC nation! During my story see if you can identify the six steps of developing initiative above and see how I used them to achieve my goals.

So, I will begin this sea story by telling you that I was a submarine sailor aboard the Los Angeles class fast attack submarine USS Memphis SSN 691.

Let me make this first statement about developing initiative before I get into the story: For me, it came from wanting something I did not have, and wanting it badly; and the only way there is to get it was to go above what was normally expected—to accomplish that which others could not do or would not do! And I figured out a way to get it done! It is crazy to me when I think back about it—this all started because I wanted to come up with a way to work less.

Aboard Memphis I was an E-5 Fire Control Technician Second Class. My job was to track enemy ships and submarines and sink them with Tomahawk torpedoes or prosecute land targets with nuclear tipped or conventional missile variants. I also operated and configured navigational and time/bearing plots, as well as provided the officer of the deck or commanding officer with real time reports on contact bearing rates, close avoidance, and contact management while the boat was on the surface (submarines are called boats by submarine sailors, typically not ships though you will hear that term used from time to time). Along with our jobs we had collateral duties necessary to keep the sub operating, in good maintenance, secure, and seaworthy.

In order to be considered at least a journeyman member of the crew you were required to "qualify" submarines within a year of your arrival to any boat. If you had previously qualified on another boat, you were given three months to qualify upon reassignment to your new submarine. In Submarine School, before you ever saw a boat, you were educated that until you got qualified you were considered a low-life, air-breathing, scum-sucking, worthless, piece of shit to the qualified crew—and they did not mind letting you know this. This was because until you were qualified you lacked the knowledge to fight casualties that might befall the boat and cause a catastrophic failure from which the submarine could not recover. A qualified sailor has studied all the combined systems onboard and knows how each basically operates, what its backup system is, how to supply power, disable power, stop flooding, fight fires, and operate emergency equipment—no matter where the casualty was located, even if it was in a space where he did not work, or was part of a group of equipment he did not operate. For instance, a submarine qualified cook could power down burning equipment in the radio room even though he knows nothing about how to send or receive a message on radio equipment. Simply put, a submarine qualified sailor has mastered basic engineering level knowledge of high pressure pneumatic, high pressure hydraulic, firefighting, flooding, shoring, electric, electronic, and high voltage systems for casualty and damage control purposes. To achieve this feat a submarine sailor would have crawled these systems hand-over-hand and traced most of them down from source to distribution and almost every inch in between. He will have read books, scoured over schematics, read piping tabs, studied hand bills, memorized procedures and emergency steps, manned oxygen breathing apparatus, operated emergency breathing systems, learned ships security systems, attended, and graduated firefighting, flooding, and damage control schools, learned how to repel intruders, qualified as a marksman with rifles, and pistols, as well as mastered a myriad of other systems that he would have never seen before in his life!

The submarine sailor was given a qualification card upon his arrival on his new boat. The qual card had a list of systems with a corresponding signature line. The sailor was expected to read, interview, question, and ask qualified crew everything he needed to know about the system. He would then go to a systems expert for an interview where the expert would grill him about his knowledge. After the examination, the expert would either sign or initial the sailor's card for that system. The initialed card meant that the young sailor did not pass and had to go and get his "look ups" and then come back to get the signature of the expert. The initial also meant that no one else could sign that card except for the expert who initialed it. This was to keep a dirtbag sailor from starting an interview with one expert and trying to finish it with another who was not quite so tough on him.

Now, a non-qual was not simply left to his own initiative to finish this card, he was given one year and a schedule (I believe two signatures per week back then) to get his card done. His card was checked weekly by his leading petty officer (LPO) and if he was not accomplishing his two signatures per week he was put on the "DELINQUENT" list and assigned "EXTRA STUDY HOURS" to be completed after his workday. These delinquent non-quals were affectionately known as Goddamned "DINKS!". Non-quals were not allowed to watch movies, play cards, or partake in any entertainment. In fact, if they were found on the submarine doing anything other than studying in their off time, they would have hell to pay from any qualified crew member that found them. (It is my understanding that in today's Submarine Navy you are no longer allowed to call any person a dink or non-qual – a sad state of affairs if you ask me.)

I've only told you about the submarine qualification card – believe it or not things got worse from there. There were perhaps as many as a dozen qual cards handed to a new person coming aboard as ship's company above and beyond the sub qual card. There were watch station cards, ship's security cards, roving watch cards, weapons handling cards, nuclear reactor operator cards, navigation cards, shore power cards, sentry cards, and every kind of card you could imagine depending upon a sailor's job classification, we called an NEC. Each card had a time frame as to when it had to be completed, and each card could get you put on the dink list, so for the first year and a half on the boat a new sub sailor's life is study, qualifying, watch standing, and hazing. That was how it was.

Submarine time is different than civilian time that you might know, and it also very different than surface or air Navy too. Underway we operate on Zulu time or 18-hour days. Basically, you are on watch six hours, off watch six hours sleeping, and then you have six hours of work time when you are performing maintenance, cleaning, training, or if you are a non-qual you are studying your brains out. The surface Navy operates differently. They have day and night and only a few people are allowed to sleep in the day—most everyone on the ship is up during the day. If you have a late watch, too bad, you are up the next day. But in the submarine Navy you can sleep almost 12 full hours after you get your quals done and if your work and training is done. You can effectively get off watch, do your after watch clean up, hit the rack, and not wake up until 11 hours and thirty minutes in time to shower and eat before your next watch. This is when submarine life is really good for the more senior guys. But if there is a shortage of watch standers, because too many guys are dink, then you must work the six hours on six hours off routine we call "port and starboard" or more affectionately "port and report." Then your days devolve from eighteen-hour days to twelve-hour days, and I can tell you that is the most grueling workloads on a submarine. This was how it was at sea.

When you came back to port and docked the submarine our days went back to regular workdays like anyone else. We mustered at 8:00 a.m. and worked until 5:00 p.m. like most professions in the world where we did maintenance, training, upkeep, cleaning, and upgrading equipment. Then every fourth day we stood twenty-four-hour duty days. On duty days you worked for the submarine standing watches necessary to keep the boat afloat, the nuclear weapons guarded, and kept enough personnel to repel attackers and get the boat underway in an emergency.

During my days in the middle of the Cold War we were deployed at sea, on station, so often that almost 80% of the crew experienced divorce one year. Crew morale was in the dirt. I often found myself depressed because we were at sea on one mission after another—but going to sea was not the worst thing for me. It was having to stand duty every four days when we were in port that depressed me the most. That meant that you almost never got a weekend off. Every four days you were stuck on the boat twenty-four-hours and there was nothing you could do about it. It was called Four Section Duty Rotation. If you were a chief, you had Twelve Section Duty Rotation and officers had something like that, but junior enlisted were on the boat all of the damned time. And I was just an E-5 so it seemed as though I lived on that boat, and I was desperate to find another way.

One day I heard a rumor from one of my shipmates that even though we were in Four Section Duty the section leader could send men home if all the watch stations were manned and there were enough security forces and emergency navigation forces aboard. He heard that was how another boat on the water was handling their watch sections. That meant that you would be in Eight Section Duty Rotation instead of four. "What the hell," I thought. "How on Earth do they do that?" I went to the Chief of the Boat (COB) and asked him if such a thing were possible. He laughed and said it would never happen on our boat because we had too many dink non-quals and not enough leadership in the duty sections for a section leader to ever get enough men qualified to make such a thing a reality. He said, "Bunch stop dreaming. One day you will make chief and then maybe you will get out of Four Section Duty—but until that day none of you swinging dicks on this boat will ever work hard enough to earn that reward!" With that he guffawed and walked off laughing so hard at what I said that he almost fell over.

It was that day that I determined I would have Eight Section Duty Rotation no matter what it took to make that happen.

At that time, aboard Memphis, the duty section leaders were only E-6 First Class Petty Officers not E-5s. So, I realized that I would have to make E-6 before I could ever lead a section and for me that was going to take too long. So, I pondered, "How could I take over a section as an E-5," and the idea came to me. I had to take over a section from an E-6!

I went to my section leader, an E-6, a guy whose name a can no longer recall, and told him that I wanted to improve the watch-standing levels of our section by aggressively pursuing all our potential watch-standers and non-quals to get them qualified to stand all their duty stations. This way we would have the best duty section on the boat. The First Class was all for it. He went to the COB to recommend me for the position of assistant section leader. He told the COB that he wanted me because I guaranteed I would get the section up to speed. The COB called me to the Goat Locker, where all of the chiefs bunked, and looked at me with an extremely jaundiced eye.

"Bunch, I do not know what you have up your sleeve, but I am going to call your bluff. You will be assistant section leader and I can promise you that it ain't gonna happen Bunch. But you are damned welcome to try!"

"I just ask one thing COB, that you do not get in my way when I throw my weight around. You make me the assistant section leader and then let me run my section."

He laughed at me again. "Bunch, that ain't your section that is the section leader's section. You follow his orders, and you will be alright with me."

He dismissed me from the Goat Locker chuckling the whole time. I could hear him mutter under his breath, "These young startups. The nerve of this one!"

I left the Goat Locker on a mission. Over the next few months, I got busy. Since we were at sea, I called a meeting of our entire duty section. I told the guys that I was the new assistant section leader, and I was going to be requiring all duty section members to be qualified all watch stations within the next 90 days at sea. Everyone kind of laughed at me and shirked me off like I had not said a word. That was when I implemented Phase I.

Phase I: Make a Plan and Put it in Motion—I got qual cards for every watch station for the duty section. We had about five or six watch stations that were manned during a duty day that included roving watches, security watches, access watches, and others. For some watches you had to be a certain rank to stand them, for other watches only junior ranks could stand them. I showed up in each section member's division and handed him all the qual cards for every watch station he could qualify all the way down to the lowliest watch station he may not have stood in four or five years. For instance, I would hand a guy who stood below decks watch (a senior watch-station) a topside sentry qual card (a junior watch station). My point was that you should be qualified to stand every watch station beneath your level so that you could be of the most significant value to the boat. This move was met by instant rejection. "What the hell do you mean you want me to qualify topside? I will never stand that watch! I am an E-6, and I will never stand that watch!" My answer was simple. "You will qualify every watch station you could possibly stand and if you do not, I am going to put your ass DINK!" Now, of course I am talking to a guy that has not been on a dink list in four or five years. Here I am, a lower rank than he was, telling him he would get qualified, or I was going to put him dink. In the Navy that is called positional authority. It is when your position gives you authority over a higher-ranking member.

There was almost a mutiny. These shipmates complained violently to their LPOs, their chiefs, and their division officers. "Bunch is power hungry! He has lost his mind! He is only an E-5 how the hell is he going to march into my space and tell my men what the hell to do?" The poor COB. He had to field all these complaints. He would just look at me when I walked past and shake his head. "I have created a monster," I once heard him mutter. But his backing was resolute. When the Executive Officer came to him to tell him about the complaints he heard, the COB said, "I will run the enlisted men sir you run the officers. And what could possibly be wrong with ensuring each man is qualified up to the highest level of watch station he could stand? I've got Bunch sir, you let me worry about him. Bunch is doing his job. Let us let him do it."

I could feel the pressure. All the brothers in my section hated me. They complained to my section leader, but he was pleased as punch. You see, I told him when I asked him to make me assistant section leader that he would not have to do anything at all. He could sleep all day on duty days and never have to lift his hand to do a thing. He could put twenty-four hours in the rack on weekends and I would handle everything for him. He was not going to rock that boat for anything. "If Bunch said get qualified I would damn sure do it, if I were you, or you will be dink bro!"

Phase 2: Build Your Team so it Can Accomplish the Task—I began holding "School of the Boat" training after watch. I would train the section on the proper ways to get qualified and stand the duty and this training I required the section members to attend. That meant instead of getting twelve hours down in your rack, you were awakened to attend Bunch's School of the Boat. I can tell you the junior guys were mad because along with qualifying submarines, qualifying in their divisions, and qualifying their at sea watch stations, they now had to endure extra training to qualify our duty section watch stations. And the complaints continued vehemently. The COB told me once, "Bunch if we were on an aircraft carrier, I would have to assign you a guard of Marines to keep your ass from being thrown overboard one night. Do you think you are going too hard on the guys?" I told him "Hell no, I want my duty section all trained the same way, the right way, my way, so I know what I have put in them and what they can withstand!" He reminded me once again, "That is not your duty section Bunch that is your section leader's duty section."

Phase 3: Dink List—Well I guess some of those guys just did not take me seriously so about a month into our deployment at sea I published the delinquent list and some of the most vehement complainers and senior guys found themselves atop the DINK list for the first time in years. Boy oh boy you should have heard them howl! No movies, no cards, no dominoes, no novels could be enjoyed. If the COB or another chief walked past you enjoying entertainment while on the dink list may God have mercy upon you because they would not. The Executive Officer took the dink list down from the bulletin board immediately when he saw it, but within two hours the COB had it reposted. And so now these fellas knew I meant business. So, their chiefs and LPOs started putting pressure on my chief and my LPO. Next thing you know my chief is assigning me all kinds of extra work, extra training, and extra cleanup. Now I had to clean up for two hours after my watch, plus turn in all this extra work, teach School of the Boat, qualify my section, and take all kinds of hell from my chief, my LPO, and my division mates. It seemed that everyone hated me. Even the cooks were screwing with my food. It was almost like the movie "Get Shorty" only everyone was out to "Get Bunch."

Phase 4: Get Everyone Qualified—I was up almost round the clock I was working so hard. I got three or four hours of sleep per day. But within about two and a half months of our three-month deployment I had everyone qualified. It was costly. Even my best friends Solo and Morris requested to be removed from my duty section. They said I had become a true dick. I lost many friends on that run. But at the end of the run everyone was qualified everything they could be qualified in the duty section.

Phase 5: Takeover the Duty Section—When we got back to port setting up the duty roster was a charm. No one in duty section 4 had to stand port and starboard watches in port because everyone was uber qualified. The guys started coming up to me and saying,

"Bunch, I am so glad everyone is qualified, I was standing port and report at sea, and I am so glad I can rest now that we are in port. I really appreciate your efforts in getting everyone up to speed. My section leader just slept on duty days. Everything that needed to be done was handled by me. Whenever someone got mad, went to his bunk to wake him, and complained, he would say, "What did Bunch say? Well then that is what you need to do. What in the hell are you waking me up for? Bunch speaks for me." Now, I had taken over the entire duty section. Not even the COB went to the section leader when he wanted something done. He came to me. The duty section was effectively mine.

Phase 6: Unify the Duty Sections—Back then in the submarine world there were really two duty sections on the boat. The forward section houses Weapons, SONAR, Machinist Mates, Torpedomen, IC men, Yoemen, Cooks, Officers, Crews berthing, etc. The aft end of the boat housed propulsion which we could sum up in one word: NUKES. The NUKES were the crew members specially trained in the various departments of nuclear propulsion to include Chemists, Nuclear Machinists, Nuclear Electrical and Electronics guys, Nuclear reactor operators, so forth and so on. We were two separate worlds that operated in independent realities. They had their own duty sections (four section) and their own section leader, kind of, they were still under the same duty section as we were, but they had a lot of independence on their side. But the key to getting the plan in place was to make sure that all their watch stations were covered so that we operated as one crew for the purposes of my plan. So, I got their leadership to go along with my strategy and when they heard what I was trying to do they were down 100%.

Phase 7: Enact the 8 Section Duty Plan—I called a meeting of all the men one morning as they came to muster for duty. I said, "Alright guys we are going to be in port and starboard duty rotation today." You should have heard the groaning and moaning! "Why did we do all this work to get everyone qualified if we are going port and starboard all day?!"

I continued, "Good question. Well, I have some good news for all of you both forward and aft duty section. Since everyone is qualified to do everything all we have to do is make sure that every watch station has a watch stander, security forces and navigational forces are manned and the rest of you can go home today! Next week the guys that stayed this week get to go home. All we have to do is make sure to muster and ensure we have the numbers we need and then you go back home. Congratulations men you are now all effectively in Eight Section Duty!"

The cheers went up! The men were so excited they screamed and jumped up and down. Now instead of having to leave your wife and children for twenty-four hours every four days, after having been at sea for four months, you only had to leave them once every eight days. The men were running through the boat, calling their wives to come and get them and the other guys were so excited that next week would be their turn.

Of course, I asked no one's permission to dismiss the men and when the Captain, the XO, and the COB were told about it by a jealous duty section the next day, I was standing before the XO and the COB who were looking at me really crazy. When the XO exclaimed "Who in the hell gave you the authority to release members of the duty section?"

"Well sir, I have met all the security requirements specified in the Ship's Operating Manual (SORM – which is why I always stress knowing your damned bylaws, if you know them no one can screw you over) and the boat is well regulated. I have trained each of these men personally. Each school of the boat training has been documented and approved and XO you even attended some of the trainings. You said you approved. Naturally, I had to let some of the men go home and enjoy their families as there was no need to hold them because the boat's requirements were met."

"And what about you Bunch, when did you go home early?"

"Never sir. What I did was for the men, not myself XO."

The XO looked at the COB and asked him what the hell he was grinning about.

"Nothing sir. I am not grinning about anything XO. Bunch you are dismissed. Carry on sailor."

The XO muttered as I left the room, "Well COB you created him you deal with him."

Phase 8: For the Men Not for Me —So, the guys were good, they were running Eight Section Duty; everyone that is except for me, I was running Four Section Duty. Even though my plan was to get myself into Eight Section Duty, I found that as the leader I could not make it happen for myself. Not yet. Instead, I stayed on the boat every four days to make sure everything was going well, and I filled in where there were gaps in coverage. I figured I would wait until we returned from another deployment before I enjoyed the benefits of Eight Section Duty, that way I would be sure the section would operate perfectly when I put myself into the rotation.

Lesson 1 : More Initiative More Responsibility I was beginning to learn that having strong initiative brought on more responsibility that may prevent you from enjoying the very thing you displayed the initiative to achieve. I was about to learn quite a bit more about the lessons of initiative.

Lesson 2: Initiative Can Cause You to Become too Important to take Leave—We went back to sea on deployment half-way round the world for the next six months. And this time at sea I did not have to force the men to qualify they did it themselves. The members of our duty section policed one another because they now knew how good they had it in the section and how cool was it going to be to be on eight section rotation while we were traveling around the world and hitting liberty ports. So, needless to say, nobody went dink, Hell, their shipmates were not about to allow that. I kept running School of the Boat so that new members to our duty section were up to speed while ensuring that everyone was learning the same techniques and operating procedures that leadership was disseminating. I realized that you had to keep doing what you did to get to the top if you wanted to stay on the top. So, we continued to work hard.

USS Memphis was patrolling the North Sea hunting down Russian submarines at the height of the Cold War and that was quite exciting. We did some really unique and top-secret things that I will never be able to repeat but we would win Navy Expeditionary medals for our accomplishments on that patrol. There were many terrifying adventures on that run that put the crew in hostile waters experiencing wartime conditions when facing the enemy. When we came off station we headed for Norway for a liberty call, some rest, and relaxation. I had been working hard, non-stop for several months and I wanted to take some vacation (we called Leave or Liberty) in Norway, the city of umbrellas, and blow some steam off.

I forwarded a request for liberty chit up the chain of command so I could take some vacation. The COB instantly denied my request. Remember my duty section was in eight section rotation but I was not. So, I was not looking forward to spending every fourth day on the boat when I could be on vacation having a good time. I stormed into the Goat Locker demanding to know why the COB denied my liberty request.

"COB, what in the hell is this? Have I not worked hard? Do I not deserve some time off? What is this with you man – you are always ten toes deep in my rear end!"

The COB seemed amused. "What is it with you Bunch you do not know how to knock? You know the protocol for entering the Goat Locker now get out and come back when you can follow the rules!"

So, I stormed out, turned around, knocked, and requested permission to enter.

"Are you going to have the correct attitude when you enter because I would hate to send you back out again not to return until tomorrow?

"Yes COB, I will have the right attitude!"

"Well please come in Petty Officer Bunch but whatever you do, I would not let my eagle mouth overload my hummingbird ass if I were you. Now, how can I help you Petty Officer?"

"I was just wondering why you denied my liberty request COB, I WANT TO GO ON LEAVE!"

"You cannot go on leave Bunch I need you. Who is going to run your duty section while you are off lollygagging and shooting the shit on the beach? The boat has needs Bunch and the boat needs you!"

"My duty section? You told me that I did not have a duty section that it belonged to my section leader. Now you say you need me. You need me? And now I have a duty section? You do not need me COB. You cannot have it both ways!"

"I can have it both ways Bunch, I am the COB, and COBs get to have it both ways! That is why God made the Navy and the Navy made COBs! Just so we could have it both ways! We are direct descendants of GOD and so like God, COBs get to have it both ways, especially on their own boats! And you still have not told me why I should let you go so these idiots you babysit can fuck up my boat while you are gone?"

"COB, I have trained the guys they will be fine under the section leader."

"Fine under the section leader—have you lost your mind? For the last six months you have allowed this man to sleep all day, every day during duty days. You give him eight section rotation and I am supposed to believe he will somehow now magically run your duty section? I doubt he even remembers how to run a duty section! Do not pout Bunch it is not manly!"

"This is absolutely unfair COB, and you know it!"

"There is no fair in Navy and submarines Bunch. Get used to it. You do what is in the best interest of the Navy, and me being able to sleep at night while you are standing duty is what is in the best interest of the Navy Bunch—way more than your liberty is believe me! But I will play your silly game Bunch. I will give you your damned liberty but if those numb nuts fuck up my submarine, I will persecute you as though you were in Hell on Earth. You get me Bunch?"

"I get you COB."

So, off on leave I went in Norway, and I had the time of my life. Met some of the most beautiful women I ever saw, spent time on a nude beach hanging out with Norwegian goddesses, made love to 6' tall Norwegian blonde headed, blue eyed super models, you know, the whole damned thing! And then as quickly as it started my leave was over. I took the launch back to my boat the USS Memphis SSN 691 that was anchored in the harbor in Bergen, Norway. Submarines were not allowed to dock in port because we carried nuclear warheads, so we were actually moored at sea a few miles off the coast. The funny thing is they let sub tenders dock in port and they were the ships that supplied an entire squadron with nuclear weapons. Hell, they had more nuclear warheads on one sub tender ship than 20 submarines. But I digress. Anyway, awaiting my arrival was the COB standing topside with his arms crossed and his face furrowed in a deep frown. I already knew there was trouble.

"So, while you were off skinning your dick with Rosey Palm and her five sisters Bunch your very fine duty section broke the stanchions in the sail by lifting the number 2 BRA 34 antenna into them! So, if we have to go into drydock before finishing this mission, I am going to drown your ass at sea! THIS IS YOUR FAULT BUNCH! I never should have let you go on leave! Now my submarine is entirely screwed up which means you've got a problem! Now, you get this mess fixed Mr. Go On Liberty!"

I was so glad that the damage was minor and did not require a trip to drydock. I was able to get the stanchions replaced from a shop on the sub tender that made us new stanchions. We survived as a duty section, and all was great. I knew I would not be getting any more leave on that deployment. I never even mentioned it again. My initiative had made me a valuable component of the boat. This was not my plan, as I was only looking to go on Eight Section Duty. Now, I could not even take leave and go on vacation.

Lesson 3: Initiative Can Make You the Go-To, by Accident—After our deployment was over we headed back to Norfolk Submarine Squadron 8 (SUBRON8), our homeport for refit. We were two days out and we would be at home for the rest of the year. Man was that going to be a good time. I would finally be in Eight Section Duty. Despite our one screw up, I felt my duty section was really tight and all would go well. That is when the COB hit me with another one of many gut punches I would experience in the Navy. I happened to walk by the bulletin board and glanced at the duty section roster. I was aghast at what I observed! Almost all of my qualified watch standers WERE removed from my duty section on the watch bill! They were all assigned to different duty sections! My hard work of the past six months was all gone down the drain. I snatched the duty section roster from the bulletin board and ran to the Goat Locker. I busted through the door without knocking and all the chiefs looked at me like… "Have you lost your damned mind?"

I screamed at the COB, "What the hell is this crap COB?"

"Is there something wrong young Petty Officer Bunch?" he asked with a wry smile.

"You took my goddamned duty section and broke it up! You stole all of my people from me COB!"

The COB elevated his voice at me for the first time ever and said, "That's my duty section bunch, not yours! in fact, last time I checked even you belong to me too bunch because this is all my shit! mine! and I will do with this shit what the hell I want to do with it sailor! and you will say, "yes cob" and you will make it goddamned happen! and you will be glad to make it happen! you get me son?"

"I get you COB."

Defeated, I turned, lowered my head, and began to walk out of the Goat Locker. I was crushed. I could not figure out why he did me and the guys so wrong.

"BUNCH," he yelled. "GET BACK IN HERE! Son, I have the responsibility to ensure that each duty section has the right number of qualified men to keep this submarine correct in port no matter what happens. The other sections were very short on qualified watch standers, and you built a duty section with a glut full of overly qualified people. So, I had to take them and divide them equally between the duty sections! The entire boat is my responsibility not just one duty section. I know you might not feel so great about it Bunch but you must understand the mission of the submarine comes first. I could fuss and fight with those other section leaders that could never qualify a section so fast, or I could balance the duty sections out using the qualified people I had in all of the sections. So that is what I did Bunch. Thank you for your contribution. But I have no doubt that you will prevail and create another superior duty section. You did it once you can do it again.

"Why should I, you will just take them again and 'balance' the duty sections."

"Because you are now in charge of building an entire boat full of duty section qualified sailors. You will run the training program for all the sections. If you put someone on the dink list, then dink they will be! There will be no pushback. You will ensure that all sections are capable of doing what you did with your section, and you have my 100% backing. You have created yourself a job Bunch, one that I know you will excel at because you have already exceled at building a huge thing aboard Memphis. Good work Bunch, I told you I needed you in Norway and I meant that. I was sick when I knew you were not going to be aboard because I knew you would never allow the guys to screw up. And just as I thought the second you were not there to look over their shoulders, they lost focus and screwed up my boat. Now carry-on Bunch and do good things."

I was not happy but from the initiative of my hard work I became a respected contributor aboard the submarine. I never actually got to participate in Eight Section Duty rotation but many men in my duty sections got to enjoy increased time at home with their young families and loved ones. I was very proud of that. I made a positive difference in the quality of life for my men.

As for me, I went in a new direction. I was so motivated from the response from the COB that I focused my gaze to qualifying the highly respected at sea duty station as Chief of the Watch, which during my time, was an almost impossible task for an E-5 to accomplish. I knew that qualifying Chief of the Watch on a submarine would put me in eight section rotation at sea (most of the crew was in three section rotation) and would put me in Twelve Section Duty rotation in port! It would also make me a legend among my crew and one of the most powerful enlisted men on the ship. You see the Duty Chief, Chief of the Watch, and Diving Officer positions were the highest enlisted positions a non-nuke could qualify. There was also the position of Contact Coordinator which on many boats was not available for enlisted men to qualify. Typically, only E6, E7, E8, E9, O1, O2, and O3 qualified those watch stations. So that was the most senior enlisted and junior officers who were mandated to complete those quals, but an E-5, that was not even a consideration. I asked a few old timers on the boat, and they told me that it was quite common during WWII and the diesel boat era but was quite uncommon aboard Los Angeles class 688 nuclear powered submarines. Still, it was not against the rules for me to qualify but it was going to be next to impossible to do. There would be no way that the XO and CO were going to let a twenty something year old E-5 sit Chief of the Watch, Duty Chief, or Diving Officer of the Watch, I was told. Well, we would have to see about that! So, I set my mind to it and the accomplishment of those goals is yet another story about using your skills in initiative that I may one day tell. But what I will say is that the journey was one of the hardest I ever faced aboard submarines. And the lessons I learned in initiative in 1987 to 1989 gave me the skills I exploited to expand the Mighty Black Sabbath Motorcycle Club Nation from a mom-and-pop San Diego MC to occupying chapters and territories from state to state across the United States some twenty-one-years later beginning in 2008, which led to my eventually becoming our second National President.

Initiative will give you the drive to move forward as a leader when everyone else doubts, hates, impedes, and lies about you. Your self-confidence will keep you steadfast and your moral compass will always point your needle true North. Use the six rules above to improve those skills and then go forth and be Prez!

"Good" Example – The club has nowhere to have meetings, make money, or gather to fellowship so you ask for someone to make a motion in the meeting for the MC to get a clubhouse, and once seconded, you ask permission to take the floor and layout a plan for getting it done. Once the club votes in the affirmative to make it happen you take the initiative to provide each committee with a set of executive plans to accomplish the mission. Then you train the VP to run the project and make weekly reports to you about the

progress, constantly reemphasizing areas of concentration for the VP to improve until the clubhouse is purchased, and the MC moves in. This plan came entirely from you, but the men believe they did it themselves.

"Bad" Example – You decide the MC needs a clubhouse, so you go out and find it with the VP and then put the club's money down without consulting any other brothers or obtaining a club vote – while also putting the lease in your name alone. The next thing the brothers know is you are telling them what day move in will be while you keep the keys to the clubhouse between you and the VP, refusing to let anyone have access until you show up after work, or they have to call you first and wait for you to show up to gain access to the "MC's" clubhouse. Sure, there was some initiative there, but it was not for the right purpose. Was it?

◊◊◊

CHAPTER TWELVE
The Leadership Principle
of Decisiveness

Decisiveness

Definition - Ability to make decisions promptly and to announce them in a clear, forceful manner.

Significance - The quality of character which guides a person to accumulate all available facts, weigh the facts, choose, and announce the best alternative. It is often better that a decision be made promptly than a potentially better one be made at the expense of more time.

As President, members will always look to you for the answer, whether you have the best one or not. Be prepared as one of the biggest burdens of leadership is the burden of being trusted with the expectation to solve any situation even if no obvious route of escape is available. It comes a part of the MC president's job. Often you will have the good fortune of having your trusted executive staff and the vote of the full patch brothers in good standing to help illuminate your path. But what about times of emergency? What do you do when there is no time to reflect, and you have to make decisions that can have long term consequences towards members' safety, health, club-longevity, and the brotherhood's freedom? How do you make decisive decisions when you have no clue as to what you are supposed to do, or when something so unexpected occurs it defies all logic, planning, and preparedness? This is when the decisiveness comes into play because an effective leader can ill-afford to be indecisive during a crisis. In the MC world an indecisive president can get his men killed. So, how does one avoid indecisiveness in battle or other urgent and life-altering situations?

Let us examine indecisiveness and get to know it for what it really is and how it can stop us in our tracks, rendering us unable to decide in dicey situations, when we most need to make decisions:

In his article "Aversive Indecisiveness Predicts Risks for and Symptoms of Anxiety and Depression Over Avoidant Indecisiveness" ([1]*https://link.springer.com/article/10.1007/s10942-018-0302-x*) July 17, 2020, Sean A. Lauderdale defines indecisiveness as "a maladaptive trait resulting in difficulty making decisions across time and situations. Indecisiveness is positively correlated with measures of anxiety, worry, and depression and has been listed as a symptom of a major depressive disorder for decades."

Sean goes on to report that indecisiveness can be represented by two distinct scopes:

> "**Aversive indecisiveness**, represented by anticipation of negative consequences as a result of decision-making, is associated with behavioral inhibition and anticipated regret about decisional choices. **Avoidant indecisiveness**, represented by a preference for decisional delay and avoidance, is associated with a withdrawal from reinforcement." [1]

Indecisiveness can lead to a mental disorder known as "aboulomania". According to the Wikipedia entry (https://en.wikipedia.org/wiki/Aboulomania), "Aboulomania (from Greek a–, meaning 'without', and boulē, meaning 'will') is a mental disorder in which the patient displays pathological indecisiveness. It is typically associated with anxiety, stress, depression, and mental anguish, and can severely affect one's ability to function socially."

Many of the same factors that contribute to aversive indecisiveness, avoidant indecisiveness, and even aboulomania are also apparent in nearly every kind of emergency or crisis a club will face. Therefore, it should not be unexpected that the effects of an emergency or a never-before-seen crisis can effectively render a normally decisive president incapable of making decisions.

Other factors that can contribute to indecisiveness include:

1. Mental Anguish
2. Anxiety

3. Stress
4. Depression

Mental Anguish:

Mental anguish can occur when the motorcycle club is confronted with a significant crisis that causes you to suffer from feelings of not knowing the repercussions of your decisions could have on the future of the club, its members lives, or that of the greater MC set.

Cornell law (*https://www.law.cornell.edu/wex/mental_anguish#*) defines mental anguish as:

> "A type of suffering that can be compensated in a personal injury case, generally meaning significant mental suffering that may include fright, feelings of distress, anxiety, depression, trauma, or grief."

Wikipedia (*https://en.wikipedia.org/wiki/Anguish*) defines mental anguish as:

> A high degree of mental pain and distress that is more than mere worry, anxiety, vexation, embarrassment, or anger of such a nature, duration, and severity that it causes a substantial disruption in the injured person's daily routine. Anguish is an emotion that is related to misery, dread, and despair.

Anguish can result in mental pain, physical pain or an emotional pain that originates from a non-physical source.

In their article "What are the Five Signs of Emotional Suffering and the Healthy Habits of Emotional Wellbeing? ", the Campaign to Change Direction identified five signs to look for to determine if you may be suffering from mental anguish
([2]*https://giveanhour.org/changedirection/*):

1. **Personality Change:** "Sudden or gradual changes in the way you typically behave. Behaving in ways that do not fit with your values, or people say you seem different."[2]

2. **Agitated:** "You seem uncharacteristically angry, anxious, agitated, or moody. You may notice that you have more frequent problems controlling your temper. You may be constantly irritable or unable to calm down. In more extreme situations of this kind, you may be unable to sleep or may explode in anger at a minor problem." [2]

3. **Withdrawn:** "You withdraw or isolate yourself from other people. You may pull away from family and friends [including your most trusted club brothers] and stop taking part in activities you used to enjoy. In more severe cases you may start failing to make it to work or [club functions.]" [2]

4. **Poor Self Care:** "You stop taking care of yourself and may engage in risky behavior. You may notice a change in your level of personal care or an act of poor judgment. For instance, you may let your personal hygiene deteriorate, you may start abusing alcohol or illicit substances or start engaging in other self-destructive behavior that may alienate trusted persons." [2]

5. **Hopelessness:** "You become overcome with hopelessness and overwhelmed by your circumstances. If you are normally optimistic and now cannot find anything to be hopeful about, this could be a sign you are suffering from extreme or prolonged grief or feelings of worthlessness or guilt." [2]

Any of these symptoms can lead you to become indecisive and incapable of making the kinds of decisions necessary to effect positive outcomes. Mental anguish can cause you to just toil in your decision painfully regretting any solution you may discover, falling ever deeply into a self-isolating hole. Do not do that to yourself. You are the president of your motorcycle club. You are the man in charge. It is upon you to guide the club's direction, confidence, and hope. You cannot convey hopelessness in the face of adversity. Recognize the symptoms of mental anguish so that you can overcome them should they befall you. You must be capable of making a decision when it is time for decisiveness. This is the difference between leaders and unqualified people who should have never stepped up in the first damned place. Remember you chose this position, now stand up and make the brotherhood proud!

Anxiety:

Having to make decisions during major club situations can cause great anxiety which can affect your decision making.

Anxiety is defined as:

> "A feeling of worry, nervousness, or unease, typically about an imminent event or something with an uncertain outcome." (*https://www.lexico.com/en/definition/anxiety*)

In psychiatry, anxiety is defined as:

> "A nervous disorder characterized by a state of excessive uneasiness and apprehension, typically with compulsive behavior or panic attacks." (*https://beechacres.org/anxious-about-anxiety/*)

Symptoms include stress that is disproportion to the impact of the event or the inability to set aside worry and restlessness. You may also experience behavioral (hypervigilance, irritability), cognitive (lack of concentration, racing, or unwanted thoughts) or whole body (fatigue, sweating) changes.

Fear of the unknown, as in, "What happens if", can also lead to anxiety.

When you find yourself in situations that cause anxiety, you may find it difficult to make decisions. You must find a way to get yourself through these situations. Try to keep a clear mind and a sense of focus, realizing you might not come up with the best solution but rather a solution that ensures the survival of the MC, even if that means a compromise that allows the brotherhood to live long enough to fight another day.

During stressful times, it is best to:

- **Avoid alcohol**: Alcohol changes levels of serotonin and other neurotransmitters in the brain, which can worsen anxiety. In fact, you may feel more anxious after the alcohol wears off. (*https://www.healthline.com/health/alcohol-and-anxiety*)
- **Reduce caffeine intake**: There's an association between caffeine consumption and anxiety including caffeine-induced anxiety disorder. (*https://www.healthline.com/health/caffeine-and-anxiety*) If you are already feeling jittery, a cup of jolt can make you feel more anxious than not.
- **Abstain from drug abuse**
- **Employ relaxation techniques.**

Symptoms of anxiety cannot be allowed to overwhelm you into indecisiveness. Afterall, you have prepared yourself to stand exactly where you are as president. This is the position you wanted, and it requires you to excel at being good under pressure.

Stress:

All troubles come with stress which adds mental pressure to a crisis and a sense of urgency that compacts situations into a pressure-cooker-like environment.

Stress is defined as:

"A physical, mental, or emotional factor that causes bodily or mental tension. Stresses can be external (from the environment, psychological, or social situations) or internal (illness, or from a medical procedure)." (*https://www.medicinenet.com/stress/definition.htm*).

Stress can have mental, physical, and emotional consequences that can negatively impact your ability to make decisions.

According to YourCenter's article "Things You Should Know About Stress" (*https://thisisyourcenter.com/stress*), stress can negatively affect your health:

"The human body is designed to experience stress and react to it. Stress can be positive, keeping us alert, motivated, and ready to avoid danger. Stress becomes negative when a person faces continuous challenges without relief or relaxation between stressors. As a result, the person becomes overworked, and stress-related tension builds. The body's autonomic nervous system has a built-in stress response that causes physiological changes to allow the body to combat stressful situations. This stress response, also known as the "fight or flight response", is activated in case of an emergency. However, this response can become chronically activated during prolonged periods of stress. Prolonged activation of the stress response causes wear and tear on the body – both physical and emotional."

Flushing Hospital's Newsletter "Stress and Mental Health: Know your Limits" (*https://www.flushinghospital.org/newsletter/stress-and-mental-health-know-your-limits/*), continues to explain:

"Stress that continues without relief can lead to a condition called distress — a negative stress reaction. Distress can lead to physical symptoms including headaches, upset stomach, elevated blood pressure, chest pain, and problems sleeping. Research suggests that stress also can bring on or worsen certain symptoms or diseases. The effects of stress usually build up over time. Taking practical measures to maintain your health and outlook can reduce or prevent these effects."

In Medcourt's blog "Stress", May 20, 2019 ([3]*http://medcourtng.com/blog/2019/05/20/stress/*), we learn:

> "Emotional problems can also result from distress. These problems include depression, panic attacks, or other forms of anxiety and worry. Research suggests that stress also can bring on or worsen certain symptoms or diseases. Stress is linked to 6 of the leading causes of death: heart disease, cancer, lung ailments, accidents, cirrhosis of the liver, and suicide."

> Stress also becomes harmful when people engage in the compulsive use of substances or behaviors to try to relieve their stress. These substances or behaviors include food, alcohol, tobacco, drugs, gambling, sex, shopping, and the Internet. Rather than relieving the stress and returning the body to a relaxed state, these substances and compulsive behaviors tend to keep the body in a stressed state and cause more problems. The distressed person becomes trapped in a vicious cycle."

Signs of Stress:

Many presidents are already under chronic stress from their job, personal life, and club-related issues that stem from trying to hold the brotherhood together and move it forward, while surviving the political battles targeted at the leader. When a major club event strikes, the compounding distress can easily manifest into indecisiveness rendering the president useless. If you find yourself in a difficult situation, it can be helpful to know the signs of stress so that you can determine if it is contributing to making you indecisive. If it is, take steps to relieve as much stress as possible to mitigate that indecisiveness.

"Chronic stress can wear down the body's natural defenses, leading to a variety of physical symptoms, including the following:

- Dizziness or a general feeling of "being out of it."
- General aches and pains
- Grinding teeth, clenched jaw
- Headaches
- Indigestion or acid reflux symptoms.
- Increase in or loss of appetite.
- Muscle tension in neck, face, or shoulders.
- Racing heart.
- Cold and sweaty palms.
- Tiredness, exhaustion.
- Trembling/shaking.
- Upset stomach, diarrhea." [3]

Reducing stress: You can mitigate the effects of stress long enough to make important decisions by keeping the following tips in mind:

- **Keep a positive attitude**. The feeling of impending doom can lower your energy level. Remember things could always be worse, even if you do not see how. A positive attitude helps you have hope for the future. Hope is a major stress reliever. Chin up! Positivity is key!
- **Accept events as they are.** There are events you cannot control. You must deal with the situation as they are rather than how you want them to be. Perhaps, you have heard the expression "It is what it is." The acceptance of situations occurring because bad things happen rather than because you are somehow bad, cursed, or should have seen it coming, helps you remain calm in the face of disaster. Keep your eye on the goal rather than the circumstances surrounding the situation. Concentrate on acting to prevent things from getting worse rather than reacting to things as they get worse. The difference is acting requires planning and thought designed to get in front of a problem to divert or block it. Whereas reacting keeps

your club as a victim to the circumstances and allows the negativity to control the situation.

- **Be assertive instead of aggressive.** Resist the urge of becoming angry, getting defensive, and assigning blame, or worse becoming passive. These tactics accomplish little towards solving the club's problems. Instead assert your feelings, opinions, or beliefs and make a decision rather than remaining indecisive. Ask yourself, "If you do not, who will," or better yet, "If you cannot, who can?"
- **Manage your time effectively.** Often during a crisis, you will have little time to make a decision. Sometimes just the lack of having the time you want is enough to cause indecisiveness. You may find yourself paralyzed, afraid to make the wrong decision so you just fail to decide. Instead manage what little time you have, effectively. Refuse to procrastinate. Start weighing the pros and cons and form an opinion. Assemble as many facts as possible and step into the decision-making mode. Don't forget to trust yourself. Afterall you are the President!
- Don't rely on alcohol, drugs, or compulsive behaviors to reduce stress.

Depression:

In a hypothetical situation where a brother is assassinated by another club, it is easy to see that along with anxiety and stress the president could also be tragically depressed while trying to come up with decisions he might not be mentally sound enough to construct. This was precisely the situation in which I found myself following the assassination of one of my presidents in 2011 while I was serving as National President of the Mighty Black Sabbath Motorcycle Club Nation. Depression can render you ineffective and indecisive. Ask me, I know.

Depression is defined as:

"A mental condition characterized by feelings of severe despondency and dejection, typically also with feelings of inadequacy and guilt, often accompanied by lack of energy and disturbance of appetite and sleep." (*https://www.riverparkpsych.com/depression*)

According to Psychiatry.com ([4]*https://www.psychiatry.org/patients-families/depression/what-is-depression*), "Depression symptoms can vary from mild to severe and can include:

- Feeling sad or having a depressed mood
- Loss of interest or pleasure in activities once enjoyed
- Changes in appetite — weight loss or gain unrelated to dieting
- Trouble sleeping or sleeping too much
- Loss of energy or increased fatigue
- Increase in purposeless physical activity (e.g., handwringing or pacing) or slowed movements and speech (actions observable by others)
- Feeling worthless or guilty
- Difficulty thinking, concentrating, or making decisions
- Thoughts of death or suicide"

Depression is different than sadness, grief, or bereavement which are common during situations like death or loss. Even though many folks describe themselves as being "depressed" during these events, it is not the same as clinical depression. People deal with loss and sadness in different ways but are generally able to get on with their lives and move forward after a time. Should these symptoms last more than two weeks there could be a clinical diagnosis of depression. And depression is bad for a president trying to lead his motorcycle club through crisis and can certainly lead to indecisiveness. There were many other factors pushing on me prior to the murder of one of my presidents, which probably had me clinically depressed long before this tragedy occurred. So, it is difficult to know whether I was just sad and grieving, or depressed.

"But being sad is not the same as having depression. The grieving process is natural and unique to each individual and shares some of the same features of depression.

Both grief and depression may involve intense sadness and withdrawal from usual activities. But they are different in important ways:

- in grief, painful feelings come in waves, often intermixed with positive memories of the deceased. In major depression, mood and/or interest (pleasure) are decreased for most of two weeks.
- In grief, self-esteem is usually maintained. In major depression, feelings of worthlessness and self-loathing are common.

For some people, the death of a loved one, losing a job or being a victim of a physical assault or a major disaster can lead to depression. When grief and depression co-occur, the grief is more severe and lasts longer than grief without depression.

Distinguishing between grief and depression is important and can help you get the help, support, or treatment you need [and allow you to recognize how your decision-making skills are being affected.]" [4]

Clearly any or all of these factors, singularly or combined, could cause a temporary condition of aboulomania and ultimately indecisiveness to any president.

The key to overcoming indecisiveness is to accept the fact that you just might not make the best decision or even the right decision necessary to resolve the situation. That's right, you may be completely wrong in whatever decision you are about to make— especially since you might not have all the facts or the luxury of time to make an informed decision. You have to accept the fact that a decision has to be made and you are the one the brothers elected to represent them and to make that decision – good or bad – no matter what. This is a great heaviness that is weighted upon the shoulders of every leader. Your decision could mean the end of the

MC as you know it or the end of its existence altogether, but it does not have to. Your decision could mean the brotherhood will prevail and ensure the survival of the MC for decades to come. You just never know for sure about these things and we will all see in the future, but right here, right now, you must decide!

The quality of decisiveness is the ability to make decisions promptly and to announce them in a clear and forceful manner. Decisiveness is the quality of character which guides a person to accumulate all available facts, weigh those facts, and choose the best path. It is often better that a decision be made promptly than a potentially better one be made at the expense of more time. That is what decision making in times of turmoil is all about. You are the one named "President," so it falls upon you to make the decision and wear the responsibility of that action. Good decision or bad the brothers will stand with you until the bitter end if they know you were brave enough to do what had to be done when it needed to be done. Never be indecisive. Learn the symptoms of indecisiveness and combat them when they appear. A successful president wins for his MC at all costs.

Example - A Sergeant at Arms is murdered in broad daylight by a rival club. The Sergeant just so happens to be the President's best friend since grade school. Immediately the club wants to take actions of retribution. International and local news agencies are pressing the president for answers. The police are tracking the MC's every move. Angry full patch brothers are threatening to remove the president if he does not act and take revenge. Facing these overwhelming odds plus his own grief and loss, the president must take the initiative to lead the club out of this trouble without losing any other brothers to violence or jail during this troublesome time.

◊◊◊

CHAPTER THIRTEEN
Leadership Principle
of Tact

Tact

Definition – The ability to deal with others in a manner that will maintain good relations and avoid offenses. More simply stated, tact is being able to say and do the right thing at the right time.

Significance – The quality of consistently treating peers, seniors, and subordinates with respect and courtesy is a sign of maturity. Tact enables a President to issue commands, guidance, and opinions in a constructive and beneficial manner that advances the goals of the MC rather than in a non-productive manner that degrades, belittles, and berates brothers ultimately stifling them.

Tact must be extended under all conditions regardless of one's true feelings. In the business of dealing with your brothers and the MC there is no benefit to allowing personal feelings to guide communications; however, the ability to communicate with sensitivity offers many benefits.

In the article *"How to Be Tactful Responding with Diplomacy and Grace"* ([1]mindtools.com/pages/article/tactful.htm), the Mind Tools Content discussed several important factors for tactfully dealing with coworkers in the business sector. I will explore these concepts as they apply to the MC world.

> "First, tact is important when you must deliver bad news or provide critical feedback. Next, communicating tactfully strengthens your reputation and builds your credibility. It allows you to preserve existing relationships and build new ones. A tactful approach shows character, maturity, professionalism, and integrity.
>
> Tact also demonstrates good manners. If you can communicate with grace and consideration, you will stand out from the crowd and be noticed for the right reasons. This can lead to unforeseen opportunities.

Finally, tact can help you avoid conflict, find common ground, and allow others to save face. Saving face can be critically important when interacting with [brothers or on the set, as interactions between alpha males can often be complex, ego-inflated, posturing events.] Tact can therefore be an important asset used in negotiations and in conflict resolution." [1]

Tact is one of those skills that can carry a President a long way and generate respect for him and his club in all spheres upon which the brotherhood operates including with councils, coalitions, confederations, outlaws, dominant MCs, and one-percenters (1%ers). Lack of tact can make a president look petty, immature, small, smug, or arrogant especially to an entity that feels superior (i.e., a 1%er club). This can lead significant repercussions that could easily been avoided with a little tact. Far worse are the challenges and inner conflicts that can arise within the family. A tactless president can evoke hate, contempt, resentment, and feelings of revenge from everyone with whom he communicates. It can also corrupt his reputation in the eyes of others not in his direct line of communication as rumors abound about his arrogance, disrespect, and lack of concern for the feelings of others. Brothers will consequently combine their intelligences and gather their forces to see him fall, then rejoice in his departure from leadership as this is the nature of these sorts of things.

Some presidents confuse so-called "absolute truthfulness" (the false assumption of "keeping it 100%" or "keeping it real") as a justification for NOT using tact, but this assumption is just that, false and is the furthest thing from the truth. The desire to be "brutally honest" does not excuse you from the responsibility of utilizing tact to communicate in a professional manner when handling club business. Honesty can be delivered deliberately without being brutal. Conveying a concise message of severity and finality using tact has more impact than being cruel and downright rude.

When someone is being brutal with their honesty, they are directly trying to be hurtful in the delivery of that so-called honesty. When you are intentionally attempting to hurt someone's feelings the outcome of that interaction is totally unpredictable — it could be something you were not prepared to deal with on any level.

My grandmother used to say, "Son, you can also kill someone with kindness." I saw her totally verbally strip grown men down to the bone without ever using one curse word or derogatory statement. The most effective was when she said, in a short and curt manner, "Bless your soul. I will pray for you." Although people knew she just insulted them, they could not get mad because she had been civil the whole time. It was a silent power she had to disarm bullies especially during the Jim Crow days when being considered a "sassy" black woman in the South with too much mouth could result in a beating or worse a lynching from angry white landowners that had power of life and death then. I saw her take on much more powerful opponents with her wit and tact and more often than not, they wound up saying, "Yes ma'am Mrs. Jackson."

I have heard presidents say "I keep it brutally honest because I am not here to care about your feelings so do not look for that sissy stuff from me! I do not coddle grown men, so I am not going to baby you," not realizing that they have set the stage for their own demise from a vengeful brother they may have embarrassed or whose reputation they may have harmed publicly. These feelings of rejection and revenge can be all consuming to a brother who feels he has been abused. I have even known presidents to be ambushed, severely beaten, or shot to death during club meetings because of their inability to employ tact when speaking foolishly to grown men! Thriving in a din of alpha males often has more to do with being tactfully astute than any other skill a president might possess. Being tactful does not mean that you have to be untruthful or any less "real," but rather that you are considerate and careful in your communications with others.

For instance, if you assigned a junior officer to complete a task that he performed poorly and during the next church you berated him in front of the entire assembly of the brotherhood—told him what an idiot he was, called him totally incompetent, or told him that you would not trust him with the charge of the MC again even if he were the last Road Captain on Earth—you have certainly been truthful and kept it "real," but what you have also done is damage his credibility, self-esteem, and consequently his loyalty to the MC. You may never realize the negative impact of keeping it "real" until you feel his knife twisting in your back when you least expect it. And believe it or not you will have brought it upon yourself.

Tact is using diplomacy and grace to respond well during communications with others. We all must deliver bad information from time to time. Diplomacy and grace allow us to communicate this information truthfully while tact allows us to preserve the other person's feelings and self-esteem, while building our own credibility.

> "Tact is the ability to tell the truth in a way that considers other people's feelings and reactions. It allows you to give difficult feedback, communicate sensitive information, and say the right thing to preserve a relationship.
>
> Tact encompasses many things, including emotional intelligence, respect, discretion, self-awareness, thoughtfulness, compassion, subtlety, honesty, diplomacy, and courtesy." [1]

Tact can save you from having to replace and retrain good people who can be easily driven away from the brotherhood, help your MC avoid pains when dealing with other MCs and could even save your life as a President.

The Mind Tools Content team suggested two tips when considering how to improve your use of tact while leading your MC nation.

Tip 1: **Be Culturally Alert When Providing Feedback**

> "Tact is strongly influenced by culture.
>
> What might be seen as open, fair feedback in some cultures might be seen as profoundly rude in others; while a message from a [99%er MC] may be seen as weak – or missed entirely – by a [1%er MC].
>
> Make sure you are culturally alert when providing feedback to people from a different background."[1]

I have observed an interesting phenomenon in many modern MC's today that directly relates to being "culturally alert". While a text message from a manager to an employee may be perfectly appropriate in corporate American culture and is considered to be an effective tool on the job, that same kind of message from a member to an officer could be seen as weak or missed altogether by a club brother in the MC culture. It could also lead an unwanted trail for law enforcement to follow and therefore would not be a welcome form of communication at all to some MCs.

I make this point because many folks are starting to come into MC culture from corporate America seeking the life they have seen on television shows or in the media. And in doing so they mistakenly assume that their corporate America speak will easily transfer to leading full patch brothers in clubs instead of taking the time to learn and apply MC protocol. When they achieve rank too quickly, we often see them trying to apply these work standards in the MC world, quickly discovering their efforts are unsuccessful and are seen as insults by the strong-minded, ego-driven full patch brothers. Be mindful to learn everything you can about MC protocol before taking over as president, since running an MC is not the same as running a business in corporate America. Being successful in this game requires a cultural awareness of our society and the rules by which we govern.

Tip 2: **Always Get Your Message Across**

> "It's great to be tactful, however, you also need to get your message across and ensure that your own rights are respected. Make sure that you handle issues assertively, not submissively, when you are being tactful." [1]

While it is great to be tactful, do not take from this lesson that the meaning of your message should ever be softened. To ensure that the rights and sovereignty of the MC should be respected at all times the circumstances and environment of each situation will dictate how tactful your response needs to be. Certain situations may require you not to be tactful at all! And in some cases, may require you to be completely tactless and downright rude. That's okay! The point is to be in control of when you will be or will not be tactful.

I will never advise any MC to lay down or accept disrespect, threats, or violence from any other MC or organization no matter what its makeup. "Tact reflects emotional sensitivity and increases the likelihood of a positive outcome," but it does not guarantee it. Never let there be any doubt about your resolve to take the MC to whatever level is necessary to protect its rights, image, safety, and sovereignty or to secure its agenda.

Depending upon the situation, you have a couple of options to get your point across. From "Go screw yourself because that shit ain't happening homie!" to "With all due respect, NO, we are absolutely resolute in the fact that we are not going to do that and there will be no further negotiations on that point. Perhaps there is another agreement we can reach before we come to a point where things devolve beyond our control creating seriously negative impacts for both of our nations." In both examples you are saying the same thing, "No!," but in the second statement, you were tactful and respectful, with hope in working out a different outcome. In the first example, you may have just started a war. Although there is no guarantee you will not start a war in either instance, using tact may provide an opportunity to move toward common ground which is your job as President.

Developing Tact

I have said this before, the biker world is a tough place wherein alpha men seek to dominate alpha men. But being a successful alpha is not always about exerting brawn and muscle to accomplish one's goals. There is absolutely nothing to be gained from a tactless tirade that leaves everyone in the room disgusted. It diminishes the respect and esteem the brothers hold for you, tarnishes your legacy, and erodes your power. Take the time to consider that the most dominate alpha is a thinking alpha who can use wit combined with his will power to inspire his men to rise to greatness rather than to intimidate them through tactless personal attacks. That being said, there is not much training available in the MC arena to develop your skills in the use of tact; therefore, if you are a tactless wonder, you will probably have to learn to improve those skills yourself. Think of the old adage "You catch more flies with honey than you do with vinegar."

The Mind Tools Content team suggests the following five strategies to hone your skills in tactful communication:

1. **Create the Right Environment by Thinking Before You Speak**
   It is useless to speak too quickly and later regret your words, so take the time to think first, speak second. Remember you are the President! Your words are magnified simply by the prestige of your position alone. Your brothers respect you as the father

and living representative and, in fact, the face of their organization. Personal attacks coming from you have a piercing effect unlike those coming from any other person in the MC. You must be tactful when engaging in adverse conversations.

Take the time to pause for one or two seconds before responding with words. If someone says, "Go to Hell jerk!" In your mind think, "One thousand one, one thousand two," while asking yourself "How can I communicate without anger to effectively craft my response?" Not knowing how to do this in the MC world could prove deadly. As I have stated before, I have been at church and seen guns pulled, knives thrown, fists fly, and shots ring out over a simple, but heated exchange. I have known of clubs wherein Presidents were killed in church for so-called "disrespectin'"; so, it behooves you to understand the importance of tact in your dealings with grown folks.

> "First, practice active listening when others speak. Then, use empathy and emotional intelligence to connect with people, and to see things from their perspective. Last, work to build trust, so that people know that your intentions are honest and compassionate."[1]

It will take time to develop this skill and you can use your daily interactions with your club brothers to build proficiency.

2. **Determine the Appropriate Time**
   Consider this scenario:

> Your club brother just found out he has been removed as Sergeant at Arms and a special committee has suspended him for a month because he was found guilty of violating the club's bylaws. Meanwhile, the National President has just informed you that you will be promoted to State Boss.

Is now the best time to talk to him about your good news? Definitely not!

> "Tact means saying the right thing at the right time, considering the situation before you speak, and being discreet. Make sure that you stay conscious of who you are with – and where you are – before you speak." [1]

Tact also means keeping some things to yourself. A wise president listens more than he speaks.

3. **Choose Your Words Carefully**
"Your choice of words can influence how others perceive your message.

> Avoid starting sentences with the word 'you.' For example, saying, 'You need to do better next time" will make the other person feel defensive.'"[1]

Instead, consider using a less confrontational tone, like, "Next time, I think your work would be more impressive and appreciated if you took more initiative to do things like clean the club or provide officer security on your own instead of always waiting around for the full patch brothers to tell you what to do, because that makes you seem less enthusiastic about prospecting than the full patches would like to see. Taking more initiative on your own will impress the brothers and likely decrease your prospecting time. What do you think?"

> "It is especially important to use "I" statements that accept blame during conflict, or even when you give constructive criticism. When you do this, you take ownership of your feelings instead of placing blame. For example, say, "I see it differently," or "I apologize for not getting back to you more quickly, but I had to go over that email several times before I understood your message."[1]

Accepting responsibility is the one time when the President should use the term "I" more than "We".

> "Think about cushioning your statements when you are angry or when you disagree vehemently with a subordinate. Cushion statements make your disagreement less personal, less emotional, and more business focused."[1]

For example, you can cushion this message:

"You are an idiot! Following my orders our brothers handled that shit perfectly you moron so, why would you want to change what I said? You think you can do it so much better? You think you know more than I know? You have only been in this club two damned years, you do not know shit! Let us see what the hell kind of decision you can make next time and not fuck it up!"

with,

"I appreciate your opinion brother and I know you always stand for what is best for the club, but the brothers were following my direct orders and I am proud of their results. Still, I value your opinion and experience in the new way clubs are handling business, and I want to know how you would do it better. Let us all sit down at church and hear out your concerns and examine your methods so that we can refine our response for next time. What do you think?"

Both messages conveyed the idea that you wanted your orders followed. But one of the messages creates an enemy whereas the other has the potential to create a great ally.

> "Also, when you are in a tense conversation, be concise. It is tempting to keep talking when you feel uncomfortable, which increases the chance that you

> will say too much or say something that you will
> regret. Be honest and assertive, and only say what
> you need to say."[1]

And only say it once. Repeating the same thing over and over
makes subordinates tend to tune you out and stop listening.
They also feel like you enjoy hearing yourself talk. Make it such
that when you speak your words echo in thunderous volumes.
Do this by speaking less! You will be amazed at how well this
actually works.

4. **Watch Your Body Language**
   Consider this scenario:

> Your Vice President is reporting on a situation that you told
> him to investigate, and he tells you that everything is just
> fine. But, as he speaks, he avoids your gaze, folds his arms
> across his chest and his voice loses confidence. Although his
> words are positive, his body language makes you question
> his honesty.

Are you sure he is telling you the truth?

> "When you are tactful, your body language matches
> your message, and you appear open when you are
> communicating, even if you are giving bad news.
> Always make eye contact and practice good posture.
> Open body language and a courteous vocal tone
> communicate your truthfulness and command of
> your subject matter."

It is okay not to know everything about what you are talking
about. It is okay to admit that you might not have all the
answers, but you know how to get it. Your men are not looking
for you to be perfect they are looking for you to have the
maturity and forthrightness to handle situations with good
judgment. Their confidence in your message can be reinforced
by your body language or just the opposite.

This reminds me of a story about body language: My club and I were in a very touchy situation with some 1%ers who were trying to regulate us. At some point their president attempted to make our club seem small, questioning the validity of our national standing. Keep in mind, in the MC world your club is not considered a National MC if it does not have five chapters in five states. Now, I have always been of the mindset that no army should ever divulge its strength to another army or potential enemy, but he really pissed me off with this line of questioning. I boldly stood and looked him in the eyes, declaring, "We have 100 chapters!" He looked at me incredulously for a second and then said, "Alright, and we will be checking, and you better have every one of those chapters." On the way home from that terrible meeting, I called him and said, "You know we do not really have a hundred chapters. You were asking me a question you knew I was not going to answer." He laughed at me and said, "Yeah, I know. But you had me going there for a minute. I really believed you by your body language. What gave it away is when a few members of your club looked up into the sky like – 'why in the hell would Dragon tell that lie right here and right now... oh my Gawd what are we going to do now?' I was so tickled I was going to tell you the next time you lie to us at least make sure your brothers are on the same damned page... damn! Their body language gave it all away!"

Teach your men if you lie under duress, they lie under duress with you—or at least they do not look up in the sky in disbelief in what you say thereby allowing their body language to give it all away.

5. **Never React Emotionally**

"It is hard to communicate tactfully when you feel angry or upset." [1]

In MC culture, your ability to react devoid of emotion is crucial to the safety of the brotherhood. As I have said before, if you do not handle emotional situations well, give yourself time to calm down before you respond. People who remain calm and non-emotional often prevail over people who do not. Remember effectively operating the presidency of an MC is a thinking man's game.

> "Learn how to control your emotions,"[1] because the brotherhood will try them!

You are dealing with people and people will bring you more problems than you could ever imagine. As president you are also a preacher, a father, or an older brother to your members. They look up to you with a kind of respect that is not given to a CEO or manager in a corporate job. Members expect you to be almost God-like in your approach to things. Your words can have the effect of a television evangelist on your brothers. Always take the time to choose them wisely! To calm down from a stressful situation, take a break from it. Go for a walk or use deep breathing techniques to regain your composure. Whatever it takes to clear your head, do it!

It is also important to understand people, words, issues, or situations that can cause you to lose your cool and communicate without tact. There is always that brother that goes out of his way to find something to ride you about. It is his mission to get you display lack of professionalism just one time to destroy your reputation, even though he has never displayed professionalism even one day since he joined the club. But then again, he is not President, is he? You are! Do not let him make you lose your temper. Do not give him that pleasure. There are other members who will try to figure out your triggers so they can pull them to get you to react. Incredibly you will find that brothers will be experts in their study of your behaviors. Do not think that they are not watching your every step. Some will almost know you better than you know yourself. But you can get the jump on them by studying your own communication habits, correcting the bad ones, and strengthening the good ones. Think back to the last time you lost your temper or said something you later regretted. Why did you react this way? What caused you to lose control? How will you keep control if confronted the same way in the future? When you understand your triggers, you will be better able to control your emotions or walk away in the future.

Common Examples in Utilizing Tact

Below are some common situations where tact can make the difference between a positive and negative experience.

1. **Kicking a Brother Out of the Club**

    "It is never easy to let people go. These situations are often emotional and tense, which is why tact is important."[1]

And though it may be the Sergeant at Arms' job to perform this function, since you are in charge—how it is handled will always fall back on you. It is important that you ensure proper and exact procedures are followed, even if you must oversee them closely yourself.

"Start by explaining clearly what is happening. This is a difficult and unpleasant message to communicate, but you owe it to your [brother] to be honest. If you allow emotion to dictate how you deliver your message, you risk "sugar coating" facts and not getting your point across [or yelling in anger turning an already bad situation worse]."

"Next, explain why [the club] has made its decision and offer emotional support. It is important to be honest in

this situation, but you can also be kind and supportive."
[1]

For some brothers, the MC is the only family they have. In fact, it can be all they have period! Losing the MC can be like losing a loved one to a death or tragedy. Even if they are the most raggedy member they deserve the best treatment possible considering the situation. Afterall, they wore the patch of your brotherhood. Also, be mindful of suicide or revenge launched at you or the club as a result of their termination. Anything is possible in this situation. Do not put anything past anyone. The more supportive and tactful you are there, the more likely this situation can be positive in a brother's life – marking a low point where the brother decided to get his act together and turn his life around. Who knows, maybe someday in the future he may be invited back.

2. **Giving Feedback**

   "It can be difficult to give feedback, especially when it is negative. The key to providing effective feedback is to give it frequently and to do it tactfully.

   A good approach can be to 'sandwich' constructive feedback between positive comments. When you start off with something positive, this helps the person to relax, and it reminds them that they are doing a good job. And, when you end with a positive, people do not walk away feeling upset."[1]

Instead, they leave with the determination to do what is necessary to improve on the good job they are already doing.

   "Avoid sandwiching the constructive feedback between too many positives, however, or people may take away the wrong message. Also, avoid using this approach too often, as people may come to mistrust positive feedback from you."[1]

Everything in its appropriate measure.

For example, you could say, "You did a good job getting the run together and ensuring the brothers had a great time. It is important, however, to always keep safety first, so although we had a great time, allowing the brothers to race in the pack, run-off and leave the pack, and perform stunts while riding in the pack is absolutely unsafe and will not be tolerated. Next time you create such a good event make sure not to let it be marred by unsafe riding practices. Keep the pack tight, keep the discipline up, and keep the pack riding together. I think the club will benefit. What do you think?"

3. **Declining an Invitation**

    "If you decline an invitation to an [MC's annual] with an outright 'no,' [you] could be viewed as crass [or arrogant].[1]

Giving sound thought to how you handle outside MCs, especially diamonds and coalitions can be crucial to the success of your MC.

> "Start with a positive comment: 'Thanks for showing us the respect of inviting our club to your annual we are honored by your invitation.' Next, tactfully decline: 'I am sorry that we cannot attend as we will be attending a national function at that time.' Last, end on a positive note: 'Hopefully, [our] schedule will be less hectic next time and we can get together.' [1]

Then, "and though we cannot attend in numbers, any of our brothers who do not go to our national function and stay in town, will be there to celebrate with you all, plus we will be sending a donation to show our respect."

Again, being tactful is not the same as kissing ass. Everyone can see through an ass-kisser. Do not be that guy! Straight forward communication is important and respected.

4. **Deflecting Gossip**

Consider this scenario: Your club brother is spreading rumors about another club brother, accusing him of stealing from the club while you are in the room.

> "You can tactfully deflect and neutralize the gossip in several ways. For instance, say something positive: 'The treasurer might struggle with his [accounting] figures, but he is damned trustworthy and since you seem to know accounting so well why don't you offer to help him with his reports during our next church so others will not believe the same vicious rumors about him that you are spreading right now?'"[1]

Or simply ask them to stop: "I do not want to talk about this, especially since we do not know the facts. Let us discuss the upcoming poker run instead," or "I do not ever engage in talking about a club brother behind his back. We can continue this discussion as soon as we get him on the phone to defend himself, or at the table next week during church," or "Let's talk about this when Smoke is here, so that he can address these issues in person and have a fair opportunity to defend himself. None of you would want someone talking like this behind your back and I know I would not either. What do you think?"

5. **Handling Disagreements**
   "Tact is particularly useful in conflict resolution, because it can relieve tension, remove blame, and allow both sides to save face."[1]

For example, conflicts between clubs notoriously set the stage for more crap in the MC world than almost any other thing you can imagine. Clubs fight over territory, women, support clubs, social clubs, image, etc. For no good reason, it at all seems to permeate our environment. As President, you will be required to navigate your club through often shark infested waters. Be thoughtful, do not react with emotion, speak clearly, concisely, and truthfully and always be professional in your approach. A good knowledge of MC protocol will be priceless in these situations therefore you should be continually striving to upgrade your MC protocol knowledge so that you can be prepared for such occasions.

During conflict resolution always try to work first from a point of where the two conflicting clubs can agree, rather than starting from a point of disagreement. Try small victories first so that both clubs can see the benefit of conversation. For example, the conversation can start out like this; "Gentlemen I am sure that we can all agree that further violence will not be good for either side so can we get an acknowledgement from both sides that we must do whatever it takes to stop the violence from this point forward?" If everyone agrees you now have your first small victory. Build from there to get to your next victory. If things start to fall apart go back to the last place everyone agreed and start again. For example, "I know we are not seeing eye to eye here gentlemen but let us all remember that we agreed to do whatever was necessary to stop the violence so let us try to get back to that space and move forward again from there."

6. **Giving Speeches**
Part of your job is motivating your brotherhood to advance the goals of the MC. So, naturally, that means you will be giving speeches or presentations. It is important to use tact during these influential times.

I once gave a eulogy of a club brother during his homegoing funeral in his church in Mississippi. During that spirited speech I told the story of when I was a prospect 30 years prior and what this brother had meant to me during my time as a prospect for the club. I started by explaining to the audience that a prospect was the lowliest position in the club and that prospects meant nothing to the club. Although I was speaking about my experience, the current prospects did not realize that and thought I was talking about them instead and not my experience nearly three decades prior. Needless to say, when we left the church, I was surrounded by sponsors at the next gas station because the National President had said prospects meant nothing to the club. We lost a prospect or two that day.

Tact is about knowing what to say and when to say it. That does not mean that you will not make mistakes but try to learn from them as quickly as possible and never repeat them again. As president everything you say will be weighed, studied, and examined for mistakes, inconsistencies, inaccuracies, marketing, and messaging. Do not speak recklessly. Have prepared speeches with talking points from which to speak. My book "Motorcycle Clubs Public Relations Officer's Bible" explains these principles in great detail.

> "To be more tactful during speeches , do not use jargon or long words that may confuse your audience. Explain complex ideas clearly, so that people do not have to ask for clarification. When appropriate, be self-deprecating to make others feel at ease; and leave plenty of time for questions, so that everyone leaves feeling informed."[1]

Example—As National President of the Mighty Black Sabbath MC Nation, I once had a brand-new president that ran into some interference from a local 1%er MC in a town where we were attempting to stand up a new chapter. The 1%er club already knew the president and knew him to be a hothead—in fact a few of them actually attended high school with him in that same small town. Before our negotiations for entering that territory had been completed, several of the new club members were seen wearing their colors around town, which can be perceived as disrespectful. The SAA of the 1%er club personally knew the president, so he stopped by his house to have a discussion with him about the situation. Now, we all know that it is improper for anyone to show up unannounced to your home, where your wife and children live, to discuss club business—especially when the conversation could be terse. The new president was therefore rightly annoyed, but it turned to outrage because he was a hot head. Instead of voicing his displeasure and letting the 1%er SAA know that he should have called before coming over, he chose to deal with that offense in a very negative way. When the SAA asked him, "Hey I wanted to speak with you about a situation for a few minutes do you have time for a chat?" He threatened the SAA's life right there on his porch and told him if he ever came over to his house again, he would not leave his porch alive. The 1%er SAA immediately apologized for being so forward as to stop by unannounced, admitted that he was not thinking properly, and promptly departed without incident. From that one encounter, it took us another four years before we got that chapter properly up and running in that area—as that once welcoming 1%er MC turned cold as ice. I cannot begin to tell you the hell his brothers suffered as a result of his prideful outburst. The sucker punch came when this same president left the club not long after because of some alleged infraction against his so-called "leadership" that pissed him off and caused him to drop his rags because the club supposedly no longer had "brotherhood." Now that he was gone the brothers still had to deal with the fallout from his piss-poor, tactless tirade years following his departure.

A president must always know that it is not just himself that he is representing, he represents the entire MC and quite possibly his MC nation. He must be mature enough to know the incredible distraction to the nation that one thoughtless outburst could cause. He must also always be considerate of the stature and makeup of the men in his brotherhood. If your men are not 1%er material, involving them in a potential conflict with a 1%er because you ran-off at the mouth is completely irresponsible. A responsible president must always consider what is best for the MC. The MC is never about "I" it is always about "WE". That means that you put the best interest of the club above your own desire to make a point that conveys some kind of message about your personal manhood. You are the president! You represent the MC whenever and wherever you speak. Maintain control of your emotions when communicating with others. You must remain tactful and professional.

◊◊◊

CHAPTER FOURTEEN
The Leadership Principle of Integrity

Integrity

Definition - Uprightness of character and soundness of moral principles. The quality of morality and honesty.

Significance - A president's word is his bond. Nothing less than complete honesty in all your dealings with your brothers and sisters is acceptable.

Award winning career coach, inspirational speaker, multi-book author, blogger, leadership coach and professional development expert Jenny Garrett OBE wrote an article entitled *"5 Top Tips to Develop Your Integrity"* ([1]*http://www.jennygarrett.global/5-top-tips-to-develop-your-integrity*). In it, she states:

> "In research on leadership, integrity is consistently rated as one of the most important character traits of a respected leader."

I suspect, this is why integrity is listed as one of the core values of just about every organization's culture statement and of course every military worldwide. But what does integrity mean in the presidency of a motorcycle club? Imagine trying to run the brotherhood without the trust of the full patch brothers you are leading. Trust is one of the most significant ingredients to success. To ensure the brotherhood knows you can be trusted, you must first establish that there is no question as to your integrity.

> "Integrity can be defined as making values-based decisions, not decisions based on personal gain. Another way to think of it is, would I behave in the same way if someone were watching me? If you were acting with integrity, you would do the same thing whether or not you were being observed because you would believe that it was the right thing to do."[1]

When speaking with MC Presidents and/or referring to the presidency of an MC, I always talk about a term I call "Presidential Integrity", which is how a president uses his integrity to run his administration and sets the tone and values of the club. To establish your presidential integrity, you must begin by building a reputation for doing the right thing, at the right time, all the time, simply because it is the right thing to do. Your men must know that you will do the right thing for the betterment of the MC even if it goes against your political ambitions, personal agenda, or the best interests of your friends and allies. No matter the political implication, whose feelings may be hurt, or what friendships must be sacrificed, you must be found doing the right thing to advance the best interests of the brotherhood, even when no one else is looking. Doing the right thing all the time is not easy especially when you are also caught up in the sticky political web of attempting to please friends and allies combined with the personal inclination of wanting to please everyone and make everyone happy under every circumstance.

One of the challenges I faced as National President was the accusation of being "wishy-washy" by some members who bitterly complained that I would say "yes" to this brother today and "no" to that brother tomorrow or tell one story today and tell a different story tomorrow. Naturally, I did not agree with them, but I had to examine myself and consider if there was any truth to what they were saying and if so, why. This is not an uncommon phenomenon as a leader. It occurs when a member or officer wants to infringe upon your presidential integrity by manipulating you into a position where you feel pressured to compromise your values to placate or appease them in some way. These members will use political-pressure, friendship-pressure, family-pressure, threat-pressure, and intimidation-pressure to cause you to change your response when dealing with similar circumstances. These kinds of pressures are far stronger than peer-pressure and are ten times harder to avoid. When you compromise your values as President, even just a little bit, you start down the slippery slope of compromising your values for all members and set yourself up for the blackmail attempt that is sure to follow. Bottom line—no matter how much you want to—it is impossible to please everyone. Draw your line where your positions are concerned and stand by it. This step alone will go far in defining your presidential integrity. Of course, this is easier said than done.

> "Aligning our internal values with our external behaviors sounds easy but putting it into practice can be a challenge."[1]

There will always be someone expecting an exception. Although exceptions are permissible, they must be exceptions not the rule. When you grant an exception, you set yourself up to have it come back to revisit you whenever someone wants to use it against you to pressure you into making an exception for them.

Having integrity as the President means more than just having "Presidential Integrity". It means possessing and expressing integrity for the standards of the MC. I call this kind of integrity "Organizational Integrity." In the MC world this could also be called "Club Integrity." A president who has a clear disdain for the rules of the MC displays to all that he cares little for club integrity or for the longevity of the brotherhood and will seek to dismantle it at any opportunity. You need to have conviction for the traditions, codes, and core values of the MC and be respectful of its time-honored processes to be successful at inspiring your brothers to greatness. When you trounce over the bylaws, or worse, start changing them to accomplish your own agenda your brothers will see you for what you are and recognize your lack of organizational/club integrity. You will lose the trust of the brothers who are loyal to the precepts of the MC's values and they will eventually turn against you.

Disastrous consequences can also occur when presidents go against organizational/club integrity even when their proposed plan is actually good for the club. That is to say I have seen presidents break the rules for reasons that greatly benefitted the club, but because they acted outside the rules, bylaws, and time-honored traditions of the club, they were still terribly punished. For example, a president – engaged in a war with a rival MC – relaxed the rules for prospecting in an effort to acquire more warriors to protect the club, but that move made longstanding brothers so mad they turned on him. Although his actions saved the club, he was still eventually thrown out for lack of club integrity.

Though your actions may be for the betterment of the brotherhood, they may be unacceptable to the most loyal core group of brothers, causing them to split from the brotherhood or eject you from it. Do not let your ideas for the club's agenda trump the long-established traditions and standard operating procedures of the brotherhood. Stay as close to the established rules and protocols as possible. Folks are not kind and can be quite unforgiving; therefore, it is important to rule every day as though it were your last. This way you will be free to do the job without fear of the consequences of making mistakes. This too is a grand part of the integrity it takes to be the leader of an MC. Finally, if you are going to change process or move away from the traditions or bylaws then do it with the vote of the body at the table. That way "we" all did it and not just you alone.

Five Tips to Develop Your Integrity

You can actively develop your skills at practicing integrity through preparation and determination.

Garrett gives us her top five tips to consider for developing your integrity:

1. **Examine your morals and ethics, create a change in behavior if necessary**

"What are your moral and ethical values and where do they come from?"[1]

Were you raised to do what is right most times, all of the time, or sporadically? Was there a high value placed on honesty and doing the right thing? Were you taught that your agenda should be accomplished before any others?

"When was the last time that you compromised your values, in a small way and why was that? Have your morals and ethics changed," [1]

perhaps based on bad experiences or failed relationships with people, loved ones, or romantic interests or from disillusionment stemmed from interactions with brothers and sisters in your MC during your career before reaching the presidency? Is your integrity solid or does it sway occasionally? For instance, you would not steal a wallet from the dashboard of a car, but if you found it lying on the ground next to that car then it would be okay to take the money out of it and throw it in the trash? If this is not acceptable, but is something you would do then are you living by your own values and morals? If not, you can begin developing your integrity by purposefully insisting that you change your behaviors to match your self-expectations. It takes a bit of work, but you can make up your mind to operate your life differently, according to your integrity, morals, and values. This is how you begin to develop your integrity by insisting upon living up to your values rather than reacting to your desires and agendas.

2. **Be a role model of integrity for your brotherhood**
   "Be consistent, open, and clear with your morals and ethics. Encourage [your brothers] to question [your actions and those of] others."

Respectfully, but critically in accordance with their understandings of the bylaws. This may mean eliminating those around you who say, "Yes" to everything you do out of hero-worship or political gain. Keep practical thinkers in your inner circle who value the agenda of the MC over theirs or yours.

> "Encourage [your brothers] to challenge you when you seem to be acting without integrity [or engaging in favoritism.]"

3. **Stand for what you believe**
   The MC has a way of testing you like no other. If the previous president made the job look easy, he cursed you and now you will discover what a trickster he was. Staying consistent and standing on your convictions under the pressure of the expectations of the brotherhood can be one of the toughest things you will ever have to do—especially when facing challenges that could split the MC or cause you to lose your most loved, trusted, and influential members.

   Not enough can be said about the strength of conviction in standing for what you believe. This does not mean that you do not have to compromise, it simply means that you will not compromise your values or integrity—EVER, for any reason!

   > "Sometimes you may have to ask, how can I satisfy my ethics while also accommodating your outcomes? With some creative thinking sometimes, you can reach a solution that creates a win for everyone."

   Having integrity does not mean, "It is my way or no way at all," but rather "We will follow the bylaws, the organizational integrity, our cultural integrity, and our personal integrity while accomplishing outcomes that are in keeping with the highest traditions, values, laws, and customs of our mighty MC nation."

4. **Keep your promises**

It has been said that "a man's word is his bond" and "the only thing a man truly has is his word." You may be born into this world rich, but not even your great fortune can buy you respect if your word cannot be trusted and you are thought to be someone who lacks integrity.

When you tell someone, you are going to do something you have given them your word. It is as simple as that! Even if you did not implicitly say, "I promise," you have implied the expectation that you will do something you said you would do and you will keep your word and make sure that to which you have committed, gets done. Every time that you do not keep your word you break a promise which erodes the trust from your brothers. It provides proof that you are a person without integrity. Treasure your relationships enough to always keep your word, even those you made to yourself. What happens when you cannot keep your word even to yourself? Then you really know you cannot be trusted! Garrett suggests

> "If you make a commitment, write it down and only
> cross it off once it is done, or let the person know if
> you can no longer fulfil it."

If for some reason you cannot fulfill a promise give a timely explanation, negotiate a new delivery date, and keep your word the second time. If you cannot keep your word at all, be quick in informing the expecting person, explain why you cannot keep your word, apologize, and make it better. Having integrity does not mean you will deliver every time—sometimes things do not go according to plan—but it does mean that you will address situations properly when you cannot keep your word. This is the basics to developing integrity.

5. **Construct your inner circle with brothers of integrity**
   I have seen all too many presidents surround themselves with sycophants and political cronies. Why not? These brothers will continue to hold up your presidency as long as you are loyal to

them, right? Wrong. Often these kinds of "advisors" are not qualified to hold the positions to which you appoint them. They make your life harder by being incompetent, petty, and self-serving. They are not your true friends; they are only along for the ride for as long as it is beneficial to them. Since they lack integrity, others will assume that you also lack integrity. When you actually need them to help you through a crisis or emergency, their lack of competence and immorality makes them useless and unreliable to help you get through the crisis. Take my word for it, they are useless. They will also be the first to turn on you or throw you out when it is no longer in their best interests to support you. Instead limit your time with them and surround yourself with brothers with solid reputations, unshakeable esteem, and unquestionable track records for handling MC business, brothers, and MC to MC interactions with integrity, competence, and loyalty—even if you do not personally like them. They will be brothers you can trust, who will keep you honest, and keep your integrity intact. They will always be about the business of advancing the best possible solutions for accomplishing the agenda of the brotherhood.

A Personal Experience with Integrity

You can also be seen to lack integrity when use your wit, skills, abilities, or position to manipulate people and cause them to do things they would not normally do.

When I was assigned as an instructor during the time I was stationed at Submarine Training Facility San Diego (SUBTRAFAC San Diego). I excelled and became one of the best, even attaining the Navy's coveted certification of Master Training Specialist—a certification that has played an integral role in every job I have had since I left the Submarine Force. I was pretty squared away and I kind of got it, but my military bearing needed improvement and my attitude was garbage. When I was instructing sailors, I was the best and everyone knew it. This is probably what got me out of trouble more than anything else. Needless to say, Master Chief Greg Houser had his hands full with me. In fact, I think I may have been one of the most difficult sailors he ever had to command.

On this particular day I was driving to work to Subbase Ballast Pointe in Point Loma, California. I was in a bad mood from all of the political and racist BS going on at the job—kind of like in motorcycle clubs these days (smile). A guy on his motorcycle was buzzing in and out of traffic behind me and I took issue with his arrogance and the way he was cutting cars off—like we folks in cars should be intimidated by this bully on a motorcycle. So, I made it up in my mind that if he got far enough up in the queue and made it to me, there was no way he would force my car out of the way to make room for his motorcycle. Now, of course, I was a biker then and that might have been another reason I was so adamant about not letting him get past me because bikers like that give bikers like me a bad reputation.

As we were getting closer to the back gate to enter the base, he finally reached my car. He tried to hog my lane and force me to move my car over on the left, but I would not budge. He tried to go around me on the right, using the bicycle lane, which really pissed me off, so I hogged the bike lane blocking his path. About the time we were making our last right to go onto the base, this fool thought he would cut in between me and the right turn, forcing me to give way and let him by. This would only work if I was the scaring kind, afraid to hit him – which was NOT the case. I timed him perfectly. I angled my car so that I would run him straight into the curb and up onto the sidewalk if he persisted. Observing the abrupt end, at the last moment he relented—just centimeters before his bike slammed into the curb. I won! I had persisted! My will power and 4,000-pound car won out over his 1,000-pound motorcycle! "Bow to me world, for I am the winner!" "The great JB Chill (my nickname back in those days) had shown himself supreme and had won the jousting contest whooaaa!"

But this was not to be the end of the joust! That biker got so pissed off that he started screaming at me and chasing my car. Now, I was a young sixth degree black belt, so I welcomed this idiot with open arms, and I could not wait to do business with him, but I realized I was now on the Navy base, where I had a reputation for getting into trouble. I thought discretion would be the better part of valor in this case and chose to let him blow off steam—after all I had won so there was no need to carry it any further. I attempted to mind my own business now and drive the rest of the way to SUBTRAFAC and get on about my day. However, the biker was not to be so easily dismissed. He followed me all the way to SUBTRAFAC and into the parking lot. I pulled in and noticed this fool had parked his bike in such a way that I could not back out. "Oh great," I thought. "I am going to kick this guy's ass so bad he will wish he had never screwed with me this morning!" I jumped out of my Toyota Celica Supra (a superior car at the time – I should have never sold that damned car) and noticed he had taken off his biker jacket, helmet, and riding pants. I was staring at a full-grown E-8 Senior Chief in dress khakis with the two stars above his anchor. For those of you who do not know there is only one enlisted rank higher than an E-8 Senior Chief and that is an E-9 Master Chief. And here I was a lowly E-5. Things went from bad to worse when this joker wanted to fist fight me right there in the parking lot!

As ignorant as I was in those days – given that my buddies and I would fight anyone at any time, and the fact that I had just started hanging out with the Mighty Black Sabbath Motorcycle Club Nation as a hang-around, which meant I was really salty – I was not so ignorant as to think I could possibly whoop a Senior Chief in the middle of SUBTRAFAC's parking lot and get away with it. Even if he was starting the fight. So, I had to think quickly and succinctly if I was going to get myself out of this jam, I had put myself squarely in with my immature and un-militaristic behavior (we called a "lack of military bearing").

"Let's go punk," screamed the Senior Chief. He threw up his "dukes" and it was funny to me. He was so open it was comical. I would have crushed through his piss-poor defenses in seconds. I wanted to do a "Billy Jack" on him—hitting him with a right inside reverse crescent kick to the right side of his face with my right foot like Billy Jack did Sheriff Posner in the town square. (I know most of you are too young to remember this scene or even the movie, but it was one of the all-time baddest kicks in any karate movie ever during the history of mankind or at least in 1971 anyway—just look up Billy Jack fight in the town square on YouTube and enjoy).

"You find something funny punk," the Senior Chief screamed! He moved to attack me but I side-stepped him and positioned myself between him and his motorcycle so he could not get to me.

"Why don't you go on to work Senior Chief, you're just gonna get your ass kicked out here in this parking lot messing around with me. You don't have what it takes to win, you can barely even ride your motorcycle and keep it on the road! Screwing with me will be a great deal more difficult I can assure you," I said pessimistically.

"Screw you that's because you ran me off the road damnit! Why don't you fight me like a man? Let's see just how tough you are when you aren't hiding behind your steering wheel"

He ran around the bike trying to catch me, but I ran around to the other side. As he threw up his fighting stance once again, I howled with laughter!

"Oh, Senior Chief you are such a hoot! You can't be serious Senior Chief with that stance! That's really how you fight? You actually won some fights like that? Man quit it before you get yourself hurt. I am a whole entire sixth degree black belt in Okinawan Karate. I will stomp you into oblivion. You need to go on before you get hurt out here in front of SUBTRAFAC and then you'll have to be trying to explain to all of the other Chiefs how you let a salty E-5 kick your old barnacle encrusted Senior Chief ass!"

By then, I had skipped over to my car to get more distance as he kept trying to get close enough to take a swing.

I knew one thing, that beating that Senior Chief up was not going to be acceptable to the United States Navy and it would never be something that they could allow to stand. I had knocked my Executive Officer flat on his ass aboard USS Memphis SSN 691 just a couple of years earlier in 1988 and the only reason I got away with that one was because the XO put his hands on me first. So, I took the liberty to tear a good piece off his rear end and roughed him up a little. Mine was the overreaction but the XO hung in there for a second. LCDR Donald J. Boland was a manly man and took getting knocked on his ass with a bit of pride. He had tussled for a heartbeat with the enlisted ranks, took it like a man, and was roundly applauded by the crew for being tough guy who had gone at it with Black Belt Bunch and looked no worse for the wear. Of course, I was prepared to go to the brig on bread and water punishment for fourteen days for striking the second in command of an operational nuclear-powered submarine underway but the XO did not take it there. Instead, he told me to walk a fine line sailor because he had his eyes on me and if I stepped out of line even one time, he was going have my butt on a silver platter. And even though he did not bust me, take a rank, or punish me for the physical confrontation, he did take special pleasure in giving me pure hell for at least six months after that incident assigning me every shit job he could imagine. I would say I won the battle, but the XO won the war! I was not about to try to see if I could get away with it again. I was not foolish enough to believe that the Senior Chief would not lie about how the whole fight took place, and that he egged it on, and there were no witnesses in the parking lot, so it would be an E-5's word against the word of an E-8's. There was no way to win that scenario, so I put a plan into motion – I had to get this situation into the view of other witnesses.

I bounced around him in a fighting stance, with my hands by my side, bouncing up and down around him like Muhammed Ali used to do. When he swung at me, I leaned back just out of reach... "Blip bop pop, pop, pop, swoosh," I thought. "Man, I could hit this guy about a thousand times! Look at that open leg kick!" I skipped backwards just out of range of each swing, until I made it to the front door, and I stepped into the building and now I was on the quarterdeck of SUBTRAFAC.

The quarterdeck is a special place that has extreme historical significance in Naval tradition that is maintained aboard ships and is the main entry and exit points of many naval buildings, especially where access is controlled by sentries or reception personnel.

> In the days of antiquity and aboard old naval sailing ships, "the quarterdeck [was] a raised deck behind the main mast of a sailing ship. Traditionally it was where the captain commanded his vessel and where the ship's colors were kept. This led to its use as the main ceremonial and reception area on board, and the word is still used to refer to such an area on a ship or even in naval establishments on land. Many such facilities have areas decorated like shipboard quarterdecks
>
> There are ancient traditions of offering special deference to the quarterdeck. Greek, Roman, and Carthaginian warships all carried shrines which were given special respect. This continued into Christian times, and in medieval British warships, the religious shrine was set up on the quarterdeck. All hands were required to salute it by taking off their hats or caps. This led to the habit of saluting whenever one entered the quarterdeck." (https://en.wikipedia.org/wiki/Quarterdeck)

And as you can imagine the quarterdeck was the most formal place in SUBTRAFAC, where one was expected to enter, present one's credentials, and move quickly to their destination. It was not a place for goofing off or messing around and everyone was expected to present their most professional behavior when there.

I knew once I made it to the quarterdeck that I could beat the Senior Chief down and he would not be able to change the story to make himself appear to be the victim. But the Senior Chief suddenly switched his bearing up as we entered the quarterdeck, which took me by surprise. Suddenly, he was calm, cool, and collected, no longer swinging at me or cursing.

He said, "Quarterdeck watch please summon the Master Chief of the Command. I have a significant problem with this Petty Officer, and I believe that I am going to have to bring charges of assault against him."

"Aye Senior Chief," yelled the quarterdeck watch and with that he immediately picked up the phone and called the COB (even though his proper title was Master Chief of the Command, in the Submarine Navy we still called the senior enlisted chief "COB" just like we did on the boat).

The COB came downstairs to the quarter deck and the Senior Chief immediately laid his complaint out.

"This Petty Officer tried to kill me out on the street. He purposely nearly ran me off the road into a curb. He then attempted to fight me in the parking lot. Your sailor is very disrespectful, and I want him officially handled at Captain's Mast (naval non-administrative court) Master Chief," he yelled to my COB.

I saw this man spinning the story and lying before my very eyes. And I could see the COB looking at me with that jaundiced eye. But I also knew I was one of the COB's shipmates and he was not likely to toss me to the wolves so quickly. The COB was seriously dedicated to protecting his men, and many times he seemed to go out of his way to save my floundering ass. But I did not trust the COB so much that I did not think I should avoid doing a little lying and spinning of my own. After all they were both Chiefs and I was not.

"Well Bunch," the COB asked.

"Well, he is a liar. I never tried to run him off the road, never tried to fight him, and I have never seen him before. I think he is off of his meds COB. The Senior Chief parked behind my car preventing me from backing out and started cussing and swinging, but I never took the bait COB. I kept my military bearing and I would not engage him fist to fist in the parking lot. I always remained respectful. Go out to the parking lot and look at his bike blocking me in. I think he probably has me mixed up with someone else. You know the Supra is a popular car COB, maybe he got mine mixed up with some other sailor's car."

"Senior Chief, the COB said." "Bunch just said he hasn't a clue of what you are talking about. Did you really block his car in with your motorcycle and try to attack him in the parking lot?"

The Senior Chief did not answer the COB's question. Instead, he started yelling.

The Senior Chief responded, "You are a goddamned liar! You know you tried to run me off the road!"

"Ahh haaa I got him to break," I thought. "Now, he is all mine..." I recognized that I could manipulate him to anger and that he could not control his emotions. All I had to do was continue to goad him and he would unwind in front of the COB and then I could stomp the shit out of him right there on the quarter deck. So, I went after him.

"I have no idea what you are talking about Senior Chief but to speak this unprofessionally on the quarterdeck of SUBTRAFAC San Diego is beneath you and goes against the standards and traditions of the

United States Naval service as well as the established conduct, good order, and discipline of steely eyed submariners that have come and gone since before your time and mine. You forget yourself Senior Chief and I kindly ask you to regather your military bearing on our esteemed quarterdeck!"

The Senior Chief took the bait. He became so enraged he could not contain himself. He started screaming at the top of his lungs right there on the quarterdeck.

He shouted, "You have no integrity you smug bastard! You are a liar, and I ought to kick your..."

And that is when I cut him off. There was something about it when he said that I had no integrity that cut me to my soul. His insult was up close and personal as it went to my character and attacked me as a man. I have never forgotten how I felt to hear him say that and no other insult has ever gotten to me quite like that one since. Even to this day that insult rings in my head, "you have no integrity!"

I looked him in the eyes and coldly said, "You call me out of my name again and I will wipe this quarterdeck up with your lame ass and I don't care what the Navy does about it. Open your mouth one more time!"

With that the COB stepped between us putting his hand on my shoulder. "Senior Chief I take it that you have no real charges that you want to bring up against Petty Officer Bunch at this time, am I right?"

"No Master Chief I don't," the Senior Chief stuttered and stammered.

"Then you are out of order Senior Chief. I would advise you to get my quarterdeck before Petty Officer Bunch wipes your ass with it."

The COB then tells my best friend Keith Corley, who had wondered down from his office to see the commotion, "Make sure Bunch gets to his office without incident."

"Yes COB!"

And with that the incredulous looking Senior Chief was left standing on the quarterdeck with his mouth agape. He could not believe the good ole boy system with the COB had not worked against me. I asked the COB later why he had taken my side when he had to know I had started the whole thing.

The COB said, "He accused you of lacking integrity for not telling the truth, but telling the truth is exactly what I expected from him as a senior enlisted naval chief. If he would have told me, "Master Chief this insolent Petty Officer pissed me off so bad I lost my cool and wanted to knock his block off in the parking lot but still we need to send a signal that his behavior will not be tolerated in the Navy," I wouldn't have written you up, but we would have designed some hellacious punishment for you. But when he tried to play me and refused to answer my question, I realized that he lacked the same integrity he demanded from you, which is not acceptable in a Senior Chief in the United States Navy, therefore I let you embarrass him to teach him a lesson he will never forget.

When I think back on it, I realize that I did lack integrity that day. If I had said, "Yes, I refused to let him bully me off the highway and if that meant he had to taste the curb then so be it. I don't apologize for that, and I am not ashamed of it. And if he tries to drive crazy in my lane putting everyone's life at stake again I would do it the same way again." I would have stood my ground and stood by my principles. I would not have manipulated him on the quarterdeck. By lying about it and manipulating him to lose his cool, I tainted my victory and cheapened myself. Master Chief Houser knew both the Senior Chief and I were lying—neither of us was worth a shit that day. But he had a bigger lesson to teach to a leader who commanded men, so I escaped his wrath. Perhaps in so doing he taught us both a lesson that day.

Integrity means you can win without cheating, manipulating, or lying. What value do you place on victory? Is it to be victorious no matter what the cost? If so, stand by to count the carcasses your presidency will leave in its wake as you sacrifice one pawn after another during your quest for power. My advice is to choose instead, to have some damned integrity.

Example - A President refuses to violate the bylaws to benefit himself, even when he knows that no one in the MC would ever discover his action.

◊◊◊

CHAPTER FIFTEEN
The Leadership Principle of Enthusiasm

Enthusiasm

Definition - The display of sincere interest and exuberance in the performance of duty.

Significance - Displaying interest in a task and optimism that it can be successfully completed greatly enhances the likelihood that the task will be done.

As president you are the leader and the face of the brotherhood. It is from your optimism, exuberance, and enthusiasm that the brothers draw their inspiration to accomplish greatness on behalf of the MC. It is sometimes difficult to understand the power of your influence over the brothers in that they key off everything you do. If you are emotionally keyed up, they are keyed up. When you are gloomy, they are gloomy. Though you may not understand all of the psychological reasons why this occurs it is important to know that your enthusiasm towards performance of duty will impact the men singularly more significantly than any other member, officer, or factor in the MC. So, learn how to develop your skills to use your enthusiasm to empower the club.

In the article "Leadership and Enthusiasm" (June 30, 2016), Michael Hopkin says that leaders inspire people to do hard things and convince them to follow because they love what they do and "have the ability to inspire and motivate people" ([1]www.aboutleaders.com/leadership.com/leadership-and-enthusiasm/). This, he says, is because leaders have enthusiasm. He quotes Simon Sinek, a leading motivational speaker and author, "People don't buy what you do, they buy why you do it." For motorcycle clubs this is especially true. Your brothers often join and follow the entire MC because they dig the vibe of the president. People often follow leaders more so than they follow an organization. Kind of like individuals who follow a religious leader more than they follow the religion, even when the leader requests his followers do something so outside the rails of normality it would seem unimaginable that any sane person would obey. For example, I am reminded of the religious leader who told his members to turn over their young, underage daughters to him to be his brides. Investigating detectives could not understand the power this leader had, but his crimes were proof he absolutely did. Similarly, during the riots on the U.S. Capitol in 2021, President Trump's supporters were so concerned with keeping him in power they were willing to fight and die to make it so, even if it meant the character of the United States would be irreparably altered should they succeed. Do not abuse this devotion over your brothers who hold you in such high esteem. Do not be shocked when you observe this behavior within your club as it can be unsettling to witness the raw power others give you, but do not become corrupted by it.

"It all comes down to attitude."[1] The enthusiasm that emanates from a president's attitude drives those he commands! It effects their behaviors, beliefs, morale, code of conduct, and much more. My club brother Ol' Skool, Original Seven Founding member of the Mighty Black Sabbath Motorcycle Club Nation, Atlanta chapter, Original Seven Founding member of the Mighty Black Sabbath Motorcycle Club Nation, Ronin chapter, Original Seven Founding member of the Mighty Black Sabbath Motorcycle Club Nation, Pensacola chapter, and Mighty Black Sabbath Motorcycle Club Nation East Coast Regional President often refers to the word attitude as "altitude!"

According to Ol' Skool, "Having the right altitude determines the outcome of any situation." I have overheard him asking members of his chapter, "Is there a problem with your altitude brother? Because if there is we can get that altitude at the right level quick, fast, and in a hurry!"

I like President Ol' Skool's characterization of altitude being the word to use in place of attitude because it points out that having a high achieving altitude in your approach to exuding your attitude before the brotherhood is the key ingredient to success in this regard. If you think of elevating your attitude to the right altitude during all situations, then you will understand how being at the right altitude with your attitude can guide the club forward during any challenge or crisis.

A brilliant president emits enthusiasm in all things where it comes to leadership. Enthusiasm can sometimes be more impactful than any other leadership quality. Club success can often come down to leadership's level of enthusiasm. When you are enthusiastic your men may describe you with words like eager, excited, inspirational, stimulating, intense, insanely passionate, zestful, ambitious, or tireless. They will seek to match you, as men are naturally competitive.

In Steven Spielberg's movie "Saving Private Ryan", a group of U.S. soldiers were tasked with going behind enemy lines to retrieve a paratrooper whose brothers had been killed in action during various battles in World War II. Since Private Ryan was the last surviving son in his family the Army decided to extract him from the war and send him home. This, of course, was a harrowing mission given to a small squad following their landing on the bitter killing fields of the beaches of Normandy on June 6, 1944, also known as "D-Day". The members of the 2nd Ranger Battalion under Cpt. Miller were tasked to find and retrieve Private James Ryan. Throughout the movie it was Cpt. Miller's enthusiasm, whose focus was on the business of the squad and the mission, that kept his men moving forward, even in the face of impending doom, to reach their goal of finding and saving the private and ultimately surviving the war so that he could get back home to his wife. From the moment they landed on Omaha beach, Cpt. Miller took one risk after another to get his men safely established on the beachhead, then against overwhelming odds to destroy the fortified bunkers to keep them alive. When tasked to take out a machinegun nest, his willingness to act on his own pushed his men forward to match his level of enthusiasm towards accomplishing the mission. No one wanted to be outdone by the leader who was willing to do more than his share of the work to always complete the mission. Eventually nearly all of his men were led to their demise and although he would not survive, the mission he fought so hard for—to save Private Ryan—had succeeded.

Though this is only a Hollywood film many WWII veterans who screened it said it was remarkably close to what they actually witnessed in combat. It stands as a classic demonstration of the enthusiastic dedicated stubbornness of a resolute leader. It does not portray enthusiasm with a fake exuberance of happiness and glee; in fact, you seldom see Capt. Miller smile, but through his resolve and uncompromising passionate pursuit of the mission no matter the cost he was able to lead his men to accomplish it against overwhelming odds. As today's modern MCs function like a pseudo military command, is not unreasonable to draw the parallel. Allow your men to see your passion for the mission of the MC and they will be compelled to follow your lead.

Enthusiasm the Secret of Success

In an article about enthusiasm written for the Leadership & Development blog([2]*www.leadership-and-development.com/enthusiasm/*), Martin Gilliard describes what he called "The Secret To Success".

> "Enthusiasm is thought to be the recognized secret of success. If you are considering two people side by side for a position of employment and both have similar intelligence, abilities, and skills. You will almost always opt for the more enthusiastic of the two.
>
> In fact, it is likely that you might choose a more enthusiastic individual over a more qualified and skilled but less enthusiastic individual."

This demonstrates how important enthusiasm is in playing a role in the success of members who are continually given increased responsibility because they possess the right "altitude" to achieve such. Equally, the leader who exhibits insatiable passion will also illicit such a response from the members of the brotherhood.

> "Enthusiasm is not a substitute for intelligence, appreciation or other qualities that you can associate with generating success. But when added to your existing skills and qualifications it can often make that extra bit of difference that is required to succeed in almost any endeavor."

Be Passionate

> "If you are passionate about something then it is generally easier to be enthusiastic."[2]

Successful MC presidents are wildly passionate about the brotherhood. They live, sleep, breathe, ingest, and consume all things MC. They are the MC, and their general countenance shows it. They wear pristine uniforms, follow the bylaws, visit sick brothers, counsel brothers, work on the mental stability of brothers, tend to the properties, wives, social clubs, support clubs, friends, and associates. Every time you see them, they are about the business of the family. Focus your passion on grooming the MC into something incredibly special. You will find that enthusiasm follows and becomes infectious among your people. Once you have it, they will have it!

Enthusiastic Presidents

> "Enthusiastic [presidents] are able to make visions come alive. They do this by being inspirational, passionate and by breathing life into the vision via their enthusiasm and energy. Enthusiasm is

> infectious and makes [presidents] more credible. It's
> the exact opposite of being dull and boring. It is the
> enthusiastic transmission of energy that brings a
> vision to life for [presidents and their members].
>
> To tap into your own energy and enthusiasm for a
> vision you have to determine what excites you most
> about the vision." [2]

What about it makes you excited? You need to have so much
excitement that you can speak to your brothers endlessly about it.

> "Get excited and then get others excited so that you
> can breathe life into the vision." [2]

Then you will see it accomplished despite all odds against it.

Improving Enthusiasm in the MC

Now that you know the importance of enthusiasm to your
presidency, consider teaching your members how to be
enthusiastic. Watch how the culture of positivity and the belief that
you all can accomplish anything spreads. Hopkin gives us some tips
below:

Tip 1: **Create the Vision**

Look introspectively at your MC and your own behavior. Are you
leading the MC in a positive direction? If not change your behavior,
because it is important in all things to lead by example. Then teach
your members how to complete their jobs competently and
successfully. When your people are confident in what they are
doing your enthusiasm now has a place to take root and grow
within them!

Tip 2: **Share Your Optimism**

Like the Marine Corps General,

"You are on the front lines. You are responsible for seeing the big picture but do not keep it to yourself. Share your vision of success with your subordinates. Communicate your optimism through your words and actions. Let them feel your passion."

In the Navy, I was a Master Training Specialist. This is the highest level of certification a Navy Trainer can achieve. It takes a Navy trainer one to two years to complete the advanced qualification process needed to attain this credential. In our training world, we had a process for generating incredible enthusiasm throughout our training culture to infect our students with success. It was called "V.E.G.A." (Voice, Eyes, Gestures and Attitude)! Not only would we shower our students with the competence of our knowledge on a subject, but we would let them feel our passion through our **V**oices, **E**yes, **G**estures and **A**ttitude.

Your spirit of accomplishment, experience, and competence must illuminate from you like a bright light. After encountering you, club members should reflect upon the meeting with the idea that they were standing with the most confident and inspirational leader on Earth. They will know they can do it because you absolutely know that they can do it. Whenever you are in front of your brothers always remember your V.E.G.A. Use it to inspire your brothers! Ask yourself, "How am I projecting my voice, eyes, gestures, and is my altitude correctly displayed in my attitude. Your men are always watching your every move every second they are in your presence. Remember, V.E.G.A.!

Tip 3: **Build a Culture of Enthusiasm**

"The greatest benefit your attitude will provide is a culture of success. Develop your [brotherhood].

Everyone wants to belong to a winning team. To expect and respect the culture of success, teach your members how to be winners by getting them used to winning.

> "Provide opportunities for them to grow. Give them direction and create structure and process to channel their growth. Create an environment where people will give their absolute best efforts.
>
> As you cultivate these behaviors within your MC family it will reap the benefits. Let enthusiasm drive your leadership."[1]

Example

The club faces a challenging situation that pits it against an enemy MC. The president exudes confidence and enthusiasm that the club will work its way out of the situation. He brings the officers together to explain the big picture and articulates each one's task to bring the plan to fruition. He details what accomplishments will constitute success and what losses will equal failure. He makes sure each officer knows his position and responsibilities intimately. Then he holds a meeting with the entire club to bring the club up to speed on his plan and his vision. He details the actions he wants from each club member while the MC is in its precarious position warning the brothers to travel in pairs when in colors and to be always on guard. He expresses his great faith and belief in the capabilities of all members and assures them of the great success they will all soon experience. He reminds them, "We are an independent nation, and we are the masters of our own fate!" The brothers know they will be successful because the Prez said so and has demonstrated a plan of action to back it up.

◊◊◊

CHAPTER SIXTEEN
The Leadership Principle
of Bearing

Bearing

Definition - Creating a favorable impression in carriage, appearance, and personal conduct at all times.

Significance - The ability to look, talk, and act like a leader whether or not these manifestations indicate one's true feelings.

There is a certain bearing folks expect from the president of a motorcycle club. In the armed forces, this may be spoken of leaders as having a "command presence." If you have ever been asked if you were ever in the military or perhaps a police officer, it is because someone sees certain presence in you that reminds them of the kind of person who would take charge in a dangerous situation. Another term for this among soldiers, seamen, and airmen is "military bearing". For instance, when you see one of the warriors guarding the tomb of the unknown soldier, just the way that they carry themselves would leave a witness with the impression that they are not messing around. The way they act is so serious that you know they are focused on the task at hand and will not be deterred from completing their job.

Just as bearing and presence are vitally important in the military, they are equally important in the MC. Perhaps we should call it "MC bearing" for the brothers and as the president you should possess a "presidential bearing" that conveys to all that you are the leader of a motorcycle club before you even open your mouth.

In the article *"Marine Corps Leadership Traits: Bearing"* ([1]*https://officercandidatesschool.com/2012/10/12/marine-corps-leadership-traits-bearing/*), the author states

> "Bearing is the way you conduct and carry yourself. Your manner should reflect alertness, competence, confidence, and control. A [president] who exhibits bearing is one who is in total control of his emotions, posture, and general outward appearance. Discipline and self-respect are the keys to bearing. Since as the

common Navy and Marine Corps phrase goes, "perception is reality," some people will form an opinion of your qualities based only on shallow impressions."

They glean from the way you present yourself.

"If you carry yourself with high standards and maintain a professional, [presidential-like], self-controlled demeanor, that perceived "reality" will not be harmed before you have a chance to make a second impression."

The article notes,

"One of the best examples of bearing in American military history is the personal conduct of General George Washington. He said, "Every action in the company of others ought to be done with some sign of respect to those present.""

Executive Bearing

In the world of corporate America bearing is often referred to among leaders as "executive bearing". In the article *"Just What is Executive Bearing, and Why Does It Matter?"* ([2]*https://rainbows.typepad.com/blog/2011/03/executive-bearing-presence-arceil-thomas-lee-impact-importance-leader-leadership.html*) on executive bearing entitled, Tomas J. Lee, notes,

"A curiously high percentage of senior executives, retired generals, three-term U.S. senators, judges, network television anchors, Cabinet secretaries, college presidents, law-firm partners, and diplomats just seem to have the ineffable bearing of leadership."

He jokes that they might not be beautiful like movie stars, "But they all definitely stand out." He goes on to say,

> "Something about them proclaims they aren't typical. Women and men alike, many of these leaders just stand an inch closer to the polished, the classy, perhaps even the distinguished."

> Whatever it is that sets them apart, it must be more than appearance or posture or anything else so insubstantial." [2]

He suggests, and I would have to agree, that bearing goes deeper than what you might see on the surface. He writes that when he thinks of bearing his mind envisions,

> "A sense of being that reaches for something profound, something important. After all, anyone could put on a neatly pressed suit and a polished pair of shoes, but not just anyone can invoke values, describe a necessary future, and inspire people to do the extraordinary. What so many highly effective leaders share is a common way of talking, behaving, and relating to other people that enables, drives, and sustains their impact as leaders." [2]

Lee laid out nine cornerstones of executive bearing believed to set highly effective leaders apart. I have adopted these cornerstones to contextualize them for motorcycle clubs:

1. *Communication (Verbal)*

"Communication is the energy of leadership. Nothing is more important than the ability to speak with clarity and to listen with interest and sincerity. Regardless of position, a putative [president] who lacks this capability is merely keeping the chair warm. You cannot expect people to read your mind, and you cannot expect to read anyone else's mind. You need not be as eloquent as Ronald Reagan or Winston Churchill, but you must learn how to express yourself and how to listen with genuine concern, intensity, and curiosity." [2]

2. *Communication (Nonverbal).*

> "By nonverbal communication, we are referring to far more than body language and facial expression. They can send messages, for sure, but they pale in comparison with the nonverbal A-B-C-D-E communication of attitudes, behaviors, character, decisions, and empathy. Every [president] must become fully aware of the myriad of ways he communicates implicitly and unintentionally, every day, all day long. Behaviors so incidental as where and with whom you eat lunch are apt to send important social cues that ricochet through your [MC]." [2]

As [president] you must be keenly aware of your non-verbal communications and manage them successfully and professionally.

3. *Appearance and Image.*

> "This part is about the visual, insubstantial as it may be. The basics are good grooming, neat and clean attire, generally looking [sharp enough to be seen as the president]." [2]

Although our uniform is generally scrappy and based in leather for protection while riding, wearing stinking, filthy leathers and presenting a disheveled appearance never serves a president well. Brothers and the extended MC family want to feel like they are being represented by an appealing president that others would respect, admire, or fear. How can a president, who cannot command his physical appearance, command the complexities and challenges of an MC?

"Impeccable manners are elementary, too. For gentlemen, that entails opening doors, yielding on entering and exiting elevators, even pulling out chairs. And do not even think of disrespecting or disregarding anyone in a position of service: waiters, chambermaids, customer-service personnel, custodians. To the contrary, be sure to greet everyone with a smile and pleasant acknowledgement. This is the ethic of reciprocity as it applies to leadership." [2]

A story I can recount is one about a president of a 99%er club that once invited his members to his home. When the brothers walked in the door of his apartment and saw the condition of his house and the filthy way he lived, with his motorcycle broken down in his living room and containers of used motor oil stinking up the bathroom, they were appalled that a man with those kinds of living conditions was the leader of their MC. Many of them had half million dollar and ¾ million-dollar homes, owned their own businesses or were senior managers or directors at their jobs. They could not believe their president lived like a hermit in a shack. This may have been okay for a 20-year-old, but this man was in his early fifties. His brothers felt foolish being led by such an irresponsible and imprudent man—who had not accomplished at least as much as they had accomplished in their lives. Needless to say, even though he was a stellar president with many years of experience on the set and in his club, he lost the next election by a landslide. Appearance and image involve everything for a president, from the condition in which you keep your motorcycle to the cleanliness of your home.

4. *Conviction and Confidence.*

"[Presidents] deal with complexity in many forms: ambiguity, nuance, multiplicity, change, and uncertainty. A [president's] self-confidence helps [members] cope with that complexity. While there is a fine line between self-confidence and arrogance, the former is a strength when borne of conviction to core principles, whereas the latter is a severe character flaw that has doomed [MC presidents for decades]. The thing to recognize and remember is the importance of core principles as the only true foundation for conviction and confidence." [2]

5. *Respect and Humility.*

   "[Presidents] have to be accountable for the actions of the [brotherhood] they lead, but no [president] deserves full credit for the [MC's] success. Indeed, without the earnest support of your [club brothers], no president is a leader. It follows that any [president] worth the title must fully respect the work of the [members]. You can accomplish just about anything as long as you accept all the blame and give away all the credit." [2]

6. *Congruence and Authenticity.*

   "It is one thing to pay rhetorical tribute to lofty values, another thing to think through their implications and then honor those values consistently." [2]

It is one thing to say the brotherhood is a democracy and everyone has the right to vote on other members' issues, but does this carry through when there is a problem that affects you and you tell the Sergeant at Arms that there will be no investigation or a vote, then you change the bylaws to suit your agenda? Remember your brothers are always watching. They will destroy your presidency the moment they discover that you are not authentic or the terms by which you run your administration are incongruent.

7. *Presence and Accessibility.*

    "There are four types of presence and four types of accessibility: the physical, the intellectual, the social, and the emotional. [Presidents] need to understand and appreciate all four. Each of the four conveys powerful messages of inclusion or exclusion."[2]

8. *Clarity of Purpose.*

    "In the private sector, most senior executives will tell you their primary purpose is to ensure a substantial return to investors. That is an essential thing, needless to say, but the organization's purpose must be viewed through the lens of the customer, not the lens of the investor." [2]

    In a motorcycle club the focus is different. The MC's purpose must be viewed through the lens of the full patch brothers, prospects, hang-arounds, properties, sisters, support clubs, and friends of the MC. The "return to investors" is actually the return to the brotherhood and the MC's extended family. This must be the focus.

    "It must drive the repeated decisions of the [brotherhood] to start or continue to address its wellbeing. Without that, the strength of the brotherhood is moot." [2]

9. *Support and Servancy.*

    "Unfortunately, few [presidents] are familiar with the concept of servant leadership. It is the notion that the leader serves the followers, not the other way around. It is President John F. Kennedy's famous dictum—"Ask not what your country can do for you;

ask what you can do for your country"—applied to [presidents] with regard to the [MC] they would lead." [2]

The president should ask not what the MC can do for him but rather what he can do to better serve the MC.

I would like to add one more cornerstone for executive bearing in the MC and that is the concept of setting high standards:

10. *High Standards and Personal Conduct.*

> The Marine Corps manual states that to develop bearing, you should hold yourself to the "highest standards of personal conduct". Never be content with meeting only the minimum requirements. If a president holds himself to this high standard of personal conduct he will remain above reproach.

There are many more things that you can concentrate on to help you develop your presidential bearing that will enable you to become an exceptional leader; however, if you get started on the things mentioned in this section you will have a good grasp of the basics. You can also consider imitating someone you greatly admire and respect. Studying someone you look up to and learning things they did to achieve success can give you a template by which you can model your own behaviors. Good luck! Move it forward.

Example

There was a guy who became National President of his MC, when the previous National President was forced to step down. The previous National was best friends with the new National but was removed from office due to a conniving lie and insidious plan concocted by the new National President. By the time the previous

National realized he had been duped, the new National was already being flown across the country to be inaugurated.

The new National became upset when he learned that his patches would not be ready for his cut in time for his first meeting in front of the brothers. He called the former National President demanding he remove the patches from his cut and turn them over just so that he could have them sewn onto his cut in time for his first meeting. The former National looked at this young fool with deep concern knowing that in all the time he had spent in the club, the new National President had not learned a damned thing about leadership or presidential bearing. He knew there would be dark days ahead for the club, so he decided to try to teach the young fool a few lessons in leadership—if he would listen. The former National explained that the new National did not need new patches sewn on his cut to lead his men and exude his command presence to get things done at his first meeting. He even reasoned that the men would probably not even expect that he would have any new patches at all since his ascension to the National Presidency had been quite sudden. He continued by explaining that everyone would quickly figure out who he was when they saw men swirling in a flurry around him, prospects escorting him as bodyguards and carrying his bags from the plane, and folks jumping to respond to his every command. No one would have to see the words "National President" on his cut to understand that he was the man in charge—and showing the men that he could command without collar devices would go a long way in establishing his credibility and confidence with the brothers. Alas the former National was unsuccessful in convincing the new National that he would not need his "I Love ME and Look at ME Patches" for his first meeting, so he relented and removed the patches from his own cut and gave them to the new National. The new National went to the first meeting with his chest pumped up, high stepping like a peacock displaying all his mating feathers.

The former National and the National before him had each served for nearly ten years each. The new National served little more than 18 months before he was forced to step down after many alcohol-fueled, drunken incidents of misconduct and missteps on the set. He left in disgrace, under scandal, and dishonor. The position he had lied, connived, backstabbed, and cheated to get remained out of his grasp to keep even after he attained it. His downfall was not caused by him being a bad president, it was that he never learned how to conduct himself with presidential bearing. He did not understand that not being able to hold your alcohol leaves you vulnerable and makes you look weak in the eyes of your men.

I have known many drug and alcohol addicted presidents whose vices have gotten them tossed from the leadership of the brotherhood. Until you can get your vices under control you are unworthy to serve in the capacity of leadership of a mighty MC Nation. Save yourself the drama of a downfall that could set the MC back 20 years with your unceremonious departure. Step down while you are ahead, get yourself together, and run for office again. The brotherhood will never be about you and if you are a distraction, then you will become the story. A president should never be the story. The story should always be about the mighty MC Nation and the good brothers who serve within.

Chapter SEVENTEEN
The Leadership Principle
of Unselfishness

Unselfishness

Definition - Avoidance of providing for one's own comfort and personal advancement at the expense of others.

Significance - The quality of looking out for the needs of your subordinates before your own is the essence of leadership. This quality is not to be confused with putting these matters ahead of the accomplishment of the mission.

An unselfish president will be a beloved president because he takes care of his people before he takes care of himself. He understands the requirements of the MC, prioritizes needs and objectives, and does not waste the club's valuable resources: people, time, money, or property. Unselfishness means you avoid making yourself comfortable at the expense of others, you are considerate of others, and give credit to those who deserve it. To be unselfish, you must keep the focus on the brotherhood and its members. The term "It's Not About You" should come to mind when referencing a president who is unselfish.

Is there anything to this idea of unselfishness? After all, you have worked your butt off to get to the top of the MC world, do you not deserve to enjoy the accolades you have achieved along with the recognition, perks, and benefits? All the hard work came from you, can you not continue forward on your path to getting to the top on your own without particularly caring about anyone other than yourself? Of course, you can. In fact, in his article, *"12 Leadership Traits: #6-Unselfishness,"* ([1]*www.geraldgillis.com/12-leadership-traits-6-unselfishness*) blogger Gerald Gillis states,

> "Selfish business and political leaders, among others, make it to the top of organizations every day, but once at the top, however, they will probably not be

effective under all conditions, both routine and demanding."

Why?

"For starters, unselfishness is a key leadership trait that is both noticed and valued by others. A leader whose personal climb is widely seen as coming at the expense of others will eventually stall and lose altitude, with the potential unpleasantness that can follow. Conversely, a competent leader who is unselfish, who has the best interests of the organization at heart, and whose employees duly recognize such, will have a level of support that could provide significant advantage in difficult times. The unselfish leader's chances of maintaining altitude and eventually resuming the climb are considerably higher given the strong support of others."[1]

To a selfish president, I would say your stay at the top will inevitably be short because members of the brotherhood will see you for what you are and begin to torpedo your command, looking for ways to undermine and erode your power and influence. A selfish president will be eliminated. You must understand the dynamics of MC culture to understand why selfish presidents are so vehemently despised by the brotherhood. Motorcycle clubs are focused on the "WE" of the organization and they are never about the "I". The survival of the MC is based upon the individual efforts of all members combined into the one collective unit. The founding principles of the tribe are the root of the MC tree, much like the behaviors of bees belonging to the hive, the full patch brothers, and extended family of the brotherhood mesh together as one to accomplish the family's agenda and ensure the long-term survival of the MC.

Father of the Mighty Black Sabbath Motorcycle Club Nation, Paul 'Pep' Perry, taught us to stop saying my, my, my, me, me, me, and mine, mine, mine. He warned us often to exclude the word "I" from all forms of our conversations, replacing "I" with "We", at every opportunity wherein it was appropriate to do so. He even went so far as to equate the word "we" with the French word "oui" (pronounced the same way as "we" but meaning "yes!") Father Paul 'Pep' Perry taught us that OUI means YES, WE CAN! We means all of us together as one and appropriately we can say OUI to anything WE want to do! You cannot be selfish if you operate in the WE. Because a motorcycle club is about us, for us, by us, and for the greater good of all of us, the culture of WE will eventually root out any selfish president who does not understand the "oui" that powers the "we" of the WEMC. In several of my YouTube videos, you may have heard me interchange references to MC with "WE-C" as I explain that the MC has never stood for "ME-C", but rather "WE-MC" ("WE-C" for short).

So, what is it that unselfishness accomplishes? How does an unselfish president behave? How does one practice unselfishness? Gillis gives us a clue in the following examples of an unselfish leader that I have adopted for this book in terms of how they would be beneficial for use for a president in an MC.

An unselfish president:

1. *Shares the credit.*
    > "[Club members of the extended family] who are recognized for their winning efforts, whether in the foreground or background, feel a sense of pride and loyalty to the [brotherhood] and their [president]. Since everyone wants to work for such a [president], a deep pool of talent very often ensues." [1]

You will notice that the turnover in the MC will sharply decline as will the cliques and internal feuding when everyone feels included and rewarded. Folks will be proud to stay and participate! You may even find that rarely seen members will once again become regulars.

2.   *Takes the time to teach.*

"Teaching is a critical role for a [president]. The unselfish [president] makes time to teach [officers and members] not only about [bylaws, rules, and traditions], but also ethical and behavioral standards that are important to the MC, the set, and the Nation." [1]

Growing chapters, resolving differences with outlaws and 1%ers, and opening up new territories are the intangibles that turn officers and members into legends as they become standouts for accomplishing the club's goals and objectives. An unselfish president does not keep these accomplishments to himself. Doing so would kill the forward momentum of the club if he was to die or is lost to the MC. Instead, he shares as much information as possible to give the club its best chance for survival.

3.   *Accepts responsibility for [members'] shortcomings.*

"An unselfish president is not quick to blame others or make excuses when [brothers] inevitably mess up. The [president] first finds the fix to the problem, followed with coaching and counseling, and then looks for ways to improve the process and the training. Learning from mistakes is critical to continuous improvement. Giving [officers and brothers] room to make mistakes and then gaining learning and confidence as a result, is an unselfish and courageous act for a [president]." [1]

In public the president blames himself, using terms like "We have made some errors here that we will examine so that we understand the error in our ways such that we can get better." In the words of my former Navy Submarine SUBTRAFAC San Diego Commander Captain Raaz, "We all deserve the right to get smarter later." But he still let us know that he was incredibly serious about us getting better from our mistakes. He could tolerate honest mistakes, but incompetence, laziness and stupidity were out of the question, as he would follow that statement up quickly with, "Now, that having been said, the stupid shall be punished!" He wasn't my only Navy commander to say those words. I guess the Navy was kind of standard in that way.

4. *Accepts and shares the ideas and input of others.*

"An unselfish [president] is open to new ideas and concepts, and from a variety of sources. So very often the [brothers, prospects, hang-arounds, properties, sisters, and supporters] who are actually doing the work have the best ideas on how a particular process can be improved. Let others be the experts. Build the bench strength by developing technical and leadership skills in the [brotherhood]. Help others to succeed and reinforce the unselfish trait." [1]

> The Father of the Mighty Black Sabbath Motorcycle Club Nation Paul 'Pep' Perry would say, "Take an inventory of your bench and those around you who are dedicated to the greater mission of the MC. Find out what skills and valuable traits each brings, then develop the talents of your best and brightest people. Empower them to be great and reward them with praise, prestige, and public upliftment. Fulfill their spirits with encouragement and high expectations of superior achievement through superior performance. Then you will notice the people under your leadership will develop and grow while the MC flourishes. And you will tell them they did it by themselves."

> Gillis summarizes this by telling us,

>> "An unselfish leader whose openness and generosity is seen by those with whom he comes into contact will very likely accrue significant benefits in both a personal and professional sense. A selfish leader who grabs all the credit and deflects all the blame will at some point find the world a very lonely place." [1]

Example

A President ensures all members of his caravan have been tented, bedded down, are dry from the rain, have electricity in the camp, communication, mosquito repellent and entertainment before he does. And if resources are scarce, he will share what he has and ensure that others do the same.

◊◊◊

Chapter EIGHTEEN
The Leadership Principle
of Courage

Courage

Definition - Courage is a mental quality that recognizes fear but enables a president to proceed with calmness and firmness. Courage is standing for what is right, even in the face of popular disfavor or eminent danger.

Significance - The importance of courage on the battlefield is obvious but the importance of courage in the everyday struggles encountered by the brotherhood is not nearly so. The pressures of politics, criticism, favoritism, and perhaps preservation can paralyze a president, rendering him incapable of exhibiting the skill of courage when most needed.

To successfully run an MC, you need to exhibit courage on two fronts of leadership: First, in the day-to-day operations to keep the brotherhood running as a well-oiled operating machine; second, to either lead your brothers into battle or avoid a battle while keeping the club's dignity intact and ensuring the MC's objectives are met.

A Point on Encouragement to Courage

Leadership of alpha males can be vexing to one's soul and trying to one's patience. A president lacking courage will have a fear-filled term that will leave him broken, dejected, and disillusioned. No matter how you try to guard against it, you will never be able to stop the backstabbing, belly-slithering, shameless, ruthless, spineless, classless, clueless, sons-of-bitches who will be out to undermine, destroy, and steal everything you have toiled to build in your MC career—from your closest officer or most trusted club brother to your most disloyal and hated member, they are out to get you. You must get used to the fact that nobody loves you when you make it to the top. Grab your ball sack, heave it into your underwear, and pull your waist band up to your navel. Stick your chest out and find the courage to lead, baby boy, because you just put on that "P" patch and shit just got real! Lead every day as though it were your last. This is the most important point of courage I share!

There is a difference between confidence and arrogance as it relates to being courageous. Too much confidence or arrogance can lead to your success, failure or even get you killed. It may be ironic to succeed at being courageous by possessing a trait others condemn but you will require either confidence or arrogance to have the strength of character to achieve victory. Which is more important? Being confident is doing what the job calls for because it must be done and no one else can do it. You use thought, reason, policy, experience, and a scientific method of deduction to form your strategy and you execute it to the best of your ability. Being arrogant is doing what the president alone thinks is right when there is no evidence or scientific method to prove or disapprove this assumption. Arrogance is more likely to cause you to fail or get you killed, shifting your odds of success from 50/50 to 80/20 against you. Arrogance may allow you to win for the day but will trick you into believing your success came from your skills rather than a manifestation of sheer luck.

For some a long history of surviving arrogant decisions gives them a sense of competency on par with having confidence. Others have no idea there is a difference, believing the arrogance is confidence. But there is a big difference between the two states of mind and how one can lead you to victory and the other to demise. Let us examine them so you can identify them in yourself when the time comes.

In her article *"Arrogance, Confidence, and Courage"* ([1]https://somaticvoicework.com/arrogance-confidence-and-courage), March 23, 2014, Jeanette Lovetri described the differences between the two.

> "The line between arrogance, confidence and courage is very tiny. It is also a perception, like everything else. I might appear very confident to someone who is self-assured, but arrogant to

> someone who is insecure. I might seem to be bold and courageous to someone who is shy, but just ordinary to another who is energized herself."[1]

The important thing to note in her observation is her focus "*on how she might appear to others.*" When making decisions for the brotherhood, as president your mindset should never be about how your thoughts and actions appear to others. Your brothers have no direct knowledge about what you feel in your heart or even what is going on in your mind. Just because others may perceive you as arrogant or confident, you must not command from their perspective. It is from your perspective that you must know from which you stand—arrogant or confident? Make your decisions accordingly. You are the one who must ultimately make presidential decisions and are held responsible for any decision you make!

Lovetri went on to say,

> "Since I wrote here about courage recently, it seems that we should investigate the characteristics of arrogance and confidence as opposites and partners to courage. An arrogant person might think that only she is right, that her ideas could never be incorrect, and that she is better than others. An arrogant person might never think of the impact of her words on others or of what others think of her words and actions. A confident person might say exactly the same things in the same way but is interested in what another person might think. She would seriously consider another person's different opinion and give it fair investigation as an alternative point of view. She would believe that she might not always be correct. Her confidence has room in it for human frailty.

> The difference is not in what is being offered, it is in the person's attitude about herself and her message.

If you do not care what others think or how they react, and if you think you can never be wrong, you are not likely to have much fear or need much courage. What would you be afraid of in the first place? You have your arrogance to protect you. If, conversely, you have great confidence, but you also have a mind that is open to the considerations of others, you might also be full of self-doubt. That would require you to gather up your courage before putting your message out, so no one else knows you are trembling in your boots the whole time." [1]

Confidence and arrogance both have a part to play in courageousness. One is a smarter way to go than the other because it gives you so many more tools to utilize to help you arrive at the appropriate decision. As President it will be up to you to decide which one you will employ. Are you confident or are you arrogant? Which will you use to arrive at the decisions that matter for your brothers? What will be the cost to the brotherhood for either characteristic that exists within you? If you do not like what you find how will you change?

As we move further into our discussion about being courageous, let us start in the context of being courageous to lead an MC in its daily obligations and ordinary standard operating procedures (courage in standard leadership), then we will talk about courageousness in terms of leading (or NOT leading) your MC into battle (courage in battle).

Courage in Standard Leadership

In a blog article entitled *"What is courageous leadership"* ([2]https://www.wework.com/ideas/professional-development/management-leadership/what-is-courageous-leadership), June 14, 2017, Samantha Pena outlines seventeen key traits of leadership that spring from what she described as the "three main buckets of courage".

Courageous leadership is what every brother hopes for and what every MC needs. A courageous president guides the club without stamping out the creativity, leads by example, and stands at the helm of the club. He gives others the confidence to work in the best interest of the brotherhood to the best of their abilities.

Three Main Buckets of Courage

Pena noted three main types of courage when it comes to being courageous:

1. Try Courage:

    "Try courage is the courage required to take the first step in something. If you are doing something for the first time, that takes courage. You might fail, you might get it wrong, or you might do something completely incredible" [2]

    But you will not do anything if you do not try. Sometimes a president will have to take big risks just to try something new. It takes courage to go against standard practices, or face something the MC has never seen before and come up with a solution completely from scratch.

2. Trust Courage:

    "This is the type of courage required to relinquish control. As a [president], you will need this courage in order to delegate to your [subordinates], to give over control to [officers and men], and to show your [brothers] that you trust them. This type of trust not only shows your [brothers] that you trust them, but also that they can trust you not to micromanage their work." [2]

3. Tell Courage:

"Tell courage is the courage you need to speak openly and with conviction about your beliefs and ideas. Often, doing this can be very scary, especially in [the clubhouse setting among alpha males]. Courageous leadership means providing your [brothers] with positive and constructive feedback on a regular basis, even if what you have to say is going to make someone feel uncomfortable or downright angry." [2]

By using these buckets of courage, you can implement the following actions to make you a stronger president for the MC:

1. Claim your courage

    "The first thing you must do is decide that you are going to be a courageous leader, no matter what may come. You must be willing to climb over obstacles, to do what is difficult, and to keep doing that every day. A courageous [president] is someone who constantly asks themselves if they are being courageous enough then making adjustments to ensure that they are. Courage is a muscle that must be strengthened day by day and exercised by choice." [2]

2. Get comfortable with being uncomfortable

    "Courageous [presidents] are [full patch brothers] who push through uncomfortable situations. They are willing to make difficult decisions and do not back down when things get too hard." [2]

3. Reveal vulnerability

> "Revealing that you are vulnerable to your [brothers] lets them see that you are human, just like them. You make mistakes and clean up after them. You understand what it is like to be in their shoes, and you want to show them that you are not just a massive walking ego."[2]

This is different than what you would employ during times of battle. For instance, you never reveal vulnerabilities to an enemy unless you are employing subterfuge.

4. Confront reality head-on

    > "Strong leadership means fully understanding the state of your [motorcycle club]. If you do not completely understand what is wrong and are not willing to admit that there needs to be change, then you face the possibility of losing good [brothers] and maybe even splitting or losing your [club] entirely." [2]

5. Seek feedback then actually listen

    > "Unfiltered feedback is often difficult to hear, but accepting it is one of the best things you can do for your [brotherhood]. Having your [brothers] give their feedback not only allows you to better understand your [club], but it also empowers them to share their thoughts and ideas. "

This practice strengthens the entire family.

> "If you encourage constructive disagreement and healthy debate over ideas, you will reinforce the strength of your [MC] and show them that you value their opinions. Allow [brothers] to give feedback not only about your ideas, but the ideas and tasks that the entire [brotherhood] is working on. Encourage invention, creativity, and risk-taking." [2]

6. Say what needs to be said

> "Real conversations are difficult to have, especially if there is conflict involved. As a [president], you need to have the courage to deal with the conflict and face issues as they arise. You must be ready to be unpopular and know that what you are doing is best for the [MC] and therefore your [brotherhood]. Letting these things fester or brushing them under the rug will only come back later to cause larger problems in the future." [2]

7. Act on performance issues

> "Confronting [alpha males] is hard. [Believe me I know!] That is why most [presidents] do not. The problem comes when you ignore these performance issues for too long. Underperforming or toxic [brothers] can quickly become a threat to your [brotherhood] and your [MC]. You cannot be afraid to [discipline a brother, take them to committee, suspend or fine them, or put them out of the club] entirely. By acting as soon as performance issues arise, you [establish yourself as a serious president]."[2]

You let all see that you are fair, but you are not playing around. Your message is that this is a way of life for you, not a hobby, not a part time thing, and you are not to be screwed with at all. In the end if you jump on performance issues immediately you are helping yourself, your brotherhood, and the entire extended family.

8. Communicate Openly and Often

"Keep the lines of communication open between you and your [officers], even when you do not know the answers. Courageous [presidents] do not hide behind their [titles]." [2]

Do not avoid answering questions by ducking behind your officers or always trying to have the brothers vote on matters they should decide themselves to avoid confronting challenges head on.

I once had a National President who thought he could cover every decision by holding a club vote. In his mind no one could hold him responsible for making a bad decision as long as he could say, "Well, that is what we decided on together." The problem came when his club had issues that required his direct leadership, experience, and in-depth understanding. It is under these circumstances he could no longer hide behind his title. The men needed him to explain the situation and guide them forward. Because he lacked the courage to even try to make an informed decision many issues stalled causing the club to step back five years from his ineptness.

I liken it to a movie based upon a true story; wherein an imposter posing as a surgeon in a teaching hospital was able to fool everyone about his capabilities because he would gather his students around a patient and take a consensus of the best course of treatment upon which they should embark. He appeared to be a brilliant doctor, his students loved him and clamored to get into his classes. His scheme worked until one day he was forced into a situation wherein his students had neither the skills or experience to make a proper diagnosis or suggest a proper course of treatment required to save the patient. The imposter could no longer hide behind his students. He had to make a decision his faked credentials would suggest he was competent to make. When he failed to save the patient's life, a formal investigation ensued and the gig was up, landing him in prison.

A courageous president ensures he is competent in everything he does. When he lacks the knowledge or experience, he backfills and learns his role, or he surrounds himself with competent members who can support him. This cannot happen if he tries to hide behind BS, process, or title. Courageous presidents use straight talk and are not afraid to say, "I do not know." They communicate openly and honestly with the MC and obtain specialized help in the areas they are weak.

> "Courageous [presidents] are open with their information. They don't hoard ideas. They maintain open lines of communication at all levels." [2]

They are not interested in so-called "job security" instead they are interested in club longevity.

9. Give Credit to Others

This is a common theme throughout each of the leadership sections in this book. Giving credit to others is an essential component of strong leadership.

> "Courageous [presidents] do not seek praise from everyone around them. Instead, they offer praise to those who deserve it. They let their [brothers] know when they have done a good job. They do not need to take the credit for the work that is done by their [officers and members] because they know it was not their work in the first place. A [president] takes more than their share of blame and less than their fair share of credit."[2]

10. Hold Yourself Accountable

> "If you expect your [officers] to perform and deliver on their commitments, then you must do the same!

> You must hold yourself accountable and be a role model for your [brothers] to emulate." [2]

You might not think this is a necessary component of being courageous, but it is actually one of the most valuable. I have known so many "Do as I say and not as I do," presidents who fail to uphold even the basic standards they require from the family. They are pompous enough to believe that no one is watching, or they should somehow not be held as accountable as those beneath them. But I reiterate – if you are selfish, you will not last long! The brotherhood has little tolerance for a president that lacks the understanding of the "We".

11. Delegate to Your Officers and Members

> "Courageous leaders have confidence in their [officers and members]. They empower them by delegating responsibility. This also means that you need to accept their mistakes. Create a working environment where brothers do not fear making errors. When errors are made, show all how everyone can learn from them too." [2]

Believe in the strength of the full patch brothers who make up the brotherhood! If they are active in training the men who will replace them, they have confidence in the skills they have developed in their brothers. You need to accept their mistakes, Prez! They are not perfect, and neither are you!

One of the saddest stories I can share pertaining to this is about a brother who was driving crazy and took out a pack of full patch brothers of the Mighty Black Sabbath Motorcycle Club Nation Macon, Georgia chapter in his Ford Expedition. He had just been patched in a few hours earlier as a Support Chief. He was so excited he took off after the pack driving ahead of him. Unfortunately, he was driving too fast to stop when the pack slowed. He ran the pack down spewing motorcycles all over the freeway, running over brothers and killing full patch brother,

Vice President "*Iceberg*". VP was the man who recruited him and stood behind him being voted into the family; in fact, he spearheaded his ascension after two years of prospecting. Our new brother had not only killed a brother but had killed a brother who had brought him in the club.

This egregious error—brothers run over from behind by another brother from our own club—was a terrible situation that left us with no one to hate, no one to blame. We were faced with a self-inflicted injury so destructive it threatened to tear the soul out of our family. Some members wanted to hate and attack our brother, the driver, but President "*Mad Dogg*" of the Macon chapter had to step forward through his grief and guide the club toward forgiveness in an effort to learn a lesson from this tragedy that could benefit our family in the future.

When tragic mistakes are made, be strong enough to guide the club back from the devastation. You are the president, and these kinds of things are never easy!

12. Stand Behind Your Brothers

> "If you know you are capable of mistakes, you must accept and stand behind your [brothers] even when they've made a mistake. Build a [brotherhood] where they know they are trusted and that if something goes wrong, you'll be in their corner."[2]

13. Change Direction When Required

> "[MCs] of all sizes need to be able to change direction on short notice. When you are faced with the need to change, you must be courageous about taking the next step. You will be leading [the brotherhood] into uncharted territory, and you need to have the confidence to guide them.

You must keep the MC nimble and capable of changing direction in an instant no matter what the tradition may suggest. The idea that, "We have always done it this way so there is no need for change," has destroyed many a powerful MC. There is a big difference in confidence, overconfidence, and arrogance. Be confident not overconfident nor arrogant when pursuing change.

> Weak [presidents] will doubt their choices, they will fear change, and they will worry. Eventually, their [brothers] will see this. If you cannot show your [brothers] that you are fully behind your own changes, how can they get behind them?" [2]

In a male dominated alpha society weakness is set upon and weak leaders are devoured.

14. Establish Higher Standards

> "Courageous [presidents] establish higher standards for themselves and their [brotherhood]. As a leader, you need to set up personal standards for yourself to reach your full potential. By demonstrating this to your [brothers], you allow them to reach their full potential too."[2]

Where you lead, they will follow. Demand more from yourself and watch them demand more from themselves.

15. Showcase your talents

> "While you want to make sure that you leave your ego at the door, showcasing your ability is an important factor in being a courageous leader. [Alpha males like those in your brotherhood] want to know they are working with [a president] who is competent and capable of getting the job done."[2]

You must remember that in all things you are often considered a God-like figure among your men. When they describe you, they say "My President" making you, in their minds, a personal possession (Wow, is that scary or what?). Make no mistake that the MC brotherhood can be almost cult-like for many members. Some brothers will even become fanatical in their hero-worship of you. Unlike a job where the president of the company is the boss, and after everyone goes home, they no longer think of him anymore, in the MC world the Prez is often considered a superhero-like figure and brothers talk about you to their wives, family members, coworkers, preachers, and uplift you to their children. It is a true burden you carry. Words from the president's mouth can destroy a person's ego more quickly than those same words coming bitterly from an enemy's mouth.

> "Showcasing your talents to your [brotherhood] energizes the [MC]. It shows [your brothers] that they can trust in you and your work. It allows [them] to learn from your example and therefore be better at their roles and in their leadership as well."[2]

During my term in office as National President of the Mighty Black Sabbath MC Nation I took great pleasure in destroying the brothers during our "Cold Ass Run to the Mother Chapter"—an annual cross-country pilgrimage from Atlanta to San Diego taken each February, the coldest time of year. During the run, we go over a mountain pass between El Centro and San Diego. Now, I have been running this pass for almost 30 years, so I know it like the back of my hand. I would get the brothers in that pass and utterly destroy them on two wheels. During one trip, a brother became so enraged I challenged him to a race through the mountain passes in the Georgia Blue Ridge Mountains. Fortunately for him, his president saved him, stepping in and taking his keys, refusing to let him race against the old man with "I don't give a damn how pissed off you get at Dragon, do not take your dumb ass up into those mountains with him. You will come back motorcycle-less. Which means one without a motorcycle title." The brother then apologized for his defiant attitude.

When you have skills that you can showcase to the men, they respect your abilities and add to the legendary mystery of your reputation. This empowers them to want to be like you, greatly admiring your skills. It spurs them to compete to be as good yet fear your legendary status.

When I was finally beaten through the pass by a brother ("Money Mike"), he was so surprised he assumed it was a fluke. He refused to accept the victory, instead telling everyone the only reason he won was because my bike was overloaded. It may have been, but others would not have cared—a win would have been a win! He added to my mystery by affirming I was not beaten. Did he best me because my bike was overloaded or because he was better than I was that day? Hell, I will never tell!

Note: "There is a difference between showcasing your talents and being a "show-off!" Remember no one admires a show-off, but most folks admire a true showcasing of talent!"

16. Remove yourself from bad situations

> "Sometimes, the most courageous thing a [president] can do is to leave a toxic [MC] environment."[2]

Though your brothers may expect one type of reaction, a courageous leader takes everything into consideration, then embarks on his own reaction which, more often than not, will be what is in the best interest of the brotherhood.

Many decades ago, father of the Mighty Black Sabbath Motorcycle Club Nation, Paul "Pep" Perry, held our annual at the mother chapter in San Diego, California. Trophies for the biggest club, the longest distance traveled, the most motorcycles, and others are always given to clubs who attend the party. On this particular night, the Black Sabbath Motorcycle Club Sgt at Arms "Scrap Iron" got drunk and took the trophies home. When it came time to hand out the trophy to the biggest club, the Persuaders MC, there were no trophies to hand out. In those days this was a big deal, and the Persuaders MC were none too happy about it! They wanted to beef, so one of their members unplugged the jukebox and announced they wanted to fight—president against president. Father took one look at the situation—with all the innocent bystanders, wives, and women sitting around the clubhouse having no idea of what was going on—and knew he was not going to allow a fist fight to escalate into a gun draw, with a possible shooting, killing one of his hundreds of guests. He instructed one of his brothers to go into the DJ booth, turn on the equipment and drown them out on the floor. No matter how mad they got and how hard they threatened no one would be able to hear them. By now the Black Sabbath brothers wanted to get at the Persuader brothers, but Father knew everyone on both sides was packing heat and he refused to allow someone to be killed over a damned trophy. His own brothers called him "yellow" and "coward." The Persuaders MC brothers were screaming for blood. Father stood his ground and told his brothers they better not start any trouble with the Persuaders; ordering both sides to stand down. He promised the Persuaders he would give them their trophy in the morning—which he did—and everything worked out. Even though his own brothers called him a coward, he had the courage to stand by his principles to extricate them from a bad situation. Conflict, in that case, would have produced no winners.

Courageous Leadership Sets the Stage for Progress and Confidence

In her article *"Robyn's blogs on Courageous Leadership"* ([3]https://robynbenincasa.com/robyns-blogs-on-courageous-leadership), January 9, 2019, Robyn Benincasa shared eight interesting steps toward building skills as courageous presidents:

1. Take Risks and Step into Character Whether you Feel like You are Ready or Not

   > "How many times in our lives have we put something off because we are not ready, we need more time, we do not feel comfortable, etc.?" [3]

   Even though she had completed 10 Ironman Triathlons and over 40 ten-day non-stop Eco-Challenge adventure races through the most remote places on Earth, Benincasa confesses she "did not feel 'ready' for any of them."

   You might not be ready, but you must be courageous enough to rely on your skills, research, knowledge, and experience when a decision must be made. Do not worry about not being ready. One way to BE ready is to STAY ready. We have a saying in the Mighty Black Sabbath Motorcycle Club Nation Atlanta chapter, "You do not have to get ready if you stay ready!" Athletes say, "If you keep yourself in competition shape you will be prepared to compete even if you have not prepared yourself to face a particular competitor."

   When underdog mixed martial arts (MMA) fighter Nate Diaz took on MMA fighter Conor McGregor during their first meeting in 2016, it was on short notice. Conor's original opponent had suffered a broken foot and had to pull out of the fight. When Nate accepted it, the fight was supposed to be an easy opportunity for McGregor and his highly anticipated win was going to allow him to be one of the first men in the MMA to win belts in two weight classes. Nate was not expected to pose much of a threat because of his past spotty performances in the octagon and not having the full six-week training camp to prepare for the fight. Even with the short notice, Nate was not afraid to take on the fight, instead jumping at the opportunity to fight against Conor. The result was an upset win, with Nate tapping Conor out and receiving a technical knockout with a rear naked choke hold midway through the second round! When Nate was interviewed by Joe Rogan after the fight he stated, "I'm not surprised motherfucker! I am an athlete, a warrior, we should always be ready to fight everybody on our worst day!" Fighters who stay in shape often accept a fight on short notice even though they have not prepared for that particular fighter. They feel confident enough in their skills and are prepared to go into the ring at any time no matter the opponent they will be facing.

Keep this in mind in your daily preparations to run your MC. Keeping yourself mentally, physically, and emotionally prepared keeps you competent so that when you need to be you will be. Stay sharp and you will stay ready!

2. Do It Anyway

> "How you feel is far less important than what you DO. Feeling scared, nervous, and uncomfortable when you're rappelling off that symbolic cliff of changing your life, starting a [club, running for office, or expanding chapters] is just a GIVEN. It is the price of admission for an exceptional life! The only difference between you and the guy or girl who is living her dream is that he or she felt the fear and 'did it anyway.' Back in the day, I played Judo. I was only a brown belt, not a black belt yet, but I was lucky

enough to do a little bit of traveling and competing on the US Team. We were at the Hungarian National Championships, and I was totally overwhelmed and scared to death in my first big international meet. And then I saw the brackets for competition and had to literally sit down on the floor because I felt nauseous."[3]

I know her feeling. Though I eventually rose through the martial arts ranks to attain my eighth-degree black belt, I too can remember when I was a brown belt and was bracketed to fight black belts. I was terrified, yet I showed up for battle. I remember one big time black belt I fought in Oklahoma back in the early 1980s. Up to this point, I endeavored to study several styles simultaneously. At 15 years old I took all the cash I made working as a dishwasher and joined several martial arts schools; Tom Haggerty's Martial Arts Academy in Midwest City, Oklahoma where I studied Wing Chung Kuen Kung Fu, Tae Kwon Do under Master Jack Hwang over on NW 10th street, and I played Judo and studied Tomiki Aikido at the Windsong Dojo under Master Chuck Caldwell on Northwest 16th street in Oklahoma City. My entire life was dedicated to work and martial arts. I think I worked out like eight hours per day seven days per week back then. I also fought a lot. I would spar from one school to another plus I fought in backyards, alleys, gyms, boxing clubs, and warehouses – anywhere I could compete (legally or illegally).

Once I attended a local tournament and was bracketed against a famous black belt fighter, I was MORTIFIED! I was supposed to be fighting a brown belt, but not enough brown belts showed up and now I had to fight one of the most notable guys in the city. He strode into that ring with so much confidence, having faced thousands of opponents, and there I was, some 15-year-old kid that he just knew he was going to destroy. I think he must have been about twenty-four. We lined up. Round one and he threw a spinning backfist that just about took my head off, followed by a round house kick to the temple and I dropped straight to the ground. The referee started counting and I was back to my feet. We were separated, and the referee shouted, "Fight!" and we were back at it. I threw three reverse crescent kicks which flew right over his head as he rolled his head and let them fly past. "Damn," I thought on the second kick, "I just barely missed!" On my third kick he timed me perfectly and just hauled off and kicked me in the testicles! I fell to my knees and the referee charged between us and sent him to his corner. This guy was meaner, quicker, and dirtier than any fighter I ever fought, plus he was a goddamned cheater! As I got to my feet the referee told me that I had five minutes to recover and that he was pausing the fight.

The most surreal thing was that I heard my mother over the rest of the cheering crowd screaming to me most clearly, "Son, you have taken his best shots! You know what he has! He cannot hurt you! Now go kill him!" The referee stopped the match right then to admonish my mother that she could not instruct me to kill someone in front of all the families and kids. My mother was a warrior in her own right. She threatened to shoot the ref! She yelled, "What are you going to do, beat me up with your black belt? I'll blow your ass from here to kingdom come! You have got the right one Mr. Black Belt!" And, of course, since my mother carried a 357-caliber pistol everywhere she went—she was not bluffing (the memory makes me laugh out loud). Well, anyway, some of the senior black belts got over to calm my mother down and after a few more minutes she was sitting down, and the fight resumed.

I felt a surge of energy rush through my body. That was because it dawned on me that my mother was right, I had taken his best blows and survived! I no longer feared him. The referee shouted "Fight!" and he came storming at me with a weird attack, but it was not new, I had seen this kind of thing before and I was not worried about his dirty fighting. In fact, my mind was alive experiencing the battle. With each blow, I blocked, countered, and parried! He could not lay a glove or foot on me. He flew in with another spinning back fist but somehow, I knew what he was throwing before he did. I ducked it with ease, saw his unguarded face and without thinking, I attacked! In seconds he was knocked out cold on the deck. To this day I do not even remember what combination of techniques I used to hit him with, but I do remember thinking that all my training, working out, schooling, education, and money invested, had prepared me for that moment!

By having the courage to fight that black belt even though I was "only a brown belt," to do it anyway, ready, or not—I gave myself the opportunity to win. From that day forward I never feared an opponent because I knew I was always in shape to fight whomever I encountered, no matter what. I won more than I lost, but when I lost, I was never disappointed because my opponents always respected my fighting abilities and battle-ready work ethic. Though there may be many challenges in running the day-to-day operations of your club, for which you will not be prepared, face them anyway. You might not realize this but the day-to-day practice of running the club actually puts you in MC fighting shape. By keeping the MC in the best shape, you will be amazed at what you can accomplish. You will not have to get ready if you stay ready.

3. Focus on the Hope of Success Versus the Fear of Failure

> "When you're driving your car or riding your bike, where is your focus? You have got a laser focus on exactly where you WANT to go, right? Where we get into the most trouble is when we start focusing on where we DON'T want to go – because that is inevitably where we will end up! So why, when we are analyzing our risks and life challenges, do we often get so obsessed with what we DO NOT want to have happen instead of envisioning what success will look like?" [3]

The lesson about focusing on what you want to avoid instead of on where you are trying to go reminds me of the guy who has yet to learn how to counter-steer his motorcycle. We bikers see this kind of thing all the time. This guy steers into the accident because he is looking at it! He is concentrating on missing it but somehow steers directly into it. It seems hard to believe but happens because no one taught him how to look at where he wanted to go instead of at what he was trying to avoid—the basic concept of counter-steering, so almost inevitably he runs into what he was attempting to miss. In motorcycle safety classes we always learn to look where you want to go instead of where you do not want to go because if you do the opposite your mind will automatically steer where you are looking without even mentally trying to do so. It is human nature to go where you are focusing, so always focus on the goal and not the challenges designed to keep you from that goal. Focusing on a goal more than the challenges is a huge part of being courageous. To hell with what "they" are talking about, you have got somewhere to go. Be about the business of getting there.

4. Back Up but Never GIVE Up!

It has often been said "discretion is the better part of valor" and "take time to choose your battles wisely". When you are in the thick of things you may find you will not be able to accomplish your goals because the cost of success will be too great, making your victory myopic. You must never be afraid to form another plan and approach a challenge from a different angle. Never be so invested in a plan you cannot change to a more appropriate course of action. The ability to make this kind of decision is perhaps the height of courage.

"Sometimes it is the setbacks in life that inspire an even better way forward. Courage means not only "enduring" those setbacks but taking yourself and the people around you to a new level in the face of those challenges." [3]

5. Far Better to Dare Mighty Things

As Theodore Roosevelt states "Far better to dare mighty things, to win glorious triumphs, even though checkered by failure, than to take rank with those poor souls who neither enjoy nor suffer much, in the gray twilight that knows neither victory nor defeat."[3]

Dare your MC to do mighty things. Reach into your brothers and pull from them the greatest things they can accomplish. Whether it is winning long distance riding trophies, building houses with Habitat for Humanity, feeding the homeless, opening charters overseas, refusing to accept support patches, or anything your brothers consider to be mighty, it does not matter. Have the courage to dare your mighty MC brotherhood to be courageous enough to do mighty things.

6. GUTS

G = Going the distance
U = Unwavering Patience and Faith
T = Taking Calculated Risks
S = Shattering the Norm

As a president you know the MC world can present dangerous waters through which the brotherhood must navigate quickly and steadfastly. Yes, much of the time our biker lifestyle is filled with fun, living out our lives in a biker's fantasy. We can be found hanging out, riding motorcycles, going to parties, attending field meets, racing, chasing women, living, and loving all things "biker life". But in this world things can go from happy-go-lucky to defecation hitting the roto oscillator in seconds. To those on the outside looking in it may appear that all we do is ride motorcycles and live life without responsibility. But when you are living this life, you quickly become aware of the dark side of MCing and the many complexities that exist within. Whether facing a hostile MC attempting to pull your brothers off a highway trying some patch police enforcement action on your club, facing the challenges of a coalition telling you, you cannot open your club in a certain town, or encountering a group attempting to impose a support patch on your brotherhood takes perseverance to accomplish the goals of the MC. When this lifestyle becomes rough, the leaders must be equally as hardened to lead alpha men into whatever may come. You will find that having the courage to be president of an MC sometimes comes down to simply having guts!

> "When I think about the word Guts, there are really two definitions. It is courageous to make that big leap or shatter the norm, but it is equally courageous to have patience and faith in your mission. So, when I talk about guts, it is an acronym....The G is: Going the Distance, quietly persevering....The U is: Unwavering in your Patience and Faith...The T is: Taking Calculated Risks...and The S is: Shattering the Norm."[3]

In 2001, I had the opportunity to interview actress, comedian, talk-show host, and author "Mo'Nique" Monique Angela Hicks during the "Queens of Comedy" tour in Atlanta. In the interview Mo'Nique told me how she had sacrificed everything for her career—which, at that time, was still up and coming. I found her story compelling and inquired about her plans in the event she failed to obtain her goals. She looked me directly in the eyes and said, "Failure is NOT an option. There is no backup plan for failure, and that is what I tell others. I am all in. There is no way

I do not make it." I thought to myself, "Damn that woman has GUTS!"

G = Going the distance

You cannot win if you pull short of the goal post. Once you have committed to a project, complete the objective. There may be plenty of times where you backup and start again but make damned sure you have the GUTS to drive the brotherhood to the finish line. Be mentally tough and resolute and never give up!

U = Unwavering patience and faith

A president pursues a goal when all others fail. He sees the bigger picture and continuously illustrates it so everyone around him comprehends. He provides the inspiration and example for his brothers to follow. He is unwavering in his faith in the greatness that is the Mighty MC Nation and has the patience to persist in making his nation great!

T = Taking calculated risks

The President makes the call, so he takes the risks. It is on his word that the MC moves, and it is equally on him if the club fails. He uses his skills, experiences, and instincts to take calculated risks but at the end of the day the duty falls on him. He has shoulders big enough to carry the brotherhood and assumes that responsibility. It is lonely at the top. He marches forward to take up that lonely position and never looks back.

S = Shattering the norm

When you have the guts to navigate the club through unchartered waters you shatter norms when you prevail, taking the MC to the next level. It takes GUTS to be the president and shatter those norms. It always has. It always will.

7. Fall Down 7 Times, Stand Up 8

Have you ever noticed how the big national clubs always seem to have everything together? They have the numbers, the chapters, the clubhouses, the dedicated brothers who stand all-for-one no matter what and seem to handle everything so super smoothly. But every top club today was once a pop-up club facing the same challenges other clubs faced, but dared to be bigger, better, stronger, and more efficient than the competition. It is safe to consider them the pros of the MC world. When you think about doing big things but talk yourself out of it because you are a small club without the resources or opportunities of the bigger clubs, you doom your brotherhood to always being mediocre because you just do not have what it takes mentally to take them to the top. It is acceptable to fall down as long as you keep getting back up. That is the only way to climb your club to the top.

> "I was at a big stand-up paddling race with my friend Bill, watching the pros battle it out for the big bucks in the sprint race. I was amazed at how deftly they could maneuver at high speed around the 8 cones on the course, zipping through 180 degree turns while simultaneously surfing 4-foot-tall waves. I was scared to death of waves and equally afraid of the turns, so I always stayed away from races that had a lot of either. As the race leaders rounded the cone closest to the beach, I asked Bill why the pros were so much better than we were, and without hesitation he said, "they're not afraid to fall in"."[3]

Do not think the big clubs did not get knocked on their asses on their way up the ladder. Do not think they do not still get knocked around today. Big MCs become pros because they got back up and continued climbing to the top each time they were knocked down. They fell down seven times but got up eight!

8. Teammates! (Brotherhood!)

> "For 15 years [Benincasa] was an Expedition Adventure Racer, which is a sport that involves 4 team members traveling 600-1000 miles, completely non-stop, running, hiking, kayaking mountaineering and navigating their own course with a map and compass for up to 10 days, across some of the most remote and dangerous terrain on earth. As you can imagine, something as daunting and crazy and difficult as an Adventure Race is something we would have NEVER done alone..."[3]

She is trying to point out the value of having teammates (brothers) you can depend on to do their jobs, contribute more than their fair share, and take responsibility to correct their failures and shortcomings. No president can do everything alone. Of course, many think they can and may even try. Some do it purposely in an effort to ensure they cannot be replaced. But failure to train your officers to be competent in their jobs only hamstrings the club, restraining it from reaching its full potential. My life partner Tahmehrah Tia "Red Bone" Perdue once said to me, "When you are a leader you are training your soldiers to be leaders. If you are not training your soldiers to be leaders, then what is it all for? You are wasting time if you are not training them to take over after you are gone!" Her sister Julianne Dunn said, "In corporate America that is called Succession Training, which is mentoring and developing individuals to assume your role as you go to higher places." You should be trying to train your brothers to carry on and be better than you were, to accomplish more, and make your MC nation greater than it was when you built it. Brotherhood, teammates, and family are the foundations upon which a Mighty MC Nation is built. If you want to accomplish something as daunting, crazy, and difficult as building a brotherhood into a Mighty MC Nation you will need teammates. Your officers and full patch brothers need to be developed into a cohesive unit capable of handling all obstacles that may impede the nation whether you are in charge, retired, or dead.

Courage in Battle

You must have the courage to lead the club on two fronts. The second is when your brothers are faced with defending themselves, their colors, their families, club business, or home (the clubhouse). No matter the makeup of your club (1%er, Outlaw, Traditional MC, Mixed Race MC, Mason MC, Veteran MC, LEMC, Family Club, Mom and Pop Club, Motorcycle Ministry, RC, RA, MSA, CoEd MC, Female MC, Gay MC) at some point you will be called upon to engage a bully or superior force to save your lives, freedom, and pursuit of happiness. As President you must have the courage to do everything in your power to keep your brothers alive, free from incarceration, intimidation, threat, coercion, shakedown, and extortion. The safety, freedom, and autonomy of the MC rests in your hands (and this can be taken quite literally). In fact, in a legal case, an MC president actually signed his club's colors away in a plea deal forcing the club to take off their colors for a time. This proves a president that lacks courage can truly damage the entire MC.

"A coward dies a thousand deaths" holds significance for me, but I do not think I truly understood all the aspects this one saying encompasses. To me it meant that a coward died a thousand times from fear before death actually came, whereas a courageous man would die but once. Although most would agree with this simplistic view of this quote, I have since come to better understand the more encompassing aspects of it.

The quote is derived from William Shakespeare's play "Julius Caesar":

> "A coward dies a thousand times before his death,
> but the valiant taste of death but once. It seems to
> me most strange that men should fear, seeing that
> death, a necessary end, will come when it will come."

Having courage neither rests in the hands of the valiant nor of the cowardly. Depending upon the situation the cowardly can become courageous and the valiant can become cowardly.

Being in charge of brothers who may have to face challenges that could lead the MC into armed conflict with other MCs can be an enormous responsibility. How can one explain to the mother of a brother that their decisions (or lack thereof) led to her son's demise? How would he look into the eyes of a fallen brother's children and explain that his lack of foresight caused them to never see their father again? How would he be able to look at his brother from across a glass window knowing his decisions took away his freedom, or worse, put him in the electric chair? Would your perception of your courage cause one of your men to pay the price for your arrogance? When it comes to courage in battle, we must look at courage differently.

For this we must go to two authors: Harriet Rubin and William Ian Miller. Rubin, founder and editorial director of the prestigious Doubleday Currency, and author of the international bestseller, *"The Princessa: Machiavelli for Women."* wrote the article *"What Is Courage"* ([4]https://www.fastcompany.com/44469/what-courage), January 31, 2002. In it, she cites:

> "What is courage? It may be the most desirable —
> and the messiest — human virtue. William Ian Miller
> wrote the book on courage, and even he calls it a
> mystery. [4]

Indicating that even a well-studied pioneering author has difficulty describing courage.

Miller, the Thomas G. Long Professor of Law at the University of Michigan Law School, honorary professor of history at the University of St. Andrews, and author of *"The Mystery of Courage"* ([5]Harvard University Press, 2000) talks about how few of us actually spend time thinking about courage but suggests that many of us assume we know it when we see it. He questions whether or not that's true. Asking if it is best displayed by marching into danger, making the charge, or by resisting, enduring without complaint? Is it physical, moral, or both? Is it fearless or does it involve subduing fear?

When looking for courage to engage your brothers in battle and deciding whether they have the fortitude to do what it takes, perhaps you should understand that finding courage for and during battle may not be as apparent as you may think. A battle can take on a form so negative it should be avoided at all costs.

> "If I had a wish it would be never to be scared, never to feel the shame of being scared. Writing this book meant trying to understand my own feelings of cowardice. Even now, in day-to-day encounters, we politely accept behavior that, if we were brave enough, we would never stand for." [5]

If you've ever witnessed an OMC dominating a family club, pulling patches, or extorting an MC you can absolutely understand where Miller's coming from. If it has happened to your club and was allowed, you have tasted the salty displeasure of politely accepting behavior that, if perhaps you were braver, or your brothers were "built like that" or "about that life", you would never have permitted. But what do you do when the pushing becomes intolerable?

> "Yet if we stood up to every opponent, we would be barbaric. So how do we live with ourselves when we

are humiliated and fearful? What form should courage take? That is the question that keeps me up at night."[5]

This in fact is the question that will keep many a president up at night. The question he asks himself when he looks into the ceiling and exclaims, "How much is too much? When is enough, enough? Am I being a coward or am I protecting my brothers and keeping us safe from harm by capitulating? Even the 1%er president must ask himself, "With all of the law enforcement forces, RICCO laws, Homeland Security, anti-terrorist squads, and FBI out to get my club is it worth it to take revenge for a brother's hit right now, or do I risk being called a coward if I tell the club to wait?" Which course of action is more courageous? In Father Pep's quandary when facing the Persuaders MC, would it have been more cowardly for him to allow his men to fight and die for nothing? At least he would not have been called a coward, but perhaps being called a coward accurately captures what he actually was. Only he could know what was in his heart.

> "While there may be no resolution to the mystery of courage. I think most men and women would say that courage is the virtue that they would most want to secure for themselves. But even though courage is the dominant theme in literature, second only to love, it is elusive. Is courage about taking pain, or is it about dishing it out? Is it about rushing into a fire when that is your job, or is it about doing something that falls beyond your job description? Is courage the same for those who are brave in war and those who are brave in sickness?
>
> Or consider this dilemma: You can be courageous and cowardly at the same time."[4]

Let us examine the case of a combat Marine stationed in Southeast Vietnam during the Vietnam conflict in the late 1960s. During his tours he won many medals for action in combat including the Purple Heart with V for valor. He survived many battles and always displayed great heroism in the field and bravery before the enemy, thus he was greatly respected by his men. I told him how proud I was to meet a walking, living legend when he abruptly interrupted me to tell me something that weighed heavy on his mind. He told me that while in the field he once observed the rape of a Vietnamese girl and her subsequent murder. He never lifted a hand to protect her. So, he never wanted me or anyone to call him a hero. Though he was courageous in battle, he did not stand up to protect that innocent Vietnamese girl.

> "It takes a certain kind of character to do certain jobs. Firemen are called upon to put their lives on the line. But doing your duty is not being courageous."[4]

We do seem to attach courage to certain occupations and often when we do, the fireman or police officer will tell us, "I am no hero, I was just doing my job! Please do not call me a hero. The real heroes are the men and women who sacrifice their lives for this country." And think about it, is not a person who is equipped, trained, and drilled in entering burning buildings or apprehending criminals just a certain character type that excels in that type of daily occupation or are they a courageous hero? For that matter is the soldier doing his job courageous or is that reserved for when he goes above and beyond the call of duty?

Miller set out to write a book about cowardice. He asked himself how many times in his life had he actually felt cowardly. Like Miller and Rubin many of us know better the emotions of cowardice than the virtues of courage.

> "I know what [cowardice] feels like, fear, shame, and self-loathing. But had I ever been courageous? What

did that feel like? I did not know. Had I never been courageous in my whole life?"[4]

Rubin studied stories of people who experienced great horrors to figure out, what was going on in their heads. She noticed that soldiers he studied, who spent time on the front lines, did not seem to know the definition of courage. Wondering,

> "If they do not know, how can I say what it is? I wanted to know what they think about what is or is not courageous."[4]

She notes that some people feel like courage means going into a "zone".

> "They become afraid of losing that zone. Others say that once you feel it, you can never lose it. You will always do the right thing, even when you are confused out of your mind."[4]

But Rubin was not satisfied with people's feelings, stating rather "feelings are mysteries; it helps to know how mysterious courage is." [4]

Rubin poses an interesting question, asking why leaders do not provide better examples of courage.

> "It's terrible how little courage our leaders have. Rudy Giuliani did the right thing on September 11. He stood out like a sore thumb. Where was the president? He was in Nebraska—and his people were putting out false reports that he was under threat. Giuliani manifested courage. He put his body on the line, even though he could have been killed in the collapse of WTC Tower 2."[4]

I wonder what Rubin would think about the once courageous Giuliani today. I wonder how she felt when a decade later he cried out to his followers for a "trial by combat" from an elevated podium only to load himself into a bodyguard protected, chauffer driven,

Suburban to flee in the opposite direction after directing hordes of followers to attack the capitol of the United States. Which brings about the obvious question: Does courage wane? Did Giuliani's? And if so, perhaps it wanes in some but not in others. For instance:

> "Why do the British love the Queen Mother? Because during the bombing of London in World War II, she refused to flee to safety. She was willing to incur the same risks as everyone else." [4]

When you think of the courage she continues to show by remaining in such a lonely position as Queen far past any human's desire to do so, even now that her rock Prince Phillip is gone, how tough must that be? Yet her courage has not waned, as she has continued to set an example since 1937. She has also been steadfast in keeping her commitment to God and country to never abdicate the throne until she is no longer capable of doing so. To me, that is courage!

Finally, Rubin came up with a way that she would profile courage to be able to determine when and where it will most likely be found.

> "You never know who's going to deliver [when it comes to courage]. Civil War soldiers would look along the line of battle and wonder who would crack and who would make it. A reliable person, good as gold, might crack just when you need him most. The pear-shaped accountant who has no physical presence could save the day." [4]

That said, here are some absolutely necessary components in profiling courage.

1. **Being lucky on the day when you are put to the test.** That turns out to be the day when you can muster the reserves of character. A person who does not scare easily can still have a bad day.

2. **Training yourself to do things that require courage.** Facing risks. Aristotle says to "train yourself to be ready when the call comes." At some point, such demands become easier to face. But it is also true that if too many demands are made on a person's courage, it runs out. Studies done after World War II showed that after prolonged fighting people simply cannot muster up any more strength from their spiritual reserves.

3. **Some people simply have a courageous nature.** Some people do not scare easily. Does that mean they have more courage than someone who has to dig deep within themselves to face danger?

4. **Feeling lucky is a source of confidence.** It can fuel courage. But do not be obsessed with luck—that is a kind of cowardice too, where you suspect that your courage is dependent upon something outside you.

Rubin ultimately concludes that courage is a mystery and calling it up during times of war is a toss-up at best. Consider this when you make plans for war because things may not go as you plan—once you commit, some things are impossible to take back.

In response to the question "How do soldiers in battles get the courage to fight when facing overwhelming odds?" on Quora:

Roland Bartetzko, former German Army, Croatian Defense Council, Kosovo Liberation Army

> "It's easier to fight against a numerically superior enemy than many people may think:
>
> First of all, when you are outnumbered, you usually don't attack but just defend your positions. Defending, however, is much easier than attacking and you can do it even when you're outnumbered by

a ratio of 1:10 or worse. If your positions are okay and the terrain is suitable for a defensive battle, you shouldn't be too concerned. I've seen a single machine gunner stopping a complete infantry brigade for most of a day. Often, your tactics and the terrain are more important than sheer troop numbers.

You also quickly get used to fighting against overwhelming odds. During the Kosovo War, my unit was once attacked by thirty-five enemy tanks while we didn't even have thirty-five soldiers. After a while, it really doesn't matter. You adapt and start using evasive tactics. Even with overwhelming numbers, the enemy can't be everywhere at the same time.

In addition to this, after you've been fighting day and night for days and weeks, all you care for is to have enough ammo, find the time and place for a nap or just to have a meal. Whether there are ten or one hundred enemies in front of you isn't your main concern."

Martin Parker, Paramedic

"It depends on the individual. For me it was a mixture of things...

1- I didn't realize how perilous it really was
2- I didn't want to look weak
3- I wanted to protect my buddies
4- I wanted to survive

In order they are, what I recall, to be the order as I got older and the longer or more tours I did. As a 19-

year-old I didn't understand what danger was. As a 26-year-old I wanted to live and see my children grow up. I guess, everyone's coping mechanisms are their individual strategies, but I'd suggest the younger you are the more it's "fun" and as you get older you become more aware of your mortality."

Rob Brown, former military

"As sad as this may sound, soldiers fighting in battle are not all heroes brimming with courage.

By far the majority fear for their lives, which is when their training takes over. Plus, of course, adrenalin. They are not individuals fighting for a cause—they are a team carrying out a plan. A team that understands that together they are much more effective than an individual. A team that knows that following orders gets the job done. Back to my original point. Not all soldiers are brave, they do not all fight for a cause, they are not all heroes. They are employees doing a job."

George Dukesh, former Researcher and Scientist at Ministry of Defence of the United Kingdom

"It's a combination of good training; making soldiers into teams that support each other, instilling pride and honour and loyalty to their unit. Personal pride; Inspirational leadership from NCOs and Officers. [It's] Human nature to defend yourself and your colleagues to the end."

In response to the question "How do some people have the courage to fight in a war when they know it could possibly kill them," on Quora:

Roland Bartetzko, former German Army, Croatian Defense Council, Kosovo Liberation Army

"There is no way to know how you'll react in combat until you are in your first fight. You might have been one of the best soldiers in training or on exercises, but it is often them who utterly fail in combat.

I remember a soldier we had in our unit in the Kosovo Liberation Army. One day we came under a massive, armored attack that was combined with infantry and supported by heavy artillery fire. I was looking for cover in a small building when I saw this guy hunkering down in a corner. He looked at me and said in a trembling voice: *"Oh man, I'm so scared!"* To be honest, that day we all were, but we continued fighting. I didn't see him again until I returned to base that evening. He then told me what had happened to him after I left him:

" I was scared that an artillery shell would hit the house, but at the same time I didn't dare to leave my hiding place as there were thousands of bullets hitting the walls of the building. I was alone; everybody else was outside fighting. I felt ashamed that I wasn't there with my comrades, but I couldn't get myself to move.

After what seemed an eternity, the fighting outside slowed down. Now another terrifying thought crossed my mind: "What if the enemy advances and finds me here?" I was still not sure what I should do, but after another minute I ran out of the building. I didn't see anybody outside and freaked out!

I kept running and running and only after I was totally exhausted did I allow myself to stop. I didn't know for how long I'd kept running, but when I looked around me, I realized that I wasn't only out of the fighting zone, but I had completely left the area where our brigade was operating!

I immediately turned around. I was very ashamed of myself and also scared that somebody would see me and would ask me what the hell I was doing there, miles away from my unit. It started to get dark and I continued my way back to our base, avoiding all villages and inhabited places."

Frankly, I was surprised about the guy's honesty. We decided that he could stay in our unit. As he obviously wasn't a fighter, we put him in our support squad which was tasked with non-combat duties, like cooking or maintenance.

As the war went on, we identified more people like him. Some of them we simply kicked out of our unit, but most of them we kept for a good reason:

When it comes to courage there is a wide spectrum. Some people have so much balls that they put themselves and all soldiers around them in unnecessary danger. It's always good to have one or two of them in your squad as you might need them in certain situations. I used to put one of those "brave" types in front of the unit and would stay right behind him to make sure he doesn't do anything stupid.

Most soldiers are somewhere in the middle of the spectrum, neither cowards nor heroes and then there are the guys who panic when the first shot is fired.

We also used to take a "panicky type" with us: They also can come in handy, for example when it comes to guard duty. They are simply more alert: When you have one of the cowards on guard duty, rest assured that he won't fall asleep.

Being afraid isn't their fault. Imagine what they must go through during the war...it must be many times harder for them than for us! Still, they did the jobs we assigned them and therefore they deserved our respect."

Robert Schumacher, former Operations Sergeant, (Team Sergeant) at U.S. Army Special Forces

"A good question, as most sane individuals prefer to avoid getting themselves into situations where they can suffer injury or even death. Combat however has its own dynamic in which sanity and normalcy don't impact. An environment, in which the chief goal is the neutralization of an opponent by violent means, cannot be considered, "normal," is one where the concepts of sanity as defined no longer apply.

How does a young, inexperienced, and presumably sane individual functionally perform in such an environment? Most nonmilitary would say that that individual possesses "courage." Most military and those having military-related experience would point to training for explaining the individual putting himself in harm's way. I would say that the answer lies in a lot of courage, tempered by a whole lot of training.

The purpose of training is to instill confidence, impart "muscle memory," as well as the technical skills needed to perform a job under combat conditions. History is full of examples where you find hordes of untrained individuals being defeated by a small number of trained troops. Generally, it is only in special, localized conditions where the untrained can defeat the trained.

Think back to when you first learned to ride a bicycle, drove a car, or asked a girl out on a date. The more you did these things, the more practiced you became and the more confidant you became. That is what training accomplished. You had to have the courage to attempt the action, but training provided the ability to accomplish it.

Training will not completely provide the individual with complete armor against every event. Soldiers still get killed and wounded, girls turn you down for dates, but the more training one has, the greater the chance of success and the greater willingness to engage in risky behavior. Some individuals, either through stress or uncertainty of their training may fail the test of combat, but that will only be seen during combat. I won't discuss out-and-out cowards as I personally have never seen any."

Justin Damani Morgan, Combat Marine

"I'm a former Marine. Short. Thin. Lifted weights and a history of some physical labor has chiseled my body. Helped condition my mind with some novice boxing training in a boxing gym—by that I mean sparring. Naturally, I have always been a timid child, teen to some extent, and lesser extent adult. Honestly, (I'm part of Gen. X) the Marine Corps made me mentally tougher and more willing to move through my fear. Yes, some if not nearly all of us have fear. Even Mike Tyson. Life events and my response has taken me backwards mentally though. Too much details to get into--some of which includes multiple gunshot wounds to the upper body by a cop and resulting permanent nerve, skeletal, damage and at times excruciating pain. Before a fight begins memory of that pain and knowledge of my limitations causes a "I can't win" in my mind. I'll admit there is a small percentage of men that move through that pain and injury in their heads and fight like tigers. They exist. But the vast, and I do mean vast, majority of men have never dealt with nor would heroically move through it. They can claim and dismiss till the cows come home. I've seen them turn or back down for lesser. There is one thing civilian and Marine--even Navy SEAL--fails to grasp. There is a difference between team sports (Marine) and gladiatorial event (boxing, wrestling, 1 on 1 prison fight in small cell or alone on a dark country road). I was never a gladiator--some, not all Marines are--but I was a solidly good team player. Some Marines or former Marines from decent areas will--in their horse shit belief "this is the greatest country of all, and bad things only happen to the bad and deserve it"--conclude in their misconception of team sports vs gladiatorial events that they would have been so much better than me. Add to this the excessive veteran veneration (far less so in inner-city) in the USA. I threw my Dress Blues and war medals and ribbons in the garbage. If you looked average or above as a man you were as pampered as a billionaire child, you don't understand. I do with becoming drug addicted about the same time my acne cleared up, had fine women flirting with me. So, looks, money, and everything "superficial" matters. And what matters to me is eating, be it another man's heart, or a steak. I give a fuck about medals or parades. And I'm not courageous. I might be a damn coward. But if armed with 9mm or 454 Casull I'm not even courageous... just can't wait, hope, and beg, for a prick SOB to give me a reason to pop him in the belly with 1 or 3 shots (recovery will be at least 1 month of excruciating hell not able to shit or fart) and to shoot his friend in the face. I don't have to be a Marine, a man, an American. I don't have to have a name. All I have to be is the end of your life. Or the memory you remember when you look at the vertical scar on your belly."

After presenting you with this information about courage when waging war with your brothers, I must implore you to weigh all available options, consider all the facts before making a final decision. If you have no other choice than to engage your brothers in battle, I recommend you train them for combat by equipping them with the skills, strategies, weapons training, and other tools necessary to triumph. In other words, a horde of untrained Bozo's showing up at an enemy's clubhouse and squeezing off rounds out of revenge and anger will never accomplish anything more than crazy jail sentences where you will most likely see one brother turn against another, at the district attorney's office, for the lightest jail terms each can wrangle for themselves. And yes, that too will be your damned fault! Lead responsibly you have people's lives in your hands.

Example - Accepting criticism for refusing to commit the club to a war after two brothers were assassinated by rivals because you knew law enforcement was watching too closely, and the result would be devastating for the club.

◊◊◊

Chapter NINETEEN
The Leadership Principle
of Knowledge

Knowledge

Definition - Understanding of a science or an art. The range of one's information, including professional knowledge and understanding of biking, biker culture, MC protocol, biker set protocol, the complex social construct of biker club set hierarchy, club bylaws, traditions, ceremonies, local laws, biker set harmonics, clubhouse management, logistics, supply, and movement of club brothers, places, people, as well as public relations management of all entities internal or external to your MC Nation.

Significance - The gaining and retention of current developments in the motorcycle club world, MC science and biker world affairs is paramount for your growth, development, and qualifications to lead the club as President.

Face it, many brothers want to be President, but most have not done the basic work to acquire the knowledge necessary to do the job successfully. Yeah, I know, I know, all one has to do is put on the patch and hold the meetings... "How hard could it be?" But if you have not done the work why in the hell are you so desperate for the job? Oh yes, I almost forgot—the women, the prestige, the adulating following, the chest puffing pomp and circumstance attributed to the president that makes the position so desirable. So, that is why so many punish their MCs with short-lived fantasies of grandeur, regressing their clubs by five years once their mirror posing legacy has come to an end.

Why does Black Dragon seem so irritated? Because I detest incompetence! But these clubs get exactly what they deserve when they vote these ill-prepared Presidents into office. I know this is sacrilege to say, but most brothers have no business voting even if they have the right as full patched brothers in good standing. That is because, sad to say, many of them are not astute enough to vote on the issues. They do not research the club's business of the day and are blind to what is even going on in the nation. They do not question their brothers running for office, inquiring about their agendas, backgrounds or experience that would lead them to do the job correctly. Instead, they unwittingly use the voting ballot to wage war against their own MC by turning the voting process into a popularity contest rather than executing an election designed towards vetting the best man most qualified to do the job. In the end they get the person "they like, they want, they think, they feel" comfortable with, often putting the club in a precarious position under an inept leader incapable of understanding the complexities of the job. Now the over-puffed ego of the non-qualified president, who knows damned well that he is absolutely unqualified, cannot be sated no matter how many bylaws he breaks in his first few weeks in office. But this is the guy everyone LIKED! HA! The terms "I think," "I like," "I want," "I feel" should be forbidden from use in the MC for any reason. These are dangerous phrases, and they are definitely not good qualifiers for establishing the order and discipline of the brotherhood. Yet, they seem pervasive as they are at the forefront of every club discussion in today's modern MCs.

Better yet are the clubs that allow an inept president to muscle his way into office without a proper vote, using his hench men to quiet those who would stand in opposition while the other brothers remain silent, too terrified to make a protest and stand for what is right! You would not think such a thing could happen among a society of alpha men, would you? But, alas, even the strongest alphas can become subservient betas like docile sheep, not wanting to cause a scene or dissent from the popular trend. When any brotherhood allows these actions to occur they get what they deserve—an unknowledgeable president.

Let us clarify even further the knowledge you should acquire if you should so desire. "I think I can" is not knowledge. "Hell, if he did it, I can do it," is not knowledge. "I am sure I can figure it out," is not knowledge. "I am the only one left to do the job," is not knowledge. "My father was the founder of the MC it is my birthright to run it," is not knowledge. Even though many folks who have uttered these words have actually turned out to be competent leaders, the overwhelming majority have not!

Dictionary.com ([1]*https://www.dictionary.com/browse/knowledge*) tells us there are four things a leader must know about knowledge:

1. "Acquaintance with facts, truths, or principles, as from study or investigation; general erudition (erudition is knowledge gained by research and study)." [1]
   The first thing we find is that knowledge is fact based. It contains truths or principles. It must be gleaned from study, investigation, erudition, and experience. Just thinking you can be President because you did not like the last guy and you worked in every way you could, behind his back, to get him removed, does not give you the knowledge to do the job!

2. "Familiarity or conversance, as with a particular subject or brand of learning." [1]
   Secondly, knowledge of something in which you have a familiarity, such that you can be conversant on the subject to lead others and discuss the pros and cons on which course of action to take. Knowledge allows you to intelligently engage brothers at church to argue convincingly to vote for the right way to do things, because you are knowledgeable about the subject at hand.

   I cannot tell you how many incompetent presidents I have seen over the years attempt to put new chapters of their clubs in areas they had no business trying to enter – neither knowing the politics of the area, the protocol necessary to accomplish such an action, nor the caliber of the men unable to stand up to the grilling administered by the local 1%ers when trying to start those chapters. Often, they end up reaching out to me on my consultation line (clarity.fm/black-dragon) asking me to help them out of the jam they should have been knowledgeable enough not to get into in the first place. As President, he should have known better! Yet, he did not have the knowledge. And do not get it twisted, incompetence is not limited to the level of hierarchy your club occupies on the political spectrum within the MC set, as I have taken many calls from members of the 1%er nations as well.

3. "Acquaintance or familiarity gained by sight, experience, or report." [1] Basically, you can gain knowledge by having spent time around those responsible for getting things done. Familiarity gained by sight (seeing things happen a thousand times before) often provides the experience needed to build a knowledge base from which to work.

4. "Knowledge or practical wisdom gained from what one has observed, encountered, or undergone."[1]

    Experience is its best teacher! Being in the MC world long enough that you know what is happening because you "feel it in your bones" can build your knowledge level and skills necessary to become President. This has nothing to do with ego, "I think," "I like," "I want," "I feel," nor some ill-conceived notion that things will come to you when the time is right. This is about knowing because it is in your bones, deep within your psyche. Bottom line, to be a successful president you must be an expert in the field of MC presidency. Blindly blustering your way along like a blithering idiot concerned with protecting your pride puts your men in danger and your MC nation at peril.

In her article "How to Become an Expert in Your Chosen Field" ([2]*www.eatyourcareer.com/2015/05/how-to-become-an-expert-in-your-chosen-field/*) May 4, 2015, Chrissy Scivicque said,

> "I'm going to make a bold statement here: In the field of professional development, I consider myself an expert. It's not just because I've been writing this blog for over 5 years (any Joe-schmoe off the street can do this, you know!). Rather, it's because I've

immersed myself in the field—soaked up knowledge and applied it at a rapid pace. And these days, I really feel it's paying off with a level of expertise few others possess. You might be wondering what that actually means, so let me tell you: It means I feel an elevated level of respect. When I speak, my ideas are listened to and considered thoughtfully. I'm sought out by others to weigh-in on topics of debate. I have an entire library of past work I can reference. In short I feel knowledgeable and empowered."

Boy-oh-boy, if all MC presidents could laude their preparations so competently, what a biker club set we would have throughout the world! Scivicque listed the preparations she undertook to prepare herself before she called herself an 'expert' at her chosen field of professional development.

- She was well-written on the subject. She had a blog about professional development she had been writing for five years.
- She immersed herself in her field, soaking up all of the knowledge she could.
- She practiced applying that knowledge at a rapid pace as she developed it.

She explains that one of the most common things professionals discuss when talking about their reputations, is their desire to be seen as 'experts' in their fields. Expertise is something to which we should all strive.

"Experts know their stuff. The have vast pools of knowledge and can be relied upon to provide accurate, insightful answers to even the toughest questions within their field of expertise. They have an abundance of wisdom, experience, and capability—and they are not afraid to use it. Colleagues at all levels sit up and take notice when an expert enters the room."[2]

As MC President, you will benefit greatly from gaining a heightened level of expertise in all aspects of the MC world.

Gaining Knowledge

How does one go about gaining knowledge on the MC set? Scivicque offers the following suggestions:

1. Practice Makes Perfect

    Do You Have Your 10,000 Hours Logged to Qualify to be president?

"Malcom Gladwell, the author of "Outliers" and many other bestselling non-fiction books, suggests that it takes 10,000 hours of practice to become an expert in any one task. That is not easy to come by! If you work a 40-hour week, and you spend every moment at work practicing that specific task at which you want to gain expertise, and you work a full 52 weeks per year, it still takes you about 5 years to hit the 10,000-hour mark." [2]

Now you know why Black Dragon is generally against the two-year wonder who enters the club and wants to be elected Regional Sergeant at Arms just because he is popular with the guys and has shown some promise with getting a few things done. "Bro! You do not have enough experience to represent our nation as Regional Sergeant at Arms, let alone Regional President! You do not even have 2,000 hours at this so what makes you think you know something about what you are doing?" Within four years he will be pushing for a national position. Sadly, being highly popular, the way clubs vote these days, he just may get it, but where is his expertise? MCs today do not demand this experience and folks pursuing presidencies do not have enough honor to wait until they are truly prepared to take the lead. Work ethic and preparation seem lacking, but do not let that be you! Get your 10,000 hours in.

Take some time to think about what I mean when I say that. I am not saying that the guy who is a two-year wonder will always do a bad job. Some do an outstanding job. But most often the successful manage to get their 10,000 hours in, even those who make it in that two-year period. Think about it—if it takes you 5 years at 40 hours per week to gain a level of expertise, what does working 80 or 100-hour weeks do for you? You've cut your time in half or more. Time-in is not always the magic formula. We all know club brothers with decades in the club that are not worth breast-feeding utensils on a brahma bull! So, I'm not saying that having time-in makes you particularly an expert either. If you have done nothing to gain knowledge during your time-in, you are not qualified to be the president either. The question is what have you done with your time, how effectively have you managed it, and is your 10,000 hours quality time or wasted time? If you get your 10,000 hours of quality expertise in two-years, so-be-it. You have done well!

2. Network with Leaders in [Other MCs]

> "Jim Rohn, personal development guru, who said, 'You are the average of the five people you spend the most time with.' Scary, huh? Think about who those 5 people are for you.
>
> If you want to 'up' your [MCing] game, you need to surround yourself with people who elevate you. Expertise is (almost always) contagious. By spending time with people who are themselves experts in [MCing], you will naturally 'catch' some of their wisdom."[2]

Look around your clubhouse. Hang around the OG who founded the club and started 20 chapters before the haters cut his legs out from under him, shunning him into a corner with a "retired" patch—he could teach you a whole lot if you just took the time to ask. Seek out those brothers people always seem to run to when the club is in trouble—folks are running to them for a reason. Do not be so afraid of the 1%er club that blessed your chapter—befriend their president and ask him about the best ways to lead men under pressure but be ready for him to try to recruit you into his club the minute he realizes you have got some sense. Believe me, that is exactly what will happen because he will understand you are building your portfolio of expertise for which he directly had a hand in developing. You may even find yourself tempted. My point is that you can discover lots of mentors and written works to build your knowledge. More and more books are becoming available, so avail yourself of the knowledge that is out there. Study to show thyself approved!

3. Mentor Someone in Your Field

> "Nothing helps to engrain knowledge as effectively as sharing it, and there is no shortage of young [club brothers, prospects, and hang-arounds inside and outside of your club] that are looking and starving for mentorship. When you see a rising star [in your brotherhood], take that person under your wing. Guide them. Share what you know—the hard-earned lessons you have collected over the years." [2]

It will make you sharp! You will have to be atop your game to educate them and hone them for theirs!

> "At the same time, keep your eyes, ears, and mind open. Afterall, the best part of mentorship is that— when it is a strong partnership—both people learn equally. As a mentor, you will gain a new perspective about the [MC world]. Your mentee's youthful inexperience can actually provide you with a wealth of powerful insight...if you are open to it." [2]

You gain the perspective of leadership without having the responsibility of being the president. In other words, you get to "practice."'" Most brothers are so busy partying, drinking, riding, or raising hell in the clubhouse they simply do not want to take the time to mentor or sponsor up-and-coming brothers. Do it! As you begin to build your communication, training, development, and educating skills you will be forced to research and improve so you can stand up to the scrutiny of the younger brothers when they question you and ask, "Why." Afterall, that is exactly what you will experience when you become President.

4.   Be a Thought Leader

> "Experts are never content with the status quo. They are always looking for the next "evolution" of [the MC]. They are constantly trying new techniques, improving on existing concepts, exploring new ideas, and adding value. They are always looking to push the boundaries and expand the limits of [the MC]. Experts are at the forefront, leading the way for the future of [their clubs].
>
> Do not simply accept 'standard practice.' As an expert, your role is to question, challenge and innovate." [2]

I have encouraged you to be a thought leader, but I also want to warn you that there can be a risk to being the person brothers consistently turn to as it can present certain challenges. People may accept or even tolerate the president as the thought leader, but what if you are not yet the president? What if you are a club brother or officer, building your 10,000 hours on your way to becoming president? What might you expect? Those higher than you in the club, like the president, may see your popularity as a threat leading to their loss of power. They will try to cancel you (cancel culture for real) by any means necessary. What if you already are the president of your local chapter and are considered to be the thought leader within your mighty MC Nation to whom all the other presidents reach out to instead of the national and regional officers to get your opinions on how things should work? The national president or other nationals and regionals or perhaps all of them may consider you a threat or an enemy (especially if your insights go against them) and they may seek to cancel you.

This, like many other things in the MC, is just how it is. Be prepared for obstacles, challenges, and insults like "know-it-all" to be slurred your way. Be mindful of those who appreciate you. They will recognize you are driving the conversations and the directions to make the club better and will want to be around you, will seek you out, and try to soak up all the information, advice, and knowledge you can give. No one wants to sit stagnant except for those fearful in their positions; terrified that new ideas, hard-charging new members, and more competent brothers will threaten their fiefdoms. That is because these are the types of leaders we all hate. The kind of president that wants to do the same old thing because he does not have enough character to inspire others to greatness, who refuses to bring in new prospects or hang-arounds and is a lackluster bump-on-a-log who is good for nothing. But yes, those guys do manage to make it to the top so when they see a thought leader all they want to do is shut him down. If you choose to be a thought leader be aware of it but do not fear it. Simply prepare yourself to go around it and multiply in spite of it. A thought leader gains more knowledge because he is involved in more discovery, research, and independent verification to establish his expertise in MC culture than anyone around him. Be prepared for the jealousy to come from all sides—even from your peers. You do not have to be the president for life to be lonely in the MC. We already know it is if you are the president.

5. Demonstrate Your Knowledge

    After you start to build your expertise by expanding your knowledgebase consider putting it to use.

    > "Experts take pride in demonstrating and sharing their skills and knowledge. They always want to be of service to their community. If you want to be seen as an expert, put your expertise out there from which all can benefit. Let your

ideas spark conversation. Be the catalyst that inspires others to think differently about [the MC].

How do you do this? The written word is always a great place to start."[2]

I first started writing on MC culture when I was a prospect for the Mighty Black Sabbath MC Nation mother chapter. The Father, Paul 'Pep' Perry came to me and asked me to rewrite the club's bylaws. I was the Editor-in-Chief of the San Diego News Link newspaper at the time and Father Pep knew that I could get the bylaws into shape, remove the grammatical errors, and make them look professional and easier to read. From there my passion grew. I wanted to know where all of these rules came from and why. I became a junkie of MC culture, consuming all that I could find written about who we were. I wrote my first articles long before I ever became a president of the Mighty Black Sabbath Motorcycle Club Nation Atlanta chapter some 10 - 12 years later. I started by posting articles on E-zines, then linked to them on all of the biker club blogs, vlogs, Yahoo, Facebook pages, and MySpace biker pages I could find. I grew tired of waiting for the publisher of Easy Rider magazine to put black female models in their magazines—celebrating white and Asian female bodies, but somehow viewing African American Goddesses as beneath them and not good enough to bless their pages, so I started my own motorcycle magazines "Black Iron Motorcycle Magazine," "Urban Biker Motorcycle Magazine," "Black Sabbath Motorcycle Magazine Online."

When I went inside white biker clubs there were fine white girls on bikes cut out of magazines, but when I went into the Black Sabbath Motorcycle Club clubhouse in San Diego, all we had were black models in some rotten beer advertisements. I thought, "Why we ain't got no pictures of our women on bikes in the clubhouse?!" When I asked Father Pep, he said, "Because there ain't none!" That made me angry! Why wouldn't "they" put "us" in "their" magazine? Then it dawned on me. "Why should I wait for "them" to do any damned thing when "we" were just as capable as anyone of putting together a magazine with whomever "we" thought was beautiful?" To wait on someone else to do right by you, when you are capable of doing it yourself, is lunacy! I was already a photographer and had already proven my ability to write could, given that my publishing career was off and running. At the time, biker magazines were just a bunch of pretty, half-naked girls bent over motorcycles, but I knew my club brothers would be interested in reading more than that. I began researching biker culture to learn what would be most useful to club bikers. Keep in mind, I was still a prospect at this time and Father Pep stood with me the entire way. I smile when I think of the first models in my first magazine, "Black Iron Motorcycle Magazine," posing on Father Pep's motorcycle. I knew I needed to know more, so I started contacting the big-time publishers of other biker magazines, including "Long Riders Magazine", "Black Biker Magazine", "Biker's Dream Magazine" and "Knight Errants Magazine", a magazine that was being published by Ringo of the Flaming Knights Motorcycle Club Nation to learn the craft. Ringo was one of the first brothers I met who was actually creating a biker magazine. He gave me great insight into the career upon which I planned to embark. Na'il Karim, publisher of "Black Biker Magazine", taught me a lot before his magazine disappeared after he went down on his motorcycle. I survived when some bozo tried to muzzle in on my magazine's name "Black Iron Motorcycle Magazine" with his own magazine with the same title—fate is interesting when I never saw his magazine make the light of day.

All of this writing and publishing eventually landed me on the set of the DreamWorks movie, "Biker Boyz," starring Laurence

Fishburn and Derek Luke, as a Technical Advisor. I worked with director Reggie Rock Bythewood on every aspect of the movie and have lived to see it make the Turner Classics and become an iconic cult movie loved by bikers all over the black biker set nationwide as well as on other biker sets. When we made "Biker Boyz" the black biker set was dying. When the movie was released, the black biker set exploded with clubs popping up across the nation. Some say this was a good thing, some say this was a bad thing, but I say make a damned impression on the world in whatever you do! Make it bigger and better when you leave it than it was before you got there.

Before I ever even made it to President, I was already considered an expert in MC knowledge, culture, and protocol. I was writing and gathering information to build, then demonstrate my knowledge. I closely responded to how folks reacted to my writings. When they responded with praise, I knew I was on the right track. When they responded with criticism or asked questions, I researched further and got back to them, increasing my knowledge. Before long I was being asked to be a guest speaker on various biker radio shows and public speaking venues. By the time I became President I had been working on expanding my MC knowledge for years. I had written about so many aspects of the culture, I eventually found myself expanding chapters, dealing with coalitions, outlaws and 1%ers, coordinating sit-downs, negotiations, territory expansion, writing of bylaws and anything else related to bettering the MC. There is a remarkably interesting phenomenon that occurs when you become a published author—whether online or in print—you are automatically afforded a certain level of authority and credibility. It is not difficult to establish a name and reputation for yourself as an expert in this way, but it does require effort.

I acknowledge that not everyone is going to write a movie or a book but that does not mean you cannot write something for your club brothers, prospects, hang-arounds, or club associates from which they can benefit. For instance, take a stab at updating your bylaws—how much could you learn about the club's bylaws if you were the one to update them? Write a procedure for prospects or what should be done during a club initiation. Help write club rules or a checklist for the road captain. Perhaps you could write down the safety procedures for guarding the president or draft the watch-bill for those on duty at the clubhouse. Write a guide for what the brothers will need to take with them on the next cross-country trip or a checklist they can use to ensure they have all that they need. Do you see how fundamental and important your writings could be to the club? And of course, after you become president your club writings will have major weight in guiding the direction of the brotherhood. Yes, I am a writer, but take my bias out of the equation, writing is just one way to demonstrate your knowledge. There are many other things you could do to prove and build your knowledge, like holding club talks, gathering prospects together to teach them how to do something, lead the brothers in a planning meeting, demonstrate a maintenance, upgrade, or modification procedure on brothers' motorcycles. The possibilities to demonstrate your knowledge are endless.

6. Stay Up to Date on Trends
   The MC world and club life are ever evolving.

   > "Experts always stay at the forefront. They explore new trends and understand where the culture is headed. They have foresight and are not afraid of the least and greatest technologies and innovations that create upheaval to the tried-and-true methods of the past. While others fight the shifting waves of

progress, experts absorb the knowledge and when appropriate, ride those waves to success."[2]

I cannot tell you how many old timers in the big clubs forbade their brothers to use the internet, social media, websites, or even Facebook for years. Some of the top clubs in the nation were held back to 18th century communications technologies because the OGs were too afraid to learn how to text and use a damned computer, forbidding their younger members from doing the same. The world grew light years past the MCs by the time we finally began using social media. How much time did the MCs lose in expanding our dynasties, communicating our messages to our publics, and managing our public relations online because of this bullheaded refusal to embrace technology? Instead, law enforcement, Hollywood, and news organizations used these very same communication modalities to destroy the reputations of bikers and biker clubs worldwide. They had years to gain a foothold in their negative slander without biker clubs even being able to defend ourselves. All because we shied away from the way the rest of the world was communicating. We must never allow this to happen again! An MC can ill afford to bury its head in the sand when confronting new trends and burgeoning technologies.

"Reading is perhaps your best tool for staying up to date on trends." [2]

There are more books written on MC protocol today than ever before. When I started, all information was delivered mouth to mouth. Not much was written. Today there are blogs, vlogs, podcasts, audio books, printed books, magazines, YouTube, Facebook, Twitch, and Instagram TV motorcycle club videos available from which you can browse, peruse, and glean. These kinds of media often discuss emerging trends and how they are shaping the future of MC club culture throughout the world. Get to know the names of the people making a literary splash in MC culture (perhaps as a thought leader, you will eventually become one of them!).

Develop and use the vast biker set network. Having bikers from all aspects of the culture, from traditional MCs to 1%er MCs, to reach out to can pay invaluable dividends and add vastly to your level of knowledge—preparing you to run an MC as president.

> "Discuss the trends and breaking events taking place within your sphere of influence. Do not jump on every bandwagon that comes along, always stick closely to the values that define your [brotherhood], but when a trend seems to really be taking hold, embrace it and share your experiences." [2]

7. Never Stop Learning

> "Your absolute best bet for expertise is to always keep an open mind and absorb new information. Read books and blogs, take classes online and in-person [in leadership, in bar/night club management], let your expertise spawn from the expertise of others. The more you learn, the more you fill your [president's] toolbox."[2]

There are lots of places from which you can learn how to become a stronger leader. Leadership principles are the same no matter what organization you are in. It requires the same principles to lead successfully. Avail yourself of the information so you can be the best you can be for the MC.

> "Remember: Experts proudly claim their expertise; they do not shy away from it."[2]

Fourteen Ways to Acquire Knowledge

James T. Mangan published the book, [3]"*You Can Do Anything*!" in 1936, during the height of the Great Depression. Can you imagine someone being so bold as to write a book about how to be successful at a time when everything in the United States was quite unsuccessful? His book was concerned with the art of living, even during the worst of times. MC presidents could learn a lot from that attitude. Among the book's highlights is a section entitled "*14 Ways to Acquire Knowledge*" wherein Mangan defines the ways in which one should go about gaining knowledge. Let us consider Mangan's fourteen ways to "get smarter later," as it is never too late to learn and acquire knowledge, even if you are already President:

1. Practice

    "Consider the knowledge you already have — the things you really know you can do. They are the things you have done over and over; practiced them so often that they became second nature. Every normal person knows how to walk and talk. But he could never have acquired this knowledge without *practice*. For the young child cannot do the things that are easy to older people without first doing them over and over and over. Most of us quit on the first or second attempt. But the man who is really going to be educated, who intends to *know*, is going to stay with it until it is done. Practice!"[3]

    I can remember practicing a mountain run in the North Georgia Blue Ridge Mountains over and over again just so I could kick the shit out of any Black Sabbath Motorcycle Club Atlanta brother that ever thought he would be bad enough to challenge my riding skills. I knew I was getting older and had to be at the top of my game so I could take the youngsters out when they came a calling. I ran those mountain passes a few times per month. I was never beaten up there by a Black Sabbath, but a youngster named "Guns", whom I had known since he was a prospect and eventually became president of the Cycle Kings MC Nation Atlanta chapter, decided to take a run at me one day. He had some kind of crazy car tire on the back of his 80's era Honda Valkyrie when he came to the mountains to get down that day. I had my '87 Honda Gold Wing which, unfortunately was not as quick as that damned Valkyrie. This kid was hitting those 15 miles per hour curves with me at 30 miles per hour. We were peg-to-peg damned near elbowing each other off the roadway! I kept thinking, "I hope that car tire does not kick his back end over into my bike or we will both be gone off of this mountain top." You could hear them pegs scraping and see the sparks flying off the road as he laid into one curve after another side-by-side edging and pushing me harder and harder. His unbridled youth against my experience and honed practice. It was his first time up there and he gave me all I could handle with that damned Valkyrie. Turns out that near the end of our run my bike simply was not faster than his. He went around me towards the last three or four turns. Not long after that loss I bought my Victory Vision. Practice helps but never forget to have the right bike because that really helps too! I have never been beaten up there again. Once I even ran down and passed a guy on his Ducati with my girl Tia on the back. When I got to the gas station the guy caught up to me and got off his Ducati and bowed to me very lowly. "Damn, I ain't never seen nobody get down on a cruiser like that man," he said humbly. "Respect, he shouted, jumped on his bike and road away. Practice!

2. Ask

"Any normal child, at about the age of three or four, reaches the asking period, the time when that quickly developing brain is most eager for knowledge. "When?" "Where?" "How?" "What?" and "Why?" begs the child — but all too often the reply is "Keep still!" "Leave me alone!" "Don't be a pest!" Those first bitter refusals to our honest questions of childhood all too often squelch our "Asking faculty." We grow up to be men and women, still eager for knowledge, but afraid and ashamed to ask in order to get it. Every person possessing knowledge is more than willing to communicate what he knows to any serious, sincere person who asks. The question never makes the asker seem foolish or childish — rather, to ask is to command the respect of the other person who in the act of helping you is drawn closer to you, likes you better and will go out of his way on any future occasion to share his knowledge with you. Ask! When you ask, you have to be humble. You have to admit you don't know! But what's so terrible about that? Everybody knows that no man knows everything, and to ask is merely to let the other know that you are honest about things pertaining to knowledge."

Everything I have ever learned in the MC world I gleaned by asking a full patch brother. I have had to humbly ask, "How do I do this?" or "How do I do that?" Sometimes people tried to make me look like a fool or have laughed at me for asking. Others lorded their information over me without doing anything to help me learn much at all. But most were willing to share everything they knew to help me learn merely because I asked. Do not be afraid to ask and certainly do not be afraid of the rejection you may get when they turn you away. Just become more determined and go ask someone else. You will be glad you did.

3. Desire

   "You never learn much until you really *want* to learn.
   A million people have said: "Gee, I wish I were

musical!" "If I only could do that!" or "How I wish I had a good education!" But they were only talking *words* — they didn't *mean* it. Desire is the foundation of all learning, and you can only climb up the ladder of knowledge by desiring to learn. If you don't desire to learn you're either a num-skull [*sic*] or a "know-it-all." [3]

The world wants nothing to do with either of these types of individuals. As I learned more about motorcycle club and biker culture I wanted to know more. It created a burning desire within me to grasp all that I could clutch. The burning desire to know more made me want to do more. The things I wanted to do were designed to better my MC nation. The more I reached out to do, the more authority Father Pep gave me. As I solved one problem, he pushed me to solve another. Soon I found myself as the National Enforcer with even more responsibilities. Before long, I was National President. My desire to learn more spurned opportunities to do more, which opened the doors that led to higher authority until I was the highest authority in my Nation.

The more you know as president the better off you will be. Let your position and office alone build in you the desire to learn more. The MC will be well protected by a wise president who knows a lot.

4. Get if From Yourself
Relying on yourself is another way to trust ourselves.

"You may be surprised to hear that you already know a great deal! It's all inside you—it's all there—you couldn't live as long as you have and not be full of knowledge. Most of your knowledge, however—and this is the great difference between non-education and education—is not in shape to be used, you haven't it on the top of your tongue. It's hidden, buried away down inside of you—and because you can't see it, you think it isn't there. Knowledge is knowledge only when it takes a shape, when it can be put into words, or reduced to a principle—and it's now up to you to go to work on your own gold mine, to refine the crude ore."[3]

I was surprised at what I knew when I started writing articles and teaching people. Sure, there were many things I did not know and had yet to learn, but my experiences in the MC world had prepared me with a lot of knowledge I never knew I had. When I became President, my entire MC life prepared me with the knowledge I needed to be one of the most successful presidents my MC nation has ever seen. There were no classes, courses, or training modules to guide me. The big things I needed were already within me. I got it from within myself.

5. Walk Around It

"Any time you see something new or very special, if the thing is resting on the ground, as your examination and inspection proceeds, you find that you eventually walk around it. You desire to know the thing better by looking at it from all angles. To acquire knowledge, walk around the thing studied. The thing is not only what you touch, what you see; it has many other sides, many other conditions, many other relations which you cannot know until you study it from all angles. The narrow mind stays rooted in one spot; the broad mind is free, inquiring, unprejudiced; it seeks to learn "both sides of the story." Don't screen off from your own consciousness the bigger side of your work. Don't be afraid you'll harm yourself if you have to change a preconceived opinion. Have a free, broad, open mind! Be fair to the thing studied as well as to yourself. When it comes up for your examination, walk around it! The short trip will bring long knowledge."[3]

If you are going to be successful in the MC business, you need to immerse yourself within it. You need to become one with the MC. It will take up all of your spare time and a lot of the time you do not have to spare. You are going to have to walk around it, climb on it, ride with it, sleep with it, dream it, live it, and love it. I hate seeing presidents take the helm knowing good and damned well they do not have time to be president. If you are working triple shifts outside the MC or are so involved in a divorce you cannot be there, give the job up and step down. The MC needs, in fact it thrives, on an engaged president who has his eyes on his flock and guards them with all he is. Do not let it be about ego or personal agenda. Always move in the best interest of the MC. Walk around it and be a part of it.

6.   Experiment

"The world honors the man who is eager to plant new seeds of study today so he may harvest a fresh crop of knowledge tomorrow. The world is sick of the man who is always harking back to the past and thinks everything worth knowing has already been learned. ... Respect the past, take what it offers, but don't live in it. To learn, experiment! Try something new. See what happens." [3]

To gain knowledge you must experiment and with experimentation comes risks.

I had no idea what it would take to expand the Mighty Black Sabbath Motorcycle Club Nation into a national club until I began trying. Each time I opened a new chapter it was yet another experiment—a different area, different 1%ers or outlaws, different coalitions, different boards, different cops, different city councils, different neighborhood associations, different ordnances. Each experiment came with a lesson to be learned; new knowledge to be obtained. But if we did not venture, we would not have gained. I am sure you have heard the expression "Nothing ventured, nothing gained." It rings true! I was never able to accomplish for the MC, dream for the MC, aspire to be great for the MC until I made a move and took a risk.

Taking risks takes guts. There are things you will try in which you will absolutely fail. The fear of failure is real. That fear traps presidents in a holding pattern preventing them from trying to do anything more than the status quo. They do not want to reach out and make great things happen because they are in fear of great failure. As I said, the fear of failure is real.

For instance, let us say, for some outlandish reason you and your club brothers want to take your club to a three-piece patch and a state rocker. You speak with a few other chapters and the idea gains popularity. You and the other presidents decide to bring this up for discussion at nationals. An unknowledgeable, lazy, and/or fearful national president may attempt to dismiss the discussion outright by swearing there is no way to do what you suggest because only outlaws and 1%ers wear three-piece patches and state rockers, refusing to even entertain the idea because he lacks the knowledge that there are plenty of 99%er clubs who wear three-piece patches and state rockers.

His arrogant obstinance and ignorant unwillingness to learn or hear anything from someone else's perspective stifles dialogue and wrests the conversation away from the intellectuals who are about advancing the condition, position, and status of the club. He acts like he knows it all but has done none of the research and does not know what the hell he is talking about! But he puffs up his chest, acts like the oracle of MC knowledge, and attempts to make the intellectuals look stupid. When someone attempts to remind him, "Yeah, but club 'X' over there did the same thing last year and they are willing to meet and instruct us on the procedure to get it done", the national scoffs and dismisses the speaker out of hand. And so, the entire MC nation is stuck! Stuck because a single nincompoop at the top. Maybe he is just plain old afraid. Afraid to attempt something for which he does not have any knowledge and therefore does not understand. Afraid to enlighten his mind and prefers the bliss of ignorance. Afraid that any failed experiment will expose his lack of knowledge and display his incompetence. Yet, he is content in himself. Satisfied and happy to keep the club at the same level it was when he took office. No growth, only losses—because a club that stops growing starts dying. There is nothing he can add because his mind has nothing to add. Terrified to acknowledge, "Really? I did not know that could be done. Let discuss it to see if it is even worth the risk. Let us get the chapter presidents together and look at this from end to end." No, instead he remains a dumb shit, "We ain't no outlaws so we won't be doing that." Refusing to even consider the pros, only viewing the cons he imagines in his mind to be true. Basically, he is afraid to experiment. He is afraid to take risks.

Risk-taking is a part of life. A baby risks falling and busting his lip wide open when he decides he will attempt to take his first steps. He gets up, he falls, he gets up again. I am sure there have been babies throughout the history of mankind that fell that one time and thought, "To hell with it. I am never going to attempt to walk again because it hurts when I fall." Consequently, that baby would never learn to walk. Instead spending his entire life crawling for fear of falling (and failing) prevailing over the advantages learning how to walk would provide. Do not be that baby! Do not be that president! Do not be that national! Risks are scary but surviving the risks empowers you with knowledge, information, education, and experience.

Taking risks for the MC has not always panned out like I planned or desired. Chapters did not open in the time framed I had planned, but we eventually got it done. The experimental part was to try. The knowledge gleaned empowered me to learn how to open more chapters. Contacts were made, connections secured, and relationships built.

> "Experiment only with your own time, your own money, your own labor. That's the honest, sincere type of experiment. It's rich. The cheap experiment is to use other people's money, other people's destinies, other people's bodies as if they were guinea pigs."[3]

Thinking about Mangun's point, I will say this about experimentation: Always keep the safety, integrity, and motives of the club in the forefront while exploring "the club's" future options. You must remember to be about the club's agenda above your own. The club has no ego it only has goals. Make the club's goals your goals and you will be alright.

7. Teach

> "If you would have knowledge, knowledge sure and sound, teach. Teach your children, teach your associates, teach your friends. In the very act of teaching, you will learn far more than your best pupil. Knowledge is relative; you possess it in degrees."[3]

You may notice that a lot of these authors say the same things when discussing how to expand your horizons. I repeat their ideas more than once in the book to drum them in your head.

When I began teaching MC protocol on my YouTube channel "Black Dragon Biker TV," I had no idea that the things I thought I knew paled in comparison to the vast knowledge I did not know but was destined to learn. When you are asked a question, research more than the question being asked to answer not only the initial question, but any follow-up questions. This process builds your own knowledge more than you will ever know. Find someone in your club to teach. It will strengthen you!

8. Read [and Read Critically]

Reading, what an interesting step. This is something we have seen before. It is funny that authors, personal coaches, and inspirational speakers around the globe say the same things. But it is interesting that they do not have the same take on the things they mention.

"From time immemorial it has been commonly understood that the best way to acquire knowledge was to read. That is not true. Reading is only one way to knowledge, and in the writer's opinion, not the best way. But you can surely learn from reading if you read in the proper manner. *What* you read is important, but not all important. How you read is the main consideration. For if you know *how to read*, there's a world of education even in the newspapers, the magazines, on a single billboard or a stray advertising dodger. The secret of good reading is this: *read critically*! Somebody wrote that stuff you're reading. It was a definite individual, working with a pen, pencil, or typewriter — the writing came from his mind and his *only*. If you were face to face with him and listening instead of *reading*, you would be a great deal more critical than the average reader is. *Listening*, you would weigh his personality, you would form some judgment about his truthfulness, his ability. But *reading*, you drop all judgment, and swallow his words whole — just as if the act of printing the thing made it *true*! If you must read in order to acquire knowledge, *read critically*. Believe nothing till it's understood, till it's clearly proven," [even what you read in this, Black Dragon's book!].[3]

Do not take what I have written at face value. Qualify me, question what I have written, compare it against your own experiences and those of presidents you know, will know, or have known. You may find whole excerpts of this book you emphatically disagree with. That is okay with me. These are my experiences, my research, my values, the club I lead. Not yours! You may find many similar situations we would not handle the same. My entire point is—Read! Read me and everything else you read, critically! Honestly, I do not mind.

9. Write

I have written extensively about writing, but it is interesting to know what Mangun says about writing:

> "To know it — write it! If you're writing to explain, *you're explaining it to yourself*! If you're writing to inspire, *you're inspiring yourself*! If you're writing to record, you're recording it on your own memory. How often you have written something down in order to be sure you would have a record of it, only to find that you never needed the written record because you had learned it by heart! The men of the best memories are those who make notes, *who write things down*. They just don't write to remember; *they write to learn*. And because they DO learn by writing, they seldom need to consult their notes, they have brilliant, amazing memories. How different from the glib, slipshod individual who is too proud or too lazy to write, who trusts everything to memory, forgets so easily, and

possesses so little real knowledge. Write! Writing, to knowledge, is a certified check. You *know* what you know once you have written it down!"[3]

10. Listen

"You have a pair of ears — use them! When the other man talks, give him a chance. Pay attention. If you listen, you may hear something useful to you. If you listen, you may receive a warning that is worth following. If you listen, you may earn the respect of those whose respect you prize. Pay attention to the person speaking. Contemplate the meaning of his words, the nature of his thoughts. Grasp and retain the truth. Of all the ways to acquire knowledge, this way requires least effort on your part. You hardly have to do any work. You are bound to pick up information. It's easy, it's surefire."[3]

11. Observe

Observation is key.

I have known presidents to enter a clubhouse, find a table in the back and put their backs up against the wall. No one in the clubhouse even knows they are there. They watch everything and everyone coming and going. They order one drink and sip on it for half the night because they want to be alert and unencumbered. They are on a mission. At the next club meeting everyone is blown away by what he knows about what is going on set wide. The best at it do not even have their colors on when they visit clubs on the set. They are in stealth mode, not hiding, but also not trying to be seen. These are not the "Look at me, I am the president," kinds of leaders. These are the leaders out reconnoitering on a reconnaissance mission.

This is one of the reasons I teach prospects and club brothers to, "Keep your big mouth shut in other people's clubhouses about club business and certainly never run your trap negatively about other clubs. You never know who is sitting next to you at the bar or is bar tending. So, running your rat trap is a good way to get your teeth kicked in later or land your club in hot water."

In fact, I can recount a story where one of my Black Sabbath brothers got frustrated with a bartender at a clubhouse and started talking shit to him, like he had dirt on him. He was very disrespectful because he did not feel the bartender was moving fast enough. The bartender asked him, "Do you know who I am?" He had something else snarky to say. You see, he thought that somehow the bartender was a prospect or someone not worthy of his respect. Turns out the bartender was a 1%er president bartending at his support club's clubhouse. Yeah, it happened.

Imagine the amount of crow eaten to smooth that incident over. My brother was not so high and mighty when he discovered he was talking shit to a 1%er president who was quite underwhelmed with his presentation of our highly esteemed club. On the biker set it is always more prudent to speak less, listen and observe more. You keep the shit down that way.

> "Keep your eyes open. There are things happening, all around you, all the time. The scene of events is interesting, illuminating, full of news and meaning. It's a great show — an impressive parade of things worth knowing. Admission is free — keep your eyes open. There are only two kinds of experience: the experience of ourselves and the experience of others. Our own experience is slow, labored, costly, and often hard to bear. The experience of others is a ready-made set of directions on knowledge and life. Their experience is free; we need suffer none of their

hardships; we may collect on all their good deeds. All we have to do is *observe*! Observe! Especially the good man, the valorous deed. Observe the winner that you yourself may strive to follow that winning example and learn the scores of different means and devices that make success possible. Observe! Observe the loser that you may escape his mistakes, avoid the pitfalls that dragged him down. Observe the listless, indifferent, neutral people who do nothing, know nothing, *are* nothing. Observe them and then *differ* from them."[3]

12. Put in Order

Before you can espouse your views on a subject, you must put your knowledge in order. Assemble it into relevant pieces so that you can have everything together.

> "Order is Heaven's first law. And the only good knowledge is *orderly knowledge*! You must put your information and your thoughts in order before you can effectively handle your own knowledge. Otherwise, you will jump around in conversation like a grasshopper, your arguments will be confused and distributed, your brain will be in a dizzy whirl all the time."[3]

13. Define

What do you know if you do not know exactly what you are talking about?

One of the interesting things about MC protocol is that it is defined differently in each area. The procedure for getting a club blessing is different in one part of the United States than another. The rules of one COC are different from another's.

The whole discussion of relevant knowledge comes down to a basic definition of the knowledge you possess.

> "A definition is a statement about a thing which includes everything the thing is and excludes everything it is not. A definition of a chair must include *every* chair, whether it be a kitchen chair, a highchair, a dentist's chair, or the electric chair, it must exclude everything which isn't a chair, even those things which come close, such as a stool, a bench, a sofa. I am sorry to state that until you can so define chair or door (or a thousand other everyday familiar objects) *you don't really know what these things are.* You have the ability to recognize them and describe them, but you can't tell what their *nature* is. Your knowledge is not *exact.*"[3]

14. Reason

All your knowledge on a certain topic boils down to how effectively you are able to use it. It gives the knowledge you attain as president value. Qualifying your presidential knowledge.

> "Animals have knowledge. *But only men can reason.* The better you can reason the farther you separate yourself from animals. The process by which you reason is known as logic. Logic teaches you how to derive a previously unknown truth from the facts already at hand. Logic teaches you how *to be sure* whether what you think is true is really true. Logic is the supreme avenue to intellectual truth. Don't ever despair of possessing a logical mind. You don't have to study it for years, read books and digest a mountain of data. All you have to remember is one word — *compare.* Compare all points in a proposition. Note the *similarity* — that tells you something new. Note the *difference* — that tells you

something new. Then take the new things you've found and check them against established laws or principles. This is logic. This is reason. This is knowledge in its highest form."[3]

So, there you have it—some principles for going about developing the expert level of knowledge you will need to become a successful president and deliver the very best service possible to your MC!

Example - The president who knows the protocols necessary to expand chapters, navigate the politics of sit downs, train junior officers and members, operate the systems of city hall to get business licenses, liquor licenses, and fire marshal safety clearances for the clubhouse, while ensuring the bylaws of the MC are being maintained and the club has a five-year growth plan for expanding across the United States—simultaneously possesses presidential knowledge.

Chapter TWENTY
The Leadership Principle
of Loyalty

Loyalty

Definition - The quality of faithfulness to the MC Nation including its full patch brothers, extended family, seniors, peers, and subordinates, placing its safety, security, aspirations, goals, and agendas above your own.

Significance – All full patch brothers owe unswerving loyalty up and down the chain of command to the MC. When you sit atop the brotherhood as a national or chapter president, it is your example of loyalty that the nation or chapter will follow. If you are loyal, among other things, you will never discuss nor expose club business with outsiders. You will never snitch on the brotherhood or sell-it-out to law enforcement for leniency in a case against you, or for any other reason. You will never talk about your club brothers unfavorably in front of subordinates or to outsiders, you will never purposely lead the MC to harm, and finally, once any legal order has been handed down by the club's authority above you, for instance from the executive board, the high council, or the national president, it is your duty to carry out that order willingly as if it were your own whether you agree with it or not. You are to never split the nation because of your own greed or self-aggrandizing.

Loyalty is the unswerving dedication to the principles, traditions, culture, and best interests of the motorcycle club, full patch brothers, and all other entities attached. It is the glue that holds the brotherhood together. Loyalty is that leadership quality that makes you continue to strive for the best interests of the MC even if all of the brothers turn on you, call you a liar, and cast aspersions upon your name or character. I am not sure that loyalty can be taught. It is a quality that one must simply possess, it is something you get from your childhood. If you are a disloyal person generally, I do not see how it will ever be possible for you to be loyal to the MC. Though loyalty can be practiced, it in my opinion, is an innate quality that cannot be learned! But we can discover loyalty based on how important a thing or entity is to us. In other words, a previously disloyal cheater who could never be faithful to his wife, may discover a love of the MC which could emerge feelings of deep respect, fealty, and loyalty that he may have never experienced before. In this way his loyalty was discovered, and perhaps where he had not the ability to be loyal before he now becomes the most loyal person on Earth towards that one entity. I do not know if this is true or not, it is often hard for a person to change their true character. But since we are discussing this topic, let us continue understanding that it is toward the study of improving our loyalty so that we may lead others who follow.

A Google search on the meaning of the word loyalty returned these seven results:

- The quality of being faithful to someone or something else.
- A feeling or attitude of devoted attachment and affection.
- Faithfulness or devotion to some person, cause, or nation.
- The state of being loyal; fidelity.
- Quality, state, or instance of being loyal.
- An obligation of support and faithfulness to a person, government, cause, duty, etc.

I think I would combine those meanings into a statement like this for the purposes of leading the MC:

There is an obligation of support and faithfulness that should come naturally to an MC president as he expresses, through his actions of leadership, the enthusiastic attitude of devoted attachment, affection, faithfulness, and fidelity through the quality of exemplary service, toward the brothers, their mission, and the best interests of the MC nation, that supersedes the personal agenda, goals, or interests of himself in every instance or situation.

But with that all being said, "What in Hell is the practical meaning of loyalty and how is loyalty best displayed by the "Prez?"

Simplistically, loyalty is the ability to put others before yourself and support them whether times are good or bad. In an article called *"How to Be Loyal"* co-authored by Kelli Miller, she said that to be loyal one must "be honest, trustworthy, supportive, and generous."

Miller broke it down to three methods:

1. Being supportive and generous.
2. Being honest and trustworthy.
3. Maintaining healthy boundaries.

We will look at these qualities she discussed as she broke them down adding, of course, our own MC equivalencies to them so that we can learn how to effectively use these principles to better ourselves for leadership:

- Being Supportive and Generous
  1. **Support the goals, ambitions, and dreams of others.** "Try to show genuine interest in the goals and dreams of the members of your [brotherhood]. Ask questions about their ambitions and goals. If they vote to reach a goal, use your office, influence, and leadership to support them in getting there."
  2. **Be a Good Listener.** "Demonstrate your loyalty to others by taking the time to listen to what they have to say. Maintain eye-contact and nod when you listen. Avoid interrupting others when they speak or talking over them. Instead, focus on them and pay attention when they confide in you."

Speaking over the top of your brothers at church or yelling over the top of them on phone meetings to bully your agenda over that of the body is NOT showing loyalty toward the MC. Making officers or members feel like they must cower before you and not ensuring that their goals are met over yours will turn them against you and make them plot towards your presidential demise. Remember you are dealing with full grown men. Never forget that members will vote with their feet and leave you to YOUR MC all by yourself if you insist on treating them like children.

3. **Offer Positive Solutions and Ideas.** "You can also be supportive and generous to others by focusing on the positives in a situation or conflict. Try to come up with solutions and ideas that make others feel optimistic and productive."

You must remember Prez that loyalty means selling out for the brotherhood. You must be "all-in" always moving in the direction of progressing the club forward. Afterall, if the president does not think it can be done or fails to show his absolute dedication to the goal then why would anybody? You must be supportive and generous to each member and always, in as much as possible, positive even when challenges seem too overwhelming to overcome. You must always believe in the MC even when it does not believe that it can overcome seemingly insurmountable obstacles. This is the strength that the conviction of loyalty brings to the brotherhood. If you always display this attitude, it builds enthusiasm and, of course, loyalty in others.

4. **Resist Judging Others for their Choices or Actions.** "Practice empathy for others so you can be there for them, rather than judge them. Replace feelings of judgement with feelings of support. If you judge people, you are basing that judgement on principles you may hold dear. Looking for them to regard your principles in the same way only sets you up for great disappointment. Accept things for how they are. Save judgements for deciding how you will fix problems. For example, instead of judging a [brother] who is struggling with addiction, support his efforts to get help. Do not let a [brother's] different lifestyle choices blind you to all the reasons why the [MC may need him, or why he may need the MC]. Try not to be scared by ideas and lifestyles that are different from yours but instead, embrace them in as much as you can. It can be most difficult to be empathetic to those most different from ourselves."

Believe me, as Prez you are going to see the best and worst displayed in your brothers—just get ready for it. As we used to say in the "Silent Service" of the nuclear-powered submarine world, "Stand by for heavy seas!" I say that because I know firsthand the ups and downs your emotions will be dragged through while demonstrating allegiance to your members. The sinusoidal emotional wave will be akin to bobbing around the ocean, up and down, like in a submarine, enduring relentless wave after wave of stormy seas! When you are voted into the office you become a father-like figure to the MC. Individuals will bring their personal issues to you from addiction, to alcoholism, from child abuse to domestic abuse. They will bring good things and accomplishments and you will see the worst of things from some of them as well. Your job is complicated. It equals being part counselor, shrink, inspirational leader, business manager, disciplinarian, public speaker, and preacher. Hell—you have got to come up with answers to many challenges for which you have not been formally trained or equipped to handle. Sometimes so much so that you will feel overwhelmed. When counseling presidents I most often hear things like, "I never knew I would be spending so many hours on the phone like this. Who would have thought this would be a twenty-four hour per day, seven day per week job that I am not even being paid for?" So, to be successful, you will have to listen and HEAR without judgement so that you can make the best calls no matter the challenge with which you may be presented.

- **Being Honest and Trustworthy**
  1. **Express how you really feel.** "Try not to sugar coat your true feelings when you speak to members. Being loyal means not being afraid to be honest and straightforward. Lying can make others distrust you and not see you as loyal. For example, you may say, "I

have to be honest with you about how I feel" or you may say, "Honestly, I am not sure if that is a good idea..." You can (and should) give your honest opinion without being judgmental. Instead of saying "that's a bad idea" or "I wouldn't do that," try something like "It's your decision to make, but if it were me, I'd ...""

2. **Don't engage in gossip.** "Talking behind someone's back is considered dishonest and disloyal. Do not believe in gossip or engage in gossip about those inside of your [club]. If you have questions or concerns, speak to the person directly rather than engaging in gossip or rumors about them. If you hear others gossiping around you, demand that they stop! You may say, "Let's not gossip or indulge in rumors" [or "I'd prefer to we talk to our brother and give him the opportunity to present his side of the story] rather than believe gossip."

I will be honest; this is perhaps one of the most difficult negative areas from which you should steer clear. There is just something about a good juicy rumor that almost reaches out and demands that you pay it some attention. Do not! You are the president. You must resist. You should have more things to do with your time than to spend any of it engaging in gossip. I have been involved in gossip against my own club brothers. Believe me if it is ever discovered that you engaged in it, member(s) will never trust you again. They will consider you the most disloyal scumbag leader the world has ever seen. I will never forget one of my club brothers asking another, "I am not concerned with what such and such said about me. What concerns me is that he felt so comfortable coming to you with the garbage rumor! Why did you fail to defend me?" And that is the question you do not ever want to have to try to answer as Prez. The terrible thing about rumors is that folks feel compelled to believe the absolute worst thing about other folks—even if what they are hearing goes generally against the character of the person the rumor is about. And they will pass this garbage on from member to member until it takes up a space bigger than the truth. Get good at shutting gossip down. If someone wants to complain about someone else, make them take it to the table. There is no place else for an accusation other than at the table during church. And another thing. The moment you put on the title of president you will become the target of more garbage gossip than you can ever imagine. You must have thick skin. If you do not you will never survive the office.

3. **Follow through on your commitments.** "Show up for events, [church, rides, and club business] when you promise you will. Follow through on commitments to [club members]. Be present for your [officers] when you say you will. Following through on what you promise others will show them they can count on you and trust you to be there for them. Avoid being flaky and try not to cancel plans last minute, as this can show others you are not trustworthy. You can quickly build a negative reputation for flaking if you are not careful with your actions. Show up on time and be present for others on time. Use your actions to prove that when you say you will be there, you mean it."

I used to have a terrible problem with being on time. It started in kindergarten when my mother got us to school late every day. She was a single mom raising three children, working three jobs, and she sent us to the nearly all white Catholic school on the other side of town. It must have been tough for her trying to drive us to school in the mornings after working 16-hour days. In first grade the nuns at the Catholic school in Lawton, Oklahoma used to beat me terribly for getting to school late. Actually, it was Sister Mary Ann Theresa who used to beat the hell out of me. She was such a mean penguin. I am glad to write her name down and expose that child-abusing witch to the world some 52 years later, even though I am sure she must be long dead. I know the Catholic church pays settlements for pedophiles, but I wonder if they pay settlements for child abusing, brutal, bullies like that rotten nun. I want the world to know how that witch beat the hell out of me with paddles and slapped the back of my knuckles with rulers and pulled my ears until I thought they would fall off and treated me like so much refuse. She was an expert at hurting you without leaving a mark and for what? I mean how in the hell is a six-year-old boy supposed to get himself to school on time? The cowardly nun never said anything to my mother. If my mother had known what she was doing to me she would not have been long for the world. I know she was a damned racist by the way she treated me differently than anyone else. I was isolated and alone and the best I can figure it she just got a pleasure and a thrill out of torturing. But I digress. Anyway, my mom's tardy ways stuck with me, and it carried on through grade school, junior high, high school, every job I had, and into the Navy. The Navy is one of those places where you can never really be late or you would be in a shitload of trouble, yet I found a way to get away with being late all of the time, even in the Navy. I became so good at my job that my Naval supervisors overlooked my constant tardiness as the cost of business— or "That is just the way Bunch is." You would be surprised how various personality quirks are accepted by crew members when they know they can depend upon you in a fight, or other areas that are more important than your quirk areas of deficiency. I mean it was ridiculous now that I think about it but aboard the submarine out on patrol, the Chief of the Watch would send the messengers to my bunk to awaken me early and then send them back every five to ten minutes to basically usher me out of bed and put me in the shower. They figured out a way to make sure that I got to my watch station on time. Now, what they were supposed to do was write me up and bust me down a rank or two and that would get the message across quickly, but a submarine crew is tight. They know the quirks of each crewmember so if you are generally squared away, they will make exceptions. My weakness was my lateness, but I handled other areas of my job impeccably. I taught school

of the boat, ran a duty section, managed the dinks (we will
have to talk about dinks – this is a word no longer used in
the submarine Navy I am told) and handled all of the
training for the junior guys.

When I became a president of my MC it was a big deal to
the members that I could not get anywhere on time. A lack
of respect for other people's time demonstrates to them
that you are not trustworthy because you are inconsiderate.
If you are inconsiderate, you are not loyal. My members
were so angry at times that they actually wanted to remove
me as president even though, like in the Navy, I was
extremely good in most other areas. It was their number
one complaint against me and sometimes my tardiness
made members mad enough to want to fight me. It was
something that I finally had to get under control after a
lifetime of not being able to make it anywhere on time. My
motorcycle club was not about to give me the same
coddling as my submarine crew. I knew I had to rebuild
credibility with my brothers so as I was working on breaking
a lifelong habit, I first started by telling the bros, "Hey, do
not wait on me. I will get there; you guys just go on."
Sometimes I had to ride alone but I got it together after a
while. You can overcome your weaknesses if you are loyal
enough to the brotherhood because you will correct your
areas of deficiencies as it will be very important to you that
you do so. Like I said about loyalty. Sometimes you have
loyalty where you did not have it before because something
means more to you than anything ever meant before. I
probably never cared about any job I ever had or even being
in the Navy as much as I cared about being a respected
president of my MC. Therefore, I developed the loyalty
necessary to change my ways and eliminate the behavior of

tardiness that had plagued me all my life and was one of the biggest sore spots with my club brothers.

- **Maintaining Healthy Boundaries**
  1. **Choose to give your loyalty to others.** Your loyalty should be something you give to others because you want to, not because you feel you have to. Do not feel obligated to be loyal to brothers who demand it and expect it because not everyone who wears your colors is your brother. Instead, choose to be loyal to those you trust and believe in. "Keep in mind being loyal does not mean blindly following what others want or expect. Instead, you should feel like you want to be loyal to others based on their character and actions."

For example, if a guy wants to sell dope at the clubhouse is it disloyal to refuse to bail him out if he gets busted behind the club caught in the act? He has an expectation that his colors should guarantee his absolute protection by the MC, yet he puts the brotherhood in jeopardy because of his deliberate exposure of it to law enforcement by breaking the law at the clubhouse. I do not believe in the blind loyalty of coming to someone's aid when they know they are wrong, and they use personal agendas to endanger the MC. Now this is a different subject if the entire MC is selling dope and the brother gets caught handling club business. The same could be said for a brother who decides to disrespect someone's old lady in their clubhouse, and he gets his teeth kicked in during the process. Should the entire club roll over to that clubhouse and beat up the other club because a brother was acting out? That is blind loyalty. It is a different story altogether if a brother gets caught up defending the interests of the MC. Then he has deserved your loyalty. There will be many who disagree with my conclusions here. I present these ideas for thought, not as some kind of overarching truth the Black Dragon has over the MC world. Do things how your club does things. These are only my ideas.

2. **Do not let others take advantage of your loyalty.** "Be aware of [brothers] who start to use your loyalty to their advantage. The relationships in your club should feel balanced and fair, where you get as much as you give. This can prevent others from taking advantage of your loyal and supportive nature. If you notice others are taking advantage of you, sit them down and explain how you are feeling. Address the issue, rather than ignoring it. Be honest and forthcoming about your feelings. It is then up to the person to change their behavior and respond positively to your concerns."

3. `Maintain your independence.** "Give yourself the chance to "do your own thing" here and there. Spend lots of time with friends and family, but also carve out time on your own. Avoid being too dependent on others, as this can start to burn you out and make you feel less self-confident. For example, you may pick one day in the week where you do something on your own, without the [club]. Or you may break up your week, so you have time to socialize with friends and time to yourself."

I know so many brothers who have lost their wives, girlfriends, sometimes entire families because they could not separate club life from personal life. Club life is not personal life. There is a difference. If your wife needs you then you need to leave the clubhouse long enough to take care of your house. This is not being disloyal to the club because how can you take care of the club if you cannot first take care of yourself? But I see this behavior most often with presidents. Sometimes you get so overwhelmed and "caught up" after you become Prez that you think the MC cannot operate without you. That is when you start over emphasizing on the club and neglecting home. "Boy, do not be no goddamned fool," as my mother used to say.

I say use the example of the airlines when you think of how to handle the club. If you have ever flown in a plane the airline stewards give a small training session before the plane takes off. In that session they explain that if the cabin ever loses pressure your breathing masks will suddenly pop out of the overhead. This is so you can plug into them and breathe even though the cabin has lost pressure. The thing they tell mothers is, "Before you put that mask on anyone else first put one on yourself!" Why do they tell them this? That is because during studies and actual incidents they discovered that mothers would try to put the mask on their children before themselves. If they had three or four kids they might pass out after only getting the mask on one or two kids. In that sad case the mother and the rest of the kids perish because she was not able to get the masks on everyone in time. But if she puts the mask on herself first, then it is okay if the other kids pass out before she gets the mask on all of them. They will be revived by the oxygen, and she would be able to save the entire family—after saving herself FIRST! The lesson here is that you cannot save anyone, and certainly not everyone, if you do not first save and take care of yourself. So, I tell presidents until you are safe, mentally sound, and healthy at home, you ain't no good for nobody period, end of story. Have some balance in your life and maintain some semblance of independence from the MC. That is healthy the other way is not.

4. **Allow time for self-care.** "Maintain healthy boundaries with the [brotherhood] by giving yourself time to focus on your needs. Have at least one hour of self-care per week where you do something you enjoy, such as painting, reading, or working out. You can also do a calming activity like taking a bath, getting a massage, or doing yoga. Giving yourself time for self-care can help prevent you from burning out on being loyal and supportive to the [MC] all the time. Guard this self-care time so you can always meet your emotional needs. Avoid readily giving it away."

Bottom line is that I know way too many of you Presidents that just become so irrationally all encompassed and insanely involved in running the brotherhood, after you make it to the top, that it truly is plain old unhealthy! You take your dedication beyond loyalty to the point that it becomes a mental illness defined by your attempted destruction of everything in your lives that are not an integral part of the MC itself. And I do mean everything to include your relationships with your wives, children, relatives, jobs, bosses, co-workers, friends, colleagues, childhood friends, freedom; you know, everything and everybody who loves, supports, and upholds you besides the club! The important thing to know is that you cannot disproportionally be good for the MC if you are not appropriately good to yourselves! Something will eventually have to give and that something will be you. The problem will be that when the breakdown occurs, if you have driven away every support system you have, you will be beyond saving because there will not be any person left to save you; especially if you should lose the support of the brotherhood and become shunned, suspended, put out bad, or otherwise separated. Be smart enough not to destroy your relationships because you are so involved with the club that you have no time for them. Do not make yourself choose between them or the club or make them choose between having an uninvolved you or moving on because the club is not a guarantee. Eventually it will move on past you, believe it or not. Eventually the MC will replace you with another president. Eventually the younger guys will move up and put you on a shelf—this happens in every organization or "so-called" extended family. Not many are "president for life" in the MC world, in fact I have only known one, Tobe Gene Livingston Founding Father of the Mighty East Bay Dragons MC. For the rest of us in the MC world your reign at the top will most likely be temporary so make sure there is something left for you to go back to after your stint at the top of your chapter, state, region, or even as national president, is over.

Example - A president displaying enthusiasm in carrying out an order from the national president even though he may privately disagree.

Chapter TWENTY-ONE
The Leadership Principles
of Endurance

Endurance

Definition - The mental and physical stamina measured by the ability to withstand pain, fatigue, stress, and hardship.

Significance – Endurance requires mental and physical focus. A toughness of mind, resilience, and determination to overcome the emotionally stressful challenges that occur when running an MC. You must also physically endure pain, exhaustion, and grueling elements such as rain, sleet, snow, and extreme heat. As president your time will be spent divided between the mental politics of running an MC on the set and the physical endeavors of riding motorcycles through the extremes of summer and winter weather while leading your men. Both traits in endurance are required—one without the other diminishes your ability to be an effective leader in the MC.

The Physical Trait of Endurance

The physical trait of endurance is typically thought of as being capable of performing the physical tasks necessary to lead an MC through demanding excursions. Riding motorcycles and leading men in the pack requires exemplary endurance. The brothers will be looking to you to be an example. Why is this so important? Because unfortunately, in many motorcycle clubs when a president is no longer capable of riding, he is no longer considered to be fit for presidency. It is crucial you maintain your physical endurance throughout your term. You will be expected to continually prove your mettle as a true biker in a traditional MC, so prepare yourself for the challenge. Stamina is another component of fitness that a president must consider when thinking about how to achieve and maintain a sustainable level of physical fitness to qualify him to lead the club. But is there a difference between endurance and stamina?

In the article "What's the Difference Between Endurance and Stamina," ([1]https://www.healthline.com/health/exercise-fitness/endurance-vs-stamina) by Daniel Yetman and medically reviewed by Daniel Bubins, M.S., NASM-CPT, NASE Level II CSS, we find out that the terms are essentially interchangeable, however there are some differences, although subtle between them.

> "Stamina is the mental and physical ability to sustain an activity for a long period. When people talk about stamina, they often use it to refer to the feeling of being peppy or energetic while doing an activity.
>
> Endurance refers to your body's physical capability to sustain an exercise for an extended period. It is made up of two components: cardiovascular endurance and muscular endurance. Cardiovascular endurance is the ability of your heart and lungs to fuel your body with oxygen. Muscular endurance is the ability of your muscles to work continuously without getting tired."[1]

I recommend you put together a physical fitness routine that builds your stamina as well as your endurance to allow you to stand up to the rigors of the job. A president should present a smart appearance and keep his conditioning a priority as the face of the brotherhood. When people see you on and off the set, they will immediately make assumptions about the club and its members based solely on your appearance. Only later do they rely on the skills and abilities you demonstrate. I discuss this in the "Bearing" section of this book.

Junior members look to you for inspiration and leadership. You will be expected to be one of the best (if not THE best) rider(s) in the club. You must be prepared handle your iron to outride men twenty or more years your junior on those long distances or cross country. Make them work hard to keep up to your standard for as long as you are president! Put together a sustainable fitness and nutrition routine that will keep you in road worthy condition. Also, and let me be frank about this, leading alpha males will be challenging, as I have said many times before in this book. As you age, younger brothers will attempt to try you, physically overpower you, or even kick your ass. By keeping yourself up, spry and fit you will be able to handle these challenges competently.

I know plenty of presidents with no more concern for their physical fitness and appearance than the man on the moon who are devastated when the club votes on the next president who may not be nearly as qualified but simply just looks a hell of a lot better, has more energy, rides harder and is more popular. Unfortunately, MC elections have become more of a popularity contest than selecting the best person for the job. Brothers prefer healthier, more physically capable men. You may get the job based upon your skills, but if you look like a slovenly, lazy, fat bastard do not be surprised if you encounter difficulties getting re-elected.

As National President of the Mighty Black Sabbath Motorcycle Club Nation, I was making a run to the National Biker's Roundup near Dallas, Texas. It was during one of the hottest summers on record, with temperatures reaching 113°F in Oklahoma City after sundown! I was in terrible physical condition with diabetes, high blood pressure, kidney disease, and gout. I was not in "riding shape" when I got out on the highway, leading the pack. As we approached Dallas, the high heat on the road finally got the better of me. My hands started cramping and it was hard to hold onto the throttle. I was getting sicker and sicker but pushed myself to make it to the next bridge to take a breather and get some shade. Now, I had already promised myself a break the last few bridges we passed, so when I crested the hill, I saw a valley 40 miles wide with no bridge in sight! That's when the heat exhaustion took over. I had gone too far to turn around and get back to the last bridge and there was no shade anywhere in front of me. I dangerously fell out of the pack and immediately pulled onto the shoulder. I was able to get the kickstand down before nearly passing out. The only shade I could find was underneath my hot motorcycle! Fortunately, I had a Hawg Cooler (invented by my good friend, Clayton Edward), but unfortunately, I was not wearing it at the time. I managed to maneuver to disconnect the return hose from the water reservoir and I turned on the pump, dumping 40-degree water on my head, shoulders, neck, and chest – immediately cooling myself down. I laid under my bike for the next hour and could see the looks in the eyes of some of my men. They did not feel sorry for the fat bastard who had not taken enough care of his health to prevent being curled up under his bike on the side of the road like an incompetent fool! Upon my return to Atlanta, I started my "get skinny" campaign, losing 100 pounds in about nine months. I was once again a king on the highway because I was back in "riding shape." Bikers all over the world started following my get skinny regime with many of my fans and brothers going on diets and getting skinny along with me! This is how a president leads! You might not start out fit, but you can get there with work and dedication.

Putting yourself into riding shape is a process of getting your nutrition and fitness together and getting into a basic exercise routine. Walking is an easy way to get your cardio—make sure to move at a brisk pace for at least 20 minutes per day to get your heartrate up. Throw in good eating habits and you are on your way.

For me, eating right was the most important part of my weight loss journey. In fact, I was so successful with my diet I lost sixty pounds in six months without exercise (I was recovering from an injury). I opted to follow a low (zero) carb diet, choosing instead to eat baked, broiled, boiled, or grilled meats, vegetables, fruits, healthy smoothies, beans, legumes, and nuts. Eliminating pasta, bread, rice, and potatoes. Naturally, I had to get creative when I went to fast food restaurants, but I made it work and selected healthier options (e.g., switching the bread buns for lettuce wraps, no fries, no soda, and no dessert). You may be surprised that if you pull up to the window at Mc Donald's and ask for a burger in shredded lettuce or wrapped in lettuce, they already have a selection for that on the menu. They call it "low carb" showing that even fast-food restaurants have gotten with the program. Encouraged by my progress, I started my "Fat Boy Getting' Skinny" Facebook page, making myself publicly accountable and allowing others to see my progress. When I could start incorporating exercise into my fitness routine, I completed the P90X and Insanity programs, twice! Even when I had to adapt some of the moves to protect my knees and back. This finally got my conditioning so on point, I was back to riding in the worst conditions—extreme heat and freezing cold—and my body responded with peak performance because it was no longer sick.

I listened to the advice of others and surrounded myself with friends and colleagues to help keep me accountable and keep me on track. Find your tribe to help you get and stay fit! My tribe taught me, trained me, worked with me, and gave me the gift of life. All I had to do was LISTEN! And that is all you have to do too. Listen to your body, listen to your heart, listen to your mind, and listen to your tribe. You cannot be a good leader until you are a good follower. My men had no idea about the strength of my team. They only saw this National President "getting skinny" before their eyes. I carried my mantra "get skinny" into my other platforms, like my daily "The Dragon's Lair Motorcycle Chaos" podcast and my "Black Dragon Biker TV" YouTube and Facebook channels. You would never believe how many of my men followed me and got skinny too! A leader leads by example. Build your physical endurance because it is important. Your men are watching and are rooting for you! Don't give them the opportunity to feel sorry for you.

Mental Toughness

How resilient are you? Are you negatively affected by setbacks? Do obstacles send you into a deep depression preventing you from moving forward? Or do you spring forward quickly and formulate new plans to keep the MC moving in a positive direction, no matter what may come?

In general, living life is a tough proposition and so too is running an MC. As president you will encounter problems you have never seen before you made it to the top position. Unfortunately, any problem in the MC can and will negatively impact your personal life, simply based on the fact that you are responsible for so many lives, jobs and well-beings. The daily pressures of leading an MC can be incredibly difficult. It will cause you stress and mental anguish to the point that it could leave you useless as a dependable decision maker. You must become mentally strong to persevere. There are several scientific methods you can implement to help build your mental resilience and mental toughness.

In her article, *"How to Become Mentally Strong: 14 Strategies for Building Resilience,"* ([2]https://positivepsychology.com/mentally-strong) certified Life Coach and Registered Yoga Teacher Michelle Ribeiro, gives us some guidance in building the mental stamina side of endurance.

> *"Mental Strength* is the capacity of an individual to deal effectively with stressors, pressures and challenges and perform to the best of their ability, irrespective of the circumstances in which they find themselves (Clough, 2002)."

Building mental strength is fundamental to leading an MC. You must develop your mental health using tools and techniques, much like you would build your physical health by exercising.

> "In order to be mentally healthy, we must build up our mental strength! Mental strength is something

that is developed over time by individuals who choose to make personal development a priority. Much like seeing physical gains from working out and eating healthier, we must develop healthy mental habits, like practicing gratitude, if we want to experience mental health gains.

Likewise, to see physical gains we must also give up unhealthy habits, such as eating junk food, and for mental gains, give up unhealthy habits such as feeling sorry for oneself.

We are all able to become mentally stronger, the key is to keep practicing and exercising your mental muscles — just as you would if you were trying to build physical strength!"[2]

In engineering "resilience" refers to the ability to spring back into shape. Similarly, "mental resilience" refers to one's ability to rebound in the face of psychological stressors, such as adversity, trauma, threat, or stress.

Running an MC is going to present you with every one of these, up close and personal. Your club could face threats from other MCs, adversity from within the brotherhood, trauma, tragic deaths, negative encounters with law enforcement, even running gun battles, and just when you think you have seen it all more sources of stress will appear on the horizon. These realities can erode your mental resilience.

A similar concept, *Mental Toughness*, refers to the ability to stay strong in the face of adversity; to keep your focus and determination despite the difficulties you encounter. A mentally tough individual sees challenge and adversity as an opportunity and not a

> threat and has the confidence and positive approach to take what comes in their stride (Strycharczyk, 2015)."

Being mentally tough is not the same as being mentally resilient. Mental toughness in the face of adversity is what will make your men respect you and trust your leadership. The ability to adapt well in the face of adversity (mental resilience) does not necessarily mean you are mentally tough. For example, accepting that your club has been threatened and as president your fearful attitude is, "it is what it is, let us pay the extortion money and move on," shows a resilience in being able to weather the storm and still hang in there, but it is not a characteristic alpha males will ever respect; however, remaining strong to establish your club's self-determination and independence without compromising the club's position and not giving up one dime shows a mental toughness your men can get behind.

Accepting fate and dealing with it or surviving despite it (e.g., "It is what it is, life goes on.") is mental resilience. Recognizing a problem, adapting to it, challenging it, and overcoming it despite all odds (e.g., "I see where you are going with this but that is not how it is going down for us") is mental toughness.

> "To be mentally tough, you must have some degree of resilience, but not all resilient individuals are necessarily mentally tough. If you think of it as a metaphor, resilience would be the mountain, while mental toughness might be one of the strategies for climbing that mountain.
>
> Strycharczyk (2015) finds it useful to think of the difference in terms of the phrase 'survive and prosper.' Resilience helps you to survive, and mental toughness helps you to prosper."
>
> Mental toughness begins when you choose to take notice of what is passing through your mind, without

identifying personally with those thoughts or feelings. Then, finding that determination to evoke optimistic thoughts about the situation at hand." [1]

Leading an MC will present many challenges demanding mental toughness. Alpha males will seldom allow you to just survive a situation. They will either see you stand mentally tough, or they will devour you from the inside. Without a leader with mental toughness, also called "internal fortitude", your brothers will be pushed around, assaulted, extorted, stripped of their colors on the side of the road, or strong armed and bullied. If you are not mentally tough, then develop your mental toughness or leave the presidency. It is really just that simple. The president's tenor leads the club. If the president is afraid the club will be afraid. If the president is a coward, he will instruct the club to move in cowardly ways. If you are a coward (and you know if you are), do the club a favor and let someone else lead. Everything WE do is for the greatness of the MC.

Strycharczyk and Cloughe (n.d.) offer the following five themes to develop your mental toughness:

1. Positive Thinking
2. Anxiety Control
3. Visualization
4. Goal Setting
5. Attentional Control

I could sum it up into one phrase: "Grow a set of balls!" but such a phrase does not help to teach you how to do that, not to mention there is much more to it, so let us get back to the scientific method.

> "As with building mental strength, developing mental toughness does require self-awareness and commitment. Generally speaking, mentally tough

individuals appear to achieve more than the mentally sensitive and enjoy a greater degree of contentment."[1]

The 4C's of Mental Toughness

Tuner (2017) describes four important traits of mental toughness:

1. Control
2. Commitment
3. Challenge
4. Confidence

The key to success is maintaining all four of these qualities.

1. Control

> "This is the extent to which you feel you are in control of your life, including your emotions and sense of life purpose. The control component can be considered your self-esteem. To be high on the Control scale means to feel comfortable in your skin and have a good sense of who you are."

> You are able to control your emotions—less likely to reveal your emotional state to others—and are less distracted by the emotions of others. To be low on the Control scale means you might feel like events happen to you and that you have no control or influence over what happens."[1]

Self-confidence is just as important as self-control. If you generally feel like you are in control of your life, your club, your men, and your surroundings you will be okay.

2. Commitment

> "This is the extent of your personal focus and reliability. To be high on the Commitment scale is to

be able to effectively set goals, and consistently achieve them without getting distracted. A high Commitment level indicates that you are good at establishing routines and habits that cultivate success.

To be low on the Commitment scale indicates that you may find it difficult to set and prioritize goals. Or adapt routines or habits indicative of success. You might also be easily distracted by other people or competing priorities." [1]

Procrastinators and those that fail to follow through do not have high levels of commitment. If this is you, fix it! It will help to build your mental toughness.

"Together, the Control and Commitment scales represent the Resilience part of the mental toughness definition. This makes sense because the ability to bounce back from setbacks requires a sense of knowing that you are in control of your life and can make a change. It also requires focus and the ability to establish habits and targets that will get you back on track to your chosen path." [1]

3. Challenge

"This is the extent to which you are driven and adaptable. To be high on the Challenge scale means that you are driven to achieve your personal best, and you see challenges, change, and adversity as opportunities rather than threats; you are likely to be flexible and agile. To be low on the Challenge scale means that you might see change as a threat and avoid novel or challenging situations out of fear of failure." [1]

Many presidents buckle under the pressure of being challenged, especially from junior members. They act out immaturely, responding by screaming, yelling, or attempting to punish any "troublemaker" who dares to challenge their authority – letting everyone see just how insecure they really are. Stay calm, cool, and collected. Challenges are part of leadership. New ideas may threaten your comfort level, but everything was new once. Embrace challenges with the positive mental attitude and spirit of accomplishment! Do not get blown out of proportion whenever you see a youngster attempting to assert himself and grow. You were that way once too. He may take your spot one day but isn't that what the MC is all about? Growth. Train him so that when he does take your spot, he will be better than you.

4. Confidence

"This is the extent to which you believe in your ability to be productive and capable; it is your self-belief and the belief that you can influence others. To be high on the Confidence scale is to believe that you will successfully complete tasks, and to take setbacks in stride while maintaining routine and even strengthening your resolve.

To be low on the Confidence scale means that you are easily unsettled by setbacks, and do not believe that you are capable or have any influence over others.

Together, the Challenge and Confidence scales represent the confidence part of the mental toughness definition. This represents one's ability to identify and seize an opportunity, and to see situations as opportunities to embrace and explore. This makes sense because if you are confident in yourself and your abilities and engage easily with others, you are more likely to convert challenges into successful outcomes." [1]

Build and Improve Resilience

Resilience is a measure of how long or how well you can withstand a challenge or perhaps "survive it;" therefore, having a strong level of mental resilience is crucial. Sometimes you must survive a situation long enough to exert enough mental toughness to overcome it.

> "Your level of mental resilience is not something that is decided upon at birth — it can be improved over the course of an individual's life."[1]

Rob Whitley, Ph.D. (2018), suggests three strategies to enhance your resilience:

1. Skill Acquisition

    "Acquiring new skills can play an important part in building resilience, as it helps to develop a sense of mastery and competency — both of which can be utilized during challenging times, as well as increase one's self-esteem and ability to problem solve." [1]

2. Goal Setting

    "The ability to develop goals, actionable steps to achieve those goals, and to execute, all help to develop will-power and mental resilience." [1]

When your club has goals, you can watch as its resilience grows with the successful accomplishment of each goal.

3. Controlled Exposure

    "Controlled exposure refers to the gradual exposure to anxiety-provoking situations and is used to help individuals overcome their fears. Research indicates that this can foster resilience, and especially so when it involves skill-acquisition and goal setting — a triple benefit." [1]

Riding in a pack is a useful club skill but also something that evokes fear in many bikers, especially hang-arounds and prospects, but I have known a few presidents and senior officers who were even too terrified to ride in the damned pack. Presidents who are afraid to ride in the pack can set goals involving controlled exposure, to develop or acquire this particular skill. Start with short rides with the road captain, eventually adding a few other brothers, progressively increasing the distance over time. Soon you will be leading the pack confidently in front of all.

This can be applied to all kinds of situations in which you may have weakness as a president. For example, as you get better at MC protocol, you will be able to be more competent in representing the club at council meetings, sit downs, coalition meetings, and club to club negotiations—especially with diamonds. Believe me—a knowledgeable president has much more resilience than an unknowing one.

11 Further Strategies from the American Psychology Association

The article "Road to Resilience," n.d. by the American Psychology Association shares the following 11 strategies for building mental resilience:

1. Make connections

> "Resilience can be strengthened through our connection to family, friends, and community. Healthy relationships with people who care about you and will listen to your problems, offer support during difficult times and can help us to reclaim hope. Likewise, assisting others in their time of need can benefit us greatly and foster our own sense of resilience." [1]

This, of course, is the greatness that is the MC. Having true brothers to stand with you through good times and bad, will inevitably help build your resilience. Just looking over your shoulder and seeing your brothers stand shoulder-to-shoulder during times of adversity spurs you on.

When I first started my "Black Dragon Biker TV" YouTube channel, I made a video entitled, "Don't Call 1%ers Brother." The intent of the video was to teach folks how to behave when going into others' clubhouses—to treat them with respect at all times, especially when visiting 1%er clubs. The crux of the lesson was that in motorcycle clubs your "brothers" are the men who wear your same patch and not to carelessly throw around the term. Never walk into a 1%er's clubhouse with a sense of familiarity calling people "brothers". *"This,"* I said, *"is disrespectful behavior."* Unfortunately, some members in a diamond club took offense with the title of the video believing I was telling people not to associate with 1%ers. They knew it was not the case but saw an opportunity to show off to the crowd that they could push the celebrity around. Shortly after the release of the video, I took twenty-two of my brothers to their clubhouse to support their venue and show respect since they had attended so many of our venues in the past and had been great friends and supporters of our club through the years. On that particular day a few of their club brothers wanted to flex. I was at the bar with my girl when a prospect tapped me on the shoulder and summoned me outside. He said someone wanted to speak to me. My brothers were interspersed throughout the event, and everyone was having a great time, so no one noticed when I stepped outside alone. When I got out the door there was a group of them and they semi-circled me in confrontation.

One yelled, *"So you're the one who made the video about not calling 1%ers brothers? Well, if you know so damned much about protocol why would you make a video like that? You are the reason not so many people have come around to see us and support our event!"*

It never dawned on him that perhaps the reason his event was so sparsely attended was because he did not know how to treat visitors who came to see him with respect, honor, and love (kind of reminded me of a Jermaine Dupree song when he said, about a local strip club to Atlanta, that he stopped going there because "They don't know how to treat you when you come in the door). You see, I had brought twenty-two brothers to spend money and fellowship and here he was on a whole lot of disrespectful BS over a video he obviously had not seen.

One of his drunk brothers interjected with, *"We can get after it right here and right now as far as I'm concerned."* Indicating that he was ready to start scrapping with me right on the spot.

It was about that time I felt my twenty-two brothers, armed to the teeth, pressing up on me shoulder to shoulder, pushing from behind, and nudging in closely as the two sides came face-to-face. I could feel them all around me with hot breath steaming up my neck. Some of my brothers, just pulling up, left their cars running in the street, scurrying to get to the scene and find out the business. None of my brothers planned on taking any whippings that day, and they clearly had my back.

After a pregnant pause the aggressor said, *"Well, we won't be getting into anything violent today."*

Both sides parted and we continued to drink and party but not like before—the mood was spoiled. I never took my brothers or myself to their clubhouse again. I always say that people vote with their feet when they do not like how they are treated. They will simply use them to walk away and never support you with their dollars and presence again. When you disrespect someone in your clubhouse, you should not wonder why you never see them again, nor should you ever blame someone else when your events are lightly attended. How people get down with you, support your events, and associate with you is 100% proportional to how you treat them. It is as simple as that. The math is easy to do. If you have a problem with someone, sit down at a table because that is the MC protocol way of doing things. Anything else can produce disastrous results that are not good for any side. I teach my presidents there is a time and a place for everything. Never handle table business at a party—it always has the capacity to go very wrong, leaving those you insulted with a bad feeling.

To be a brother worthy of that kind of support my brothers gave me that day you have to BE a president/brother who gives that same support during whatever crisis your brothers face. Be the kind of leader that exemplifies this type of brotherhood.

2. Avoid seeing crises as insurmountable problems

"We cannot change the external events happening around us, but we can control our reaction to them. In life, there will always be challenges, but it is important to look beyond whatever stressful situation you are faced with and remember that circumstances will change. Take notice of the subtle ways in which you may already start feeling better as you deal with the difficult situation." [1]

3. Accept that change is a part of living

"They say that the only thing constant in life is change. As a result of difficult circumstances, certain goals may no longer be realistic or attainable. By accepting that which you cannot change, it allows you to focus on the things that you do have control over." [1]

4. Move toward your goals. (*also suggested by Whitley, 2018)

"It is essential to make sure your goals are realistic. Creating small, actionable steps makes our goals achievable, and helps us to regularly work towards these goals, creating small "wins" along the way. Try to accomplish one small step towards your goal every day." [1]

5. Take decisive actions

"Instead of shying away from problems and stresses, wishing they would just go away, try to take decisive action whenever possible." [1]

6. Look for opportunities for self-discovery

"Sometimes tragedy can result in great learnings and personal growth. Living through a difficult situation can increase our self-confidence and sense of self-worth, strengthen our relationships, and teach us a great deal about ourselves." [1]

7. Nurture a positive view of yourself

"Working to develop confidence in yourself can be beneficial in preventing difficulties, as well as building resilience. Having a positive view of yourself is crucial when it comes to problem-solving and trusting your own instincts." [1]

8. Keep things in perspective

"When times get tough, always remember that things could be worse; try to avoid blowing things out of proportion. In cultivating resilience, it helps to keep a long-term perspective when facing difficult or painful events." [1]

9. Maintain a hopeful outlook.

"When we focus on what is negative about a situation and remain in a fearful state, we are less likely to find a solution. Try to maintain a hopeful, optimistic outlook, and expect a positive outcome instead of a negative one. Visualization can be a helpful technique in this respect."
[1]

10. Take care of yourself

"Self-care is an essential strategy for building resilience and helps to keep your mind and body healthy enough to deal with difficult situations as they arise. "[1]

11. Additional ways of strengthening resilience may be helpful.

"Resilience building can look like different things to different people. Journaling, practicing gratitude, meditation, and other spiritual practices help some people to restore hope and strengthen their resolve." [1]

We have talked about some of the mental and physical attributes you will develop to focus on building your presidential endurance traits. Life as the leader of the MC can vex your spirit and your soul. You will need patience and solid will power to resist temptation and overcome obstacles. Prepare yourself president for you will need those skills.

Example - A president realizes in April that he has a cross country ride to the mother chapter coming up in February. He knows that he is not in riding shape and does not ride well in the pack. He is wary of the challenge but puts together a fitness and diet program to prepare him for the run. He also begins practicing with the road captain his pack riding skills. He takes several short trips each increasing in distance while learning hand commands, signals, positioning and moving the MC element on the highway. Simultaneously, he must mentally focus on putting down a split within the club by a brother who has been causing trouble for years. He exercises patience and resilience in handling the issue with the club brother always keeping his patience when the brother tries to test his mettle. Eventually he gets the political problems solved and is physically prepared to make the run in February because he had built up his endurance, skills, and traveling chops to make the trip.

Thank you for reading my book President's Bible Chronicle I Principles of Motorcycle Club Leadership!

John E. Bunch II

Appendix A:
Bibliography

1. *Authors: Norman, John: SFE: Science Fiction Encyclopedia* www.sf-encyclopedia.com/entry/norman_john. *Retrieved 2020-7-11]*

2. *Gracen, Julia "Chaingangsalon"* www.chaingangsalon.com. *Retrieved 2020-7-11*

3. *"Gor-Wikipedia"* https://en.m.wikipedia.org/wiki/Gor. *Retrieved 2020-7-11*

4. *Langford, David (1988) "The Kink in Space" SFX. Future Publishing (39)* https://ansible.uk/sfx/sfx039.html *Retrieved 2020-7-11 "No More Gor: A Conversation with John Norman", David Alexander Smith, The New York Review of Science Fiction, #92, April, 1996*

5. *E-Reads "Are John Norman's Gors "Boy Books"? Richard Curtis* http://web.archive.org/web/20121031111019/http://ereads.com/2007/10/are-john-normans-gors-boy-books-2.html

6. *https://www.mbassett.com/blog/how-greater-leaders-dont-allow-to-corrupt-them*

7. *https://www.procsi.com/resources/articles/change-management-methodology*

8. *https://blog.prosci.com/avoid-these-change-management-obstacles*

9. *www.scu.edu/ethics/ethics-resources/ethical-decision-making/justice-and-fairness/*

10. *https://scholarlycommons.law.wlu.edu/wlulr/vol50/iss4/8*

11. *https://link.springer.com/article/10.1007/s10942-018-0302-x*

12. *https://meliuscareers.com/blog/six-ways-to-improve-personal-judgement*

13. *https://en.wikipedia.org/wiki/Aboulomania*

14. *https://en.wikipedia.org/wiki/Anguish*

15. *https://www.law.cornell.edu/wex/mental_anguish#*

16. *https://en.wikipedia.org/wiki/Anguish*

17. *https://beechacres.org/anxious-about-anxiety/*

18. *https://giveanhour.org/changedirection/*

19. *https://www.lexico.com/en/definition/anxiety*

20. *https://beechacres.org/anxious-about-anxiety/*

21. *https://www.healthline.com/health/alcohol-and-anxiety*

22. *https://www.healthline.com/health/caffeine-and-anxiety*

23. *https://www.medicinenet.com/stress/definition.htm*
24. *https://thisisyourcenter.com/stress*
25. *https://www.flushinghospital.org/newsletter/stress-and-mental-health-know-your-limits/*
26. *http://medcourtng.com/blog/2019/05/20/stress/*
27. *https://www.riverparkpsych.com/depression*
28. *https://www.psychiatry.org/patients-families/depression/what-is-depression*
29. *http://www.jennygarrett.global/5-top-tips-to-develop-your-integrity*
30. https://en.wikipedia.org/wiki/Quarterdeck
31. *https://officercandidatesschool.com/2012/10/12/marine-corps-leadership-traits-bearing/*
32. *https://rainbows.typepad.com/blog/2011/03/executive-bearing-presence-arceil-thomas-lee-impact-importance-leader-leadership.html*
33. www.aboutleaders.com/leadership.com/leadership-and-enthusiasm/
34. *www.leadership-and-development.com/enthusiasm/*
35. *www.geraldgillis.com/12-leadership-traits-6-unselfishness*
36. https://somaticvoicework.com/arrogance-confidence-and-courage
37. https://www.wework.com/ideas/professional-development/management-leadership/what-is-courageous-leadership
38. https://positivepsychology.com/mentally-strong
39. https://robynbenincasa.com/robyns-blogs-on-courageous-leadership
40. https://www.fastcompany.com/44469/what-courage
41. *https://www.dictionary.com/browse/knowledge*
42. *www.eatyourcareer.com/2015/05/how-to-become-an-expert-in-your-chosen-field/*
43. https://www.healthline.com/health/exercise-fitness/endurance-vs-stamina

These are the bibliography QR codes. They are not guaranteed to work especially several years after this book has been published as we do not manage the servers upon which they reside. These are the links to those sites as they exist as of the writing of this book. Use you the QR code scanner on your mobile device to launch the links.

Appendix B:
President's Readiness Test

This is an essay test that requires you to answer the questions in written or essay form. That means you will not find yes or no questions. The purpose of this exam is to test your knowledge and look up your answers in this book.

If you email your completed test to me (blackdragon@blacksabbathmc.com) I will grade them. If you get an 80% or better grade, I will send you our Bachelor of Science Degree in Motorcycle Club Presidency from our Motorcycle Education division, after you pay the associated $150.00 fee. You will get two attempts to pass this test for your $150.00. If you fail two times you will have to wait four months and submit again with another $150.00 fee.
Send $150.00 payment to: PayPal = jbunchii@aol.com
Cashapp = BikerPrez
Check or money order to:
Bunch Media Group
P.O. 931792
Norcross, GA 30003
If you complete the tests in all of my books and email them in, if you pass them all with 90%; I will send you a Master's Degree in Motorcycle Club Protocol and Social Construct along with each Bachelors of Science associated with each book. The fee is $300.00.

Note: The degrees are printed on attractive parchment with our official seal affixed. They are suitable for framing.

1. Why does the practice of brotherhood not always pay a dividend?
2. What is the purpose of doing what is right?
3. Why should the president never handle the club's money?
4. What are six things the president should not do with the club's money?
5. What kind of system should be employed for the club's checks, credit cards, and money apps?
6. What should the president do if he finds he must deal with club funds directly?
7. What are the three P's?
8. What is the dark seduction of the three P's?
9. Who is Dr. Dacher Keltner?
10. What is "The Power Paradox"?
11. What enables presidents to have the most influence over others?
12. What is the fourth "P" and what should a president do to avoid be corrupted by it?
13. Why is it important to have sexual harassment policies as part of the bylaws?
14. If the MC owns a bar and has women working there what are the implications for the MC if a president or members violate the tenets of the fourth "P"?
15. What are the five liabilities of romance?
16. What does the lesson of Tarl Cabot of Ko-ro-ba teach us about absolute power?
17. Name a couple of US Supreme Court cases that might come into place for an MC caught up in sexual harassment shenanigans.
18. Name six major obstacles to changing behaviors and policies in an MC.
19. Name the highlights in change management for each obstacle.
20. What are six techniques you should use to know yourself and seek improvement?

21. What are six steps you can take to improve your tactical proficiency?
22. What are six ways to practice the principle of knowing your people and looking out for their welfare?
23. What are four techniques you can apply to the principle of keeping your brothers informed?
24. What are sex things you can practice to improve the principle of setting the example?
25. What are six things you can practice to improve the principle of ensuring that tasks you assign are understood, supervised, and accomplished?
26. What are six things you can do to improve the principle of training your brothers like a team?
27. What are four things you can do to improve the principle of making sound and timely decisions?
28. What are nine ways you can improve the principle of developing a sense of responsibility among your members?
29. What are four ways that you can ensure you always employ your MC within its capabilities?
30. What are seven ways that you can improve the principle of seeking responsibilities and responsibility before you become president?
31. What are the 14 leadership principles of the ACRONYM JJ-DIDTIEBUCKLE?
32. What is the definition of the principle of justice?
33. What is the significance of being able to administer justice within the MC?
34. What are the types of justice as identified in this book?
35. Define each type of justice and give an example of how it is used.
36. Author Karen Newman wrote of justice, "One of the most enduring _____."

37. How many types of judgements are made in determining procedural justice?
38. What are the six criteria for judging objective procedural correctness as stated by Professor Gerald S. Leventhal?
39. What are nine ways to improve the opportunities for fairness and justice to be a strong part of your MC culture?
40. What is the definition of judgement?
41. What is the significance of exercising sound judgement within the MC as the president?
42. What are six ways to improve personal judgement as per the article "Six Ways to Improve Personal Judgement" from the leadership development team at Melius?
43. How does Sir Andrew Likierman define judgement?
44. What are six basic components to good judgement and how do you improve upon each?
45. Why is success not a reliable proxy for judgement?
46. What does Sir Andrew Likierman caution us to ponder if we have to make fast judgements?
47. What are three questions you should ask yourself about your judgement should the MC wind up in a bad situation?
48. What is the definition of dependability?
49. What is the significance of a president who can assign tasks within an MC where dependability is stressed?
50. Name three practical ways to become more dependable.
51. What is Susan Keller's first axiom of dependability?
52. What is Susan Keller's second axiom of dependability?
53. What is Susan Keller's third axiom of dependability?
54. What are six ways to increase dependability in others?
55. What is the leadership principle of initiative?
56. What is the significance of a president being a self-starter?
57. What are six steps you can use to develop your initiative?
58. What is the definition of the leadership principle of decisiveness?
59. What is the significance of the character trait of a decisive president in an MC?
60. What are the two distinct scopes of decisiveness?

61. Define aboulomania and why it is important for an MC president knowing about it?
62. Name four factors that can contribute to indecisiveness and their causes.
63. What is the definition of mental anguish?
64. Name five signs to look for to determine if you may be suffering from mental anguish.
65. What are the definitions of anxiety?
66. What are the symptoms of anxiety?
67. What are four things to avoid when you find yourself suffering from anxiety?
68. What is the definition of stress?
69. What are twelve physical symptoms of stress?
70. Name five ways you can mitigate stress.
71. What are the definitions of stress?
72. How is depression different from sadness or grief?
73. What is the definition of Tact?
74. What is the significance of treating peers, seniors, and subordinates with respect and courtesy?
75. What is the importance of being culturally alert when providing feedback?
76. What is meant by "still get your message across," when using tact?
77. Name five strategies that you could employ to hone your skills in tactful communications.
78. Name six common examples in utilizing tact.
79. What is the definition of integrity?
80. What is the significance of a president keeping his word in the MC and on the set?
81. Name five tips you could use to develop your integrity.
82. Define the leadership principle of enthusiasm.
83. What is the significance of displaying enthusiasm towards accomplishing tasks within the MC?

84. Why is enthusiasm considered the secret of success?
85. How does being passionate about something help being enthusiastic.
86. What are three tips you can use to create enthusiasm.
87. What is V.E.G.A. and how is it used?
88. What is the definition of the leadership principle of bearing?
89. What is the significance of a president who exhibits bearing?
90. How does the Marine Corps define bearing?
91. What is executive bearing?
92. What is 'MC' bearing?
93. What are nine cornerstones of executive bearing and how is each used?
94. Define the leadership principle of unselfishness.
95. What is the significance of a president who practices unselfishness in the club?
96. What are four tenets of unselfishness?
97. What is the definition of the leadership principle of courage?
98. What is the significance of both showing leadership on the battlefield and in the day-to-day operations of the MC?
99. Discuss the line between arrogance, confidence, and courage and how that effects decisions within the MC.
100. Name three main buckets of courage and define each.
101. Using three buckets of courage, what are sixteen actions could you implement to make yourself a stronger president for the MC? Elaborate briefly on the merits of each one.
102. What are eight steps presidents can use to build skills in courageousness? Elaborate briefly on each.
103. What does the acronym GUTS stand for?
104. What does William Shakespeare's quote, 'A coward dies a thousand deaths" mean to the ?
105. What are four necessary components in profiling courage? Briefly elaborate on each.
106. Define the leadership principle of knowledge.

107. What is the significance of a president learning and retaining knowledge?

108. Name four things a leader must know about knowledge.

109. Name and elaborate on the seven ways a president can go about gaining knowledge.

110. Name the fourteen ways James T. Mangan book "You Can Do Anything!" states that you can acquire knowledge. Elaborate on each.

111. Define the leadership principle of loyalty.

112. What is the significance of an MC that practices loyalty?

113. What are three methods one can use to build loyalty and what are the steps within each method? Elaborate on how they are used.

114. What is the definition of the leadership principle of Endurance?

115. What is the significance of endurance as it refers to how it is used within the MC?

116. What is the physical trait of endurance?

117. What is the difference between endurance and stamina?

118. What are five themes to developing your mental toughness? Elaborate on each.

119. What are the 4C's of mental toughness? Elaborate on each.

120. Name three strategies to enhance your resilience. Elaborate on each.

121. What are 11 strategies from the American Psychology Association for building mental resilience? Elaborate on each.

◊◊◊

Appendix C: Biker Set Readiness Test

A President should have a firm knowledge of the MC Biker Set. Test your knowledge with the following test. This test is by no means all-inclusive, but you can use it as a guide to begin your research:

1. In what city, state, and year was your MC Nation founded?
2. In what neighborhood was your MC Nation founded?
3. How many members comprised the founding fathers of your MC Nation and local chapter?
4. What were the names and occupations of the founding fathers of your MC Nation?
5. What is the motto of your MC Nation, and what does it mean?
6. How did your MC Nation obtain its first clubhouse?
7. What are the addresses of your MC Nation's mother chapter and your local chapters?
8. What is the birthday celebration of your MC Nation and all of your local chapters?
9. What is alarm code to get into the clubhouse?
10. What is mascot of your MC Nation?
11. What were the first motorcycles, makes, and models, owned by the founding fathers of your MC Nation?
12. How did the founding fathers of your MC Nation learn to ride?
13. Describe your MC Nation's colors and explain the meanings, origins, and symbols of all of the elements of the patch.
14. What was the name of the first brother killed on a motorcycle in your MC Nation? What year did he die, and how was he killed?
15. Who are the racing heroes of your MC Nation? Why?
16. What is the history of the first MC split in your MC Nation and what happened to the members who split off?
17. What is the preferred bike color and style of your MC Nation?
18. How many years must you be in the MC before you are

authorized to wear the MC's colors as a tattoo?

19. What is your MC's policy for the removal of their tattoo if you should leave your MC Nation?

20. How many years must you be in the MC before you are authorized to wear the MC's medallion or ring?

21. What are the bike nights of all your MC Nation's clubhouses?

22. What are the names of the Presidents of all of the chapters within your MC Nation?

23. When did the President of your local chapter join your MC Nation? What are the telephone numbers and contact names for all of the chapters within your MC Nation?

24. How often are club meetings generally held throughout your MC Nation and when?

25. How many members are necessary to hold a quorum in your local MC?

26. What is the order procedure for how church is conducted in your MC Nation?

27. What are the monthly dues owed to the National Headquarters by all chapters in your MC Nation?

28. What are the real names, phone numbers, email addresses and emergency contact numbers for every member in your chapter?

29. What are the steps to becoming a Prospect in your MC?

30. Who can be a Prospect sponsor within your MC?

31. What are a sponsor's responsibilities?

32. When does a chapter President vote on a motion?

33. How long can your motorcycle be inoperable before you are required to buy a new one or turn in your colors?

34. What are the main responsibilities of the Road Captain?

35. Who are the Regional Presidents in your MC Nation?

36. How many miles one-way must a member ride to be recognized as a Nomad Rider in your MC Nation?

37. What are all of the award patches a rider can earn in your

MC Nation?

38. If a MC member suspects that a brother is too drunk to ride what is their obligation to that drunken member according to your MC's bylaws or policies?
39. What is the MC's procedure for one member borrowing money from another member?
40. What is the procedure for solving a physical altercation between two members in your MC Nation?
41. What member of your MC is allowed to physically strike another other member?
42. What members in a local chapter can actually fine other members?
43. What members in your local chapter can actually fine the chapter President?
44. Under what specific circumstances may your colors be taken from you for an infraction against the bylaws?
45. If a local chapter president requests your colors what must be done before the president can keep your colors forever?
46. Who comprises your MC's governing Council?
47. Is your MC coed?
48. What can your wife or girlfriend wear to support the MC if she is not a member?
49. What is the status of women associated with your MC?
50. Does your MC have a First Lady and if so, who is she?
51. What is the definition of a member in good standing?
52. What are the main responsibilities of a Prospect within your MC Nation?
53. What are the basic rules of conduct for a Prospect within your MC Nation?
54. Where are required patches to be worn on the vest of a Prospect and full patched brothers?
55. What is the quickest way to tell if you are dealing with a 1% outlaw MC Nation member if you greet him face to face and have not seen the back of his vest?
56. How can you distinguish outlaw colors from the back?
57. What is the definition of an Outlaw MC?
58. What is a 99%er MC?

59. What is a 1%er MC?
60. Is there a difference between an outlaw MC and a 1%er MC and if so, what is that difference?
61. Where did the term 1%er come from?
62. What is the philosophical definition that sets 1% MCs apart from traditional MCs?
63. Who was the first person to lose his life in a clubhouse altercation within your MC Nation?
64. What criminal or civil actions, if any, have been brought against your local or national MC by city, local, or national law enforcement agencies in an attempt to shut down, prosecute, and/or fine your MC during its history, and what were the outcomes of those charges?
65. What were the lessons learned from question 64?
66. What were the names of any members that have been murdered or accosted while representing your MC Nation?
67. What caused any second or subsequent MC splits within your MC Nation?
68. To whom do the colors, insignia, designs, patches, logos, and other paraphernalia of your MC belong?
69. How many MCs has your MC Nation flipped or patched over, and to what MC Nation did those chapters belong before they were flipped/patched over?
70. Does your MC Nation wear support patches for a 1%er MC Nation? If so, which one?
71. If your MC Nation wears support patches for a 1%er MC Nation, who are their enemies?
72. If your MC Nation wears support patches what areas of town, cities, or states is it unsafe for you to ride in your colors without being in the company of your brothers?
73. Why is it important to always remember that you are representing every MC member within your Nation when you are operating out in public?
74. What is your MC's consequence to you if you rip your patch

off of your vest?

75. What is the consequence for striking another brother of your MC?

76. What is the consequence for stealing from your MC?

77. What is the consequence for discussing MC business outside of the MC?

78. What is the consequence for posting MC business on social media?

79. What is the consequence for cyber-banging on social media?

80. What is the consequence for losing your colors?

81. What is the consequence for disrespecting your colors?

82. Should your colors ever touch the ground?

83. Should you ever let anyone outside of your MC hold your colors?

84. What is another term for the vest used to hold your colors?

85. What does the term backyard mean?

86. What is the 80/20 rule?

87. What is the AMA?

88. What is ABATE?

89. What is a boneyard?

90. What are broken wings?

91. Why is it against protocol to burnout in front of another MC's clubhouse?

92. What is a cage?

93. What is the rule about wearing your vest in a cage?

94. What does going to church mean in the MC world?

95. What is the proper procedure for dating the property of a 1%er MC?

96. What is the biggest no-no about parking in front of another MC's clubhouse?

97. What happens if you put your helmet on the bar of a MC you are visiting?

98. What does the term "Club Hopping" mean?

99. If your President wants to Prospect a hang-around who was first a member of another MC, what is the proper protocol

to accomplish this?

100. What is the proper protocol for approaching a girl with another MC's patch on her back to ask her to dance or go out?

101. What is the proper protocol for passing an outlaw or senior MC on the open highway when your pack is traveling faster than theirs?

102. What does counter steering mean and how is it done?

103. To what does the term "Slow, Look, Lean, and Roll" refer?

104. What is the proper hand signal to flash to the pack when a cop/highway patrol vehicle is spotted?

105. What is the proper hand signal flashed to the pack when debris is in the road on the left side of the bike?

106. What is the proper foot signal flashed to the pack when debris is in the road on the right side of the bike?

107. What is the proper hand signal flashed when the Road Captain wants the pack to assume a single file formation?

108. What is the proper hand signal flashed when the Road Captain wants the pack to assume a staggered formation?

109. What is the proper hand signal flashed when the Road Captain wants the pack to assume the suicide (two abreast) formation?

110. When the Road Captain lifts his hand up to indicate a left or right turn what does the rest of the pack do?

111. What is the proper hand signal flashed when the Road Captain wants the pack to slow down?

112. What is the proper hand signal flashed when the Road Captain wants the pack to continue on while he drops out of the pack to view it for safety?

113. What is the proper hand signal flashed when the Road Captain wishes to change places with the Assistant Road Captain in the back of the pack?

114. What is the best way to cross railroad tracks in an intersection?

115. During a rainstorm when is the road the slickest?

116. When braking a motorcycle, what is meant by the term "reaction time?"
117. When traveling twenty mph how many feet does it take to bring a motorcycle to a complete stop including reaction time?
118. When traveling 80 mph how many feet does it take to bring a motorcycle to a complete stop including reaction time?
119. Why does the front brake have more braking power than the rear brake?
120. According to distribution of impact locations on motorcycle helmets during collision studies conducted by Dietmar Otte, Medizinische Hochschule Hannover, and Abteilung Verkehrsunfallforschung in Germany, where are most head injuries concentrated for motorcyclists?
121. What does DOT stand for and why is it important when purchasing a motorcycle helmet?
122. What is a flash patch?
123. What is a freedom fighter?
124. What does FTW mean?
125. What does KTRSD mean?
126. What does LE/LO mean?
127. What is an OMC?
128. What is an OMG?
129. Are cell phones allowed in your church meetings?
130. What is the consequence for secretly taping your church meetings?
131. What is an MRO?
132. What does the term "On Ground" mean?
133. What does the term "On Two" mean?
134. What does the term "Patch Over" mean?
135. What does the term "Flipping" mean?
136. What is a PRO?
137. What is a probie?
138. What are the major differences between an RC and a MC?
139. What is the RICO act?
140. What is a rocker?
141. What is a run?

142. What is a gypsy run?

143. What is special about a mandatory run?

144. What is a tail gunner?

145. What does the diamond "13" mean?

146. What is the significance of the three-piece patch?

147. What is the significance of turning your back on another MC or patched person?

148. What does BSFFBS mean?

149. What does DILLIGAF mean?

150. What is a 5%er?

151. What is a lick and stick?

152. What does the term "Running 66" mean?

153. What is a vested pedestrian?

154. What is a hang-around?

155. What is a civilian?

156. What is a "Property of"?

157. What is a House Mamma?

158. What is an ink slinger?

159. How often should the financial report be given at your MC's club meeting?

160. Where must your MC's colors be purchased?

161. What are your rights if you ever face your MC's disciplinary committee?

162. What is necessary for you to be found guilty of a charge in your MC?

163. Who are the closest MCs to your MC Nation who can be considered to love your MC like brothers and where your MC will always have a home away from home (allies)?

164. What is a dominate MC?

165. It is possible to Prospect for your MC without owning a motorcycle?

166. If you don't like the direction your MC pack is going you can simply leave the pack and take a shortcut and catch up to the pack later? Y/N

167. Folks can join your MC without prospecting? T/F
168. It is okay to pop a wheelie in the pack? T/F
169. It is okay to leave a brother in trouble? T/F
170. It is okay to screw a brother's old lady or wife? T/F
171. Can the Road Captain fine a member without a trial for infractions committed in the pack?
172. When can the Road Captain order a member not to ride their bike?
173. Does the Road Captain have the right to see a member's license, registration, and insurance in your MC?
174. When is it okay to give out personal information about a MC member to someone outside of the MC?
175. It is okay for an MC President to attend a function thrown by your MC without being searched for a weapon if everyone else is being searched?
176. What is the ranking order for the way your MC rides in formation?
177. Where does a Prospect ride when escorting a senior member of the MC Nation?
178. What is the first responsibility a Prospect is assigned after he learns to ride in the pack?
179. What is 'packing', and is a Prospect ever allowed to pack?
180. Who was the first Godfather of your MC Nation, and what was his contribution to the MC?
181. When did the original Godfather die?
182. Who is the Godfather of your MC Nation today?
183. When is the Road Captain considered the President of a local chapter?
184. What is required to take a leave of absence from your MC?
185. When are you allowed to retire from your MC?
186. Where are standard business cards ordered?
187. What is the email address of any MC member in the nation?
188. How do you get a MC email address?
189. What duties must a Prospect perform daily in your chapter?
190. Can a Prospect crossover without speaking with the National President, National VP, or the High Council President

in your MC Nation?

191. What is the name of the most honored veteran within your MC Nation?

192. When was the office of National President created within your MC Nation?

193. How many MCs operate in your town and what are the names of twenty-five of them?

194. What is the C.O.C.?

195. What is meant by the term "Top 5" when talking about MCs?

196.

197. Name the OMCs in every state surrounding yours.

198. What is a supporter MC?

199. It is okay to walk into a MC representing your MC Nation without wearing your colors?

200. Should you have a Set of colors with you no matter where you travel?

201. What is the mission statement of your MC Nation?

202. Does handling a problem internally within the MC relive you of your legal responsibility to call law enforcement if you think a crime has been committed?

203. What are the rules for all members to stand duty at the clubhouse should your chapter have a clubhouse?

204. What are your MC's national and local website addresses?

205. Does your MC have a women's auxiliary?

206. Does your MC have a Support Crew?

207. What is the phone number and password used for your MC's conference calls?

208. How do you jump start a motorcycle?

209. When would you jump start a motorcycle?

210. Can you use a car to jump start a motorcycle safely?

211. How can one battery man on a motorcycle push another man on a motorcycle without a strap or rope or chain?

212. How do you pick up a heavy motorcycle like a Gold Wing or

a Hog if it falls over and you are by yourself?

213. Does your MC ride in staggered or suicide formation?

214. Where is lane splitting legal in the United States?

215. When encountering a tornado on the open road should you take refuge under a bridge? Why or why not? (Refer to http://www.srh.noaa.gov/oun/?n=safety-overpass, especially slide 22 – this may save your life!)

216. What should be done to avoid tornadoes in open country?

217. If riding on the open highway and you encounter sudden heavy fog, how should you seek to protect yourself?

218. When riding across country in extreme heat (100° F or higher) degrees what is one of your greatest mechanical concerns?

219. When riding across country in extreme heat (100° F or higher) degrees how can you quickly cool off if you feel overwhelmed by the heat?

220. When traveling cross country through various OMC territories what should your MC do before entering their territory?

221. If riding cross country what auto parts store will always carry motorcycle batteries?

222. How does the AAA 'club motorcycle towing package' differ from your motorcycle insurance coverage towing plan?

223. When riding with another MC, where should your MC pack be located?

224. What is your local chapter's responsibility to your MC Nation?

225. If your MC chapter needs a bank account, is it okay for a member to put that account in his name?

226. What is the purpose of the website www.praying24hours.com?

227. Why do you want to be a member of your MC Nation?

228. What do you bring to your MC Nation?

229. What do you want from your MC Nation?

◊◊◊

Appendix D:
Brief History of the
Mighty Black Sabbath Motorcycle Club Nation

Mighty Black Sabbath Motorcycle Club Nation

The Mighty Black Sabbath Motorcycle Club Nation is a national, traditional motorcycle club whose members ride all makes of street legal motorcycles (cruisers at least 750cc and sport bikes at least 600cc). The Mighty Black Sabbath Motorcycle Club Nation does not belong to any governing organizations like the AMA. It is an independent MC nation that does not wear support patches or coalition support insignia. The Black Sabbath MC derived its name from the Original Seven African American male founders who rode on Sundays after church. When the Original Seven were looking for a name to call themselves—they said, "We are seven black men who ride on the Sabbath after worship, so let us call ourselves Black Sabbath MC!" Though we have been asked many times throughout the decades our founders had never heard of the band named Black

Sabbath when they started the MC.

History

The Original Seven founding fathers of the Mighty Black Sabbath Motorcycle Club Nation taught themselves to ride on one Honda 305 Scrambler in the hills of a neighborhood called Mount Hope in San Diego, California in 1972. That bike, given to 'Pep' by a close friend, was shared between them. The founding fathers mostly worked at the San Diego Gas and Electric Company or were enlisted in the US Navy, some were merchant marines. They practiced evenings and weekends on the Honda 305 Scrambler, until they eventually learned how to ride, and each bought a motorcycle.

Faithfully, they gathered at each other's garages after church on Sundays to ride, tell tall tales, and drink beers. By 1974, their wives united and revolted, demanding that no more club meetings be held in their garages on Sundays because the neighbors kept complaining and the wives felt threatened by the strength of the brotherhood. Undaunted, the founding fathers rented an abandoned bar at 4280 Market Street; where they remained one of the most dominant, influential, and successful MCs on the African American Biker Set since 1974 (nearly fifty years at the time of this writing).

Founding Fathers

The seven original founding fathers were:

- First Rider: Robert D. Hubbard 'Sir Hub' (SDG&E Electrician)
- VP: William Charles Sanders 'Couchie'(SDG&E Electrician)
- Sgt-at-Arms Alvin Ray 'Stretch'
- Road Capt: Paul Perry 'Pep' (SDG&E Meter Reader)
- Asst Road Capt: Solomon 'Sol'
- Secretary: John Kearny 'Black'
- Clayton Mitchell "Mitch" (Designer of our colors)

Note: Originally the leader of the BSMC was called "First Rider." We did not adopt the term "President" for many years later.

Racing roots

The Black Sabbath MC was not complicated in its mission during the early years. It was comprised simply of seven men who loved to ride, mostly on Sundays, who were similarly possessed with an insatiable appetite for custom building "Choppers" and unbeatable drag race bikes. This is still true today. All bike styles are welcomed, and racers are still most cherished in the Mighty Black Sabbath Motorcycle Club Nation.

Battle cry "I came to race"

The MC's battle cry was fathered by Black Sabbath MC legend-fabled racer, Allen 'Sugar Man' Brooks, who once wrecked Pep's motorcycle (early 1970's), on the way to the Salton Sea bike run/race event, without a helmet at over one hundred ten mph. Pep had warned Sugar Man that his bike was not operating properly and was excessively vibrating when it got to one hundred mph—so he told him not to exceed one hundred mph on the bike. Sugar Man still insisted that Pep let him test it. Needless to say, he exceeded one hundred mph and the bike went into a high-speed wobble. He crashed and destroyed Pep's bike. After the accident, Sugar Man was forbidden to compete as the MC deemed that he was too injured to race. The President threatened to take his colors if he attempted to compete in the drag racing the next day. Sugar Man said, "You can take these damned colors if you will, but I came to race!" Sugar Man consequently won the drag racing competition despite his injuries; thereby etching himself into the Black Sabbath MC's history books. His battle cry has been echoed by Black Sabbath racers from that time until now; "I came to race!"

San Diego Mother Chapter

The Mighty Black Sabbath Motorcycle Club Nation's mother chapter clubhouse stood at 4280 Market Street on the corner for forty-three years. During most of that time the MC reined dominant as the most successful MC in San Diego and is the oldest surviving MC on the black Biker Set there. For decades, the Black Sabbath MC clubhouse was the only clubhouse on the black Biker Set in the city.

During that time, all San Diego and Los Angeles MCs came to San Diego to celebrate the Black Sabbath MC's yearly anniversary, which grew to be called "The First Run of the Year." Even to this day, West Coast MCs gather in San Diego for the first run which generally happens around the second or third weekend in February. These days Mighty Black Sabbath MC Nation chapters around the country send their riders on this great pilgrimage across the United States braving freezing winters to this annual celebration. This run was named by Black Dragon as "The Cold Ass Run to The Mother Chapter."

Nationwide chapters

The Mighty Black Sabbath Motorcycle Club Nation has chapters across the United States from coast to coast. Growth was initially slow as the MC never envisioned itself a national MC from its inception in San Diego in 1974. The Black Sabbath MC is also the oldest surviving MC born in San Diego. The second charter was not given until 1989 some fifteen years after the MC started. Club racing legend, Allen 'Sugar Man' Brooks, took the colors to Wichita, Kansas where Knight Rider and Lady Magic (previously members of the Penguins MC) developed the chapter; subsequently becoming the oldest surviving MC on the black Biker Set there.

In 1999, then National President Pep, launched the Denver, Colorado chapter. Not long after, he assigned veteran member, Leonard Mack, to head up the Minneapolis, Minnesota chapter. Two years later, Pep ordered Dirty Red to launch the St. Paul, Minnesota chapter. In 2004, Pep launched the Little Rock, Arkansas chapter with his nephew, Lewis 'Doc' Perry, who became the first East Coast Regional President. Once again, two years later Doc launched the Oklahoma City, Oklahoma chapter with his high school buddy, James 'JB' Baker, as President. In 2008 former mother chapter President, Dewey 'Jazz' Johnson, launched the Phoenix, Arizona chapter. By then, the Wichita, Kansas chapter was all but dead with only a few active members.

Exponential growth was not seen until 2009 when then National Enforcer John E. 'Black Dragon' Bunch II was given the mandate by

Father Pep to build the club into a national powerhouse. Pep's dream, as intimated to him all the way back in 1997 was to construct a legendary national MC known worldwide for hard riding on iron that could one day become a household name. Black Dragon accepted the assignment. His first move was to convince Sugar Man to come out of retirement and together they launched the Tulsa, Oklahoma chapter. Black Dragon then rebuilt the Wichita, Kansas chapter over the next three years, but despite his best efforts could not sustain the re-launch until Lady Magic tapped her son, 'Pull-it', and grandson, Chris 'Chill' Hill. With the addition of those two brothers the Wichita chapter again soared. Black Dragon simultaneously launched the Atlanta, Georgia chapter with former Oklahoma City member, Pappy, who had also grown up with Doc Perry. Later, in 2009, Black Dragon launched the Houston, Texas chapter with Bernard 'Krow'Augustus who became the first Midwest/Central USA Regional President.

In 2010, the Atlanta, Georgia chapter was taken over by Black Dragon's former submarine shipmate, Leon 'Eight Ball' Richardson, who also became the first East Coast Regional President. Black Dragon became National President in 2010, and patched over the Macon, Georgia chapter under Curtis 'Ride or Die' Hill from the Zulus MC Nation under a negotiation with 'Wolverine' then the Zulus National President. 'Ride or Die' became the third East Coast Regional President and eventually rose to become the fourth National President of the Mighty Black Sabbath MC Nation. Black Dragon then patched-over Sic Wit' It MC in Rome, Georgia under President G Man to make Black Sabbath MC among the few clubs to achieve three chapters in Georgia at that time.

Sugar Man's first cousin, Jamel 'Huggy Bear' Brooks, launched the San Antonio, Texas chapter by the end of 2010, and became the first West Coast Regional President assuming command of the Phoenix, Arizona chapter. Black Dragon instructed then National Vice President Tommy 'Hog Man' Lewis and Huggy Bear to patch over the Inland Empire, California chapter under the leadership of former

Regulator 'Big Dale' in 2011. Big Dale eventually became the second West Coast Regional President. In 2012, National Vice President Tommy 'Hog Man' Lewis received a blessing from the Chosen Few MC to open the Las Vegas, Nevada chapter with then West Coast Regional President Huggy Bear. In 2012, Black Dragon launched the Jacksonville, Florida chapter under President 'Prime'. In 2014, Black Dragon instructed West Coast Regional President Big Dale to patch over a former 1%er club that had been shut down due to west coast external conflicts. It launched in Riverside, California as the Riverside chapter under President Bob 'Bob O' Rinaldi. In 2015, Black Dragon opened the Hutchinson, Kansas chapter under President Dizzle. External problems with local 1%ers caused them to have to fly "West Wichita" colors for nearly three years, but eventually, through continued negotiations the Hutchinson chapter finally flew their rightful city once again. In 2015 Black Dragon launched the Colorado Springs, Colorado chapter under President 'G-Ride' which flies under the Olympic City flag. In 2016 Black Dragon opened the Topeka, Kansas chapter under President Cliff 'Big Red Dog'. Consequently, the chapter bounced up and down for nearly four years and never fully opened until about late 2019. In 2017 Black Dragon launched the Beaufort, South Carolina chapter under President Homesick after nearly three years of negotiations with local 1%ers. In 2017 Black Dragon gave President Jason 'Ol' Skool' Monds the mandate to open the Pensacola, Florida chapter but it took until 2019 to secure all necessary agreements to bring it online. Also in 2017, after nearly four years of work Black Dragon opened the Fort Worth, Texas chapter under President Big Mixx who was the second longest prospecting member of the Mighty Black Sabbath MC Nation. In late 2017 early 2018 Black Dragon launched the RONIN chapter of the Mighty Black Sabbath MC Nation. Shortly after he stepped down from the position of National President. In 2020 Black Dragon consulted with President Big Mixx to open the West Fort Worth chapter and in 2021 Black Dragon launched the North Shore Louisiana chapter under President Cuban and the Frederick Maryland chapter under President Devil. In April 2021 Black Dragon began prospecting the Lagos Nigeria chapter, his third attempt in Africa. Perhaps this time those efforts will succeed. Hail to the forefathers of the Mighty Black Sabbath Motorcycle Club

Nation! We hope they are proud of what their dreams have become. Amen.

Membership

A prospective member is allowed into the Black Sabbath Motorcycle Club as a "hang-around," indicating that the individual is invited to some MC events or to meet MC members at known gathering places. This period could last several months to several years. It is the time for the hang-around to evaluate the MC, as well as for the MC to evaluate the hang-around. If the hang-around is interested, and the Black Sabbath Motorcycle Club likes the hang-around; he can request to be voted in as a Prospect. The hang-around must win a majority vote to be designated a Prospect. If he is successful he will be given a sponsor and his prospectship begins. The prospectship will be no less than ninety days, but could last for years, depending upon the attitude and resourcefulness of the Prospect. Former National President Black Dragon prospected for nearly five years before he crossed over. The Prospect will participate in some MC activities and serve the MC in whatever capacity the full patched brothers may deem appropriate. A Prospect will never be asked to commit any illegal act, any act against nature, or any physically humiliating or demeaning act. The Black Sabbath Motorcycle Club never hazes Prospects. A Prospect will not have voting privileges while he is evaluated for suitability as a full member but does pay MC dues.

The last phase, and highest membership status, is "Full Membership" or "Full-Patch". The term "Full-Patch" refers to the complete one-piece patch. Prospects are allowed to wear only a small thirteen-inch patch with the letters of the local chapter (i.e., BSSD) and the black cross on it. To become a full patched brother the Prospect must be presented by his sponsor before the MC and win a one hundred percent affirmative vote from the full patched brothers. Prior to votes being cast, a Prospect usually travels to every chapter in the sponsoring chapter's geographic region (state/province/territory) and introduces himself to every full patched brother. This process allows all regional chapter members to become familiar with the Prospect. Some form of formal induction follows, wherein the Prospect affirms his loyalty to the MC and its members. Often the Prospect's sponsor may require him to make a nomadic journey on his motorcycle before crossing over, sometimes as far as 1,000 miles that must be completed within twenty-four hours to ensure that the Prospect understands the Black Sabbath Motorcycle Club is a riding motorcycle club. The final logo patch is then awarded at his swearing in and initiation ceremony. The step of attaining full membership can be referred to as "being patched", "patching in" or "crossing over."

Command Structure
- National President
- National Vice President
- High Council President
- High Council
- National Business Manager
- National Ambassador
- Regional President
- President
- Vice President
- Secretary
- Sgt-at-Arms
- Road Captain
- Treasurer
- Business Manager
- Public Relations Officer
- Media/Web Design Officer
- Full Patch Member
- First Lady S.O.T.C.
- Full Patch S.O.T.C.
- Head Goddess
- Full Patch Goddess
- Support Crew

- Prospect
- S.O.T.C. Prospect
- Goddess Prospect
- Hang Around
- Special officers include Disaster Chief, Nomad/Ronin, National Sgt-at-Arms, Enforcer, Support Crew Chief, Father, Godfather, and Godmother.

Colors

The Black Sabbath Motorcycle Club patch is called the "Turtle Shell". The colors are set out on a white background inside a black circle, inside a black crested shield, with the words Black Sabbath MC encircling the riding man. The crested shield on the sixteen-inch back patch gives the appearance of a turtle's shell when worn as it covers most members' entire back. The MC's colors are white, yellow, black, and blue.

In the forty-plus year history of the MC the colors have remained untouched except for the addition of the shield in 1975 and the enlargement of the patch to nineteen-inch by sixteen inch in 2009. The adherence to the original patch mirrors their adherence to the core values of the Original Seven founding forefathers.

Racial Policies

Because the Black Sabbath Motorcycle Club was started by African Americans and its membership is primarily African American (90%) it is considered to be on the 'Black Biker Set" by biker clubs across America. However, the Black Sabbath Motorcycle Club states that even though it was started by seven African American men who rode on Sundays, today it is a multi-racial organization that is accepting of all religions, with chapters across the United States from coast to coast. The Mighty Black Sabbath Motorcycle Club Nation is a brotherhood based on a unified lifestyle centered on riding motorcycles, living the biker lifestyle, and embracing one another as extended family- as close as any blood relatives.

Neutrality

The Mighty Black Sabbath Motorcycle Club Nation has followed all MC protocol in setting up its chapters nationwide. To that end, it has secured negotiations to operate by dominants in every area in which it has chapters. As a neutral elite traditional motorcycle-enthusiast riding MC the Mighty Black Sabbath Motorcycle Club Nation wears no support patches as it takes no political sides and does not align itself with OMC politics.

Women in the Black Sabbath MC Nation

A male dominated organization, the Mighty Black Sabbath Motorcycle Club Nation men belong to the brotherhood of the cross. Women fall into two unique categories. Women who do not ride motorcycles belong to the female support social club known as "Goddesses of the Mighty Black Sabbath Motorcycle Club Nation". Women who ride motorcycles belong to the "Sisters of the Cross MC of the Mighty Black Sabbath Motorcycle Club Nation".

Sisters of the Cross

The Sisters of the Cross MC of the Mighty Black Sabbath Motorcycle Club Nation (SOTC) is a female motorcycle club that rides under the full patched brothers of the Black Sabbath Motorcycle Club. The SOTC was established in 2011 by National President, Black Dragon. SOTC Prospects must be eighteen years old, own a motorcycle and have a motorcycle driver's license. The SOTC are called the "First Ladies of the Black Sabbath Motorcycle Club", and the ranking SOTC is called First Lady. The SOTC MC was created to recognize the achievements of many of the Goddesses of the Black Sabbath Motorcycle Club who were buying, learning how to ride, and getting licenses for motorcycles at an incredible rate. The Mighty Black Sabbath Motorcycle Club Nation sought to reward the hard work and passion to ride these women displayed by giving them their own MC under the auspices of the Mighty Black Sabbath Motorcycle Club Nation.

Goddesses of the Club

The Goddesses of the Mighty Black Sabbath Motorcycle Club Nation is the social club auxiliary that supports the MC. Goddess

Prospects must be eighteen years old, be of exceptional character and devoted to serve the best interests of the Mighty Black Sabbath Motorcycle Club.

Mission Statement

1. "To become the greatest riding motorcycle club in the world by pounding down great distances on two wheels, bonding on the highways and byways as family, camping out while riding to biker events or cross country, enjoying the wilderness, racing, competing, winning, and experiencing our extended family by tenderly loving each other more and more each day!

2. To become the greatest motorcycle club family in the world by encouraging diversity within our MC, building strong, lasting friendships among members, instilling a sense of love, pride, and togetherness within our communities, helping those in need through volunteerism, and cultivating a mindset of moral and social responsibility amongst our members; also, by inspiring our youth to achieve beyond all limitations which will leave a legacy of hope and boundless dreams for future generations of the Mighty Black Sabbath Motorcycle Club Nation to come."

National President

The office of the National President was created by Tommy 'Hog Man' Lewis then President of the mother chapter and former mother chapter President Dewey 'Jazz' Johnson in the summer of 2000. Paul 'Pep' Perry, the last original founding member left in the chapter, was elected the first National President. Curtis 'Mad Mitch' Mitchell was appointed first National Vice President one year later. Pep also created the office of National Ambassador to which he assigned Jazz. The National Vice President position was eventually terminated. In 2010, Godfather Washington of the Mighty Black Sabbath Motorcycle Club Nation died, and Pep retired to become Godfather. National Enforcer and President of the Atlanta chapter,

Black Dragon, was summoned to the mother chapter in San Diego and was elected as the second National President of the Mighty Black Sabbath Motorcycle Club Nation during the February mother chapter annual dance. Black Dragon recreated the National Vice President office and recruited then retired former San Diego President Hog Man for the position. Black Dragon created the High Council President office to which he assigned Sabbath racing legend Sugar Man. He also created the High Council which consists of the President and Vice President of every chapter. Black Dragon also created the National Sgt-at-Arms, National Business Manager, Nomad/Ronin, Disaster Chief, Support Chief, and Public Relations Officers (PRO) offices.

Riding Awards and Designations

In order to challenge his MC members to ride harder and to distinguish the Mighty Black Sabbath Motorcycle Club Nation as a superior elite motorcycle-enthusiast riding MC, Black Dragon created the Nomad Rider program. In an article written in the Black Sabbath Magazine, Black Dragon stated, "A historic traditional MC Nation is nothing if its members do not ride!" The Nomad Rider program recognizes and awards Black Sabbath Motorcycle Club nomad riders for their achievements. Some of the awards include:

- Nomad Rider = 1,000 miles one-way (N1)
- 1 K in 1 Day Nomad = 1,000 miles one-way ridden in twenty-four hours or less (N124)
- Nomad Traveler = 2,000 miles one-way (N2)
- Nomad Warrior = 3,000 miles one-way (N3)
- Nomad Adventurer = 4,000 miles one-way (N4)
- Nomad Wanderer = 5,000 miles one-way (N5)
- Snow Bear Disciple Nomad = one hundred miles traveled in sleet, snow, or 18° F (SBN)
- Poseidon's Disciples Nomad = traveling through three states during continuous driving rain (PSN)
- Great Plains Nomad = riding across the Oklahoma or Kansas great plains (GPN)
- Panhandle Nomad = riding across the great state of Texas (TPN)

- Great Winds Nomad = riding through fifty mph windstorm (GWN)
- 1,000-mile bull's horn = eleven-inch bull's blowing horn, awarded to all Nomad Riders
- 2,000-mile Kudu's horn shofar = twenty-three-inch Kudu antelope's blowing horn, awarded to all Nomad Travelers
- 3,000-mile Kudu's horn shofar = thirty-three-inch Kudu or Blesbok antelope's blowing horn, awarded to all Nomad Warriors
- 4,000-mile horn shofar = forty-inch Kudu, Blesbok or Impala antelope's blowing horn, awarded to all Nomad Adventurers; can be Kudu, Blesbok or Impala
- 5,000-mile horn shofar = fifty-inch antelope's blowing horn, awarded to all Nomad Wanderers; can be any horned cloven-footed animal.

Violence

Violent incidents have occurred in and around nationwide clubhouses.

- In 2002, President 'Bull' of the Zodiacs MC was killed after he pulled a gun on his former Prospect, who was partying at the mother chapter with a new MC in which he was interested. The former Prospect slashed Bull's throat with a knife when he looked away during the confrontation. This was the first killing ever committed at a Black Sabbath MC clubhouse and brought the city of San Diego down on the club. The City Attorney initiated a campaign to shut down the clubhouse nearly finishing the Black Sabbath MC. The clubhouse was subsequently firebombed in retaliation for Bull's killing.

- In February 2010, the mother chapter at 4280 Market Street was again targeted by arsonists who attempted to burn it to the ground right before the 2010 annual. They were unsuccessful.

- In 2010, a man was fatally shot in a hail of gunfire near the Phoenix chapter of the Black Sabbath MC clubhouse during an altercation over a woman. He died a block away while fleeing the scene. This incident caused the closing of the Phoenix chapter

Page | 401

clubhouse.

- On 11 May 2012, San Diego mother chapter President, 'Wild Dogg', was murdered in front of the Black Sabbath Motorcycle Club clubhouse at 4280 Market Street during a drive by assassination. The case is still unsolved and open.

Epilogue

"Everything that I stand so firmly against today, I once was! It is only through experience, pain, suffering, and being blessed to learn life's lessons that I have evolved to whom I've become. "

John E. Bunch II

◊◊◊

Glossary

1%er: Initially a description falsely attributed to the AMA to describe some of the MCs that attended Rolling Gypsy race meets. It was alleged that the AMA stated that 99% of the people at their events were God fearing and family oriented. The other 1% were hoodlums, thugs, and outlaws. Non-AMA sanctioned MCs, thus being seen as outlaws, adopted the 1%er moniker and embraced it as an identity. Over time the 1%er designation became exclusively associated with OMGs, criminal biker syndicates, and some OMCs. Though not all 1%ers are criminals it is certain that the 1% diamond designation attracts law enforcement scrutiny like no other symbol on a biker's cut.

5%er: A member of an MRO. Only five percent of motorcyclists are involved with MROs that are dedicated to protecting the rights of the other ninety-five percent of bikers by spending money, dedicating time, and championing pro-biker legislation.

80/20 Rule: A requirement held by some MC councils requiring all blessed MCs within a council's region to demonstrate, via a bike count, that 80% of the MC's members have operational motorcycles at all times.

AMA: American Motorcyclist Association

ABATE: An organization started by Easy Rider Magazine to fight against discrimination toward motorcyclists, mostly helmet laws originally. Once called "A Brotherhood Against Totalitarian Enactments" or "American Bikers Against Totalitarian Enactments", ABATE now has many other names including "American Brotherhood (or Bikers) Aimed Toward Education." ABATE fights for biker rights and champions many issues well beyond helmet laws. Members often help charities. Membership comes with yearly dues and officers are elected from the active membership.

Ape Hangers: Tall handlebars that place a biker's hands at or above his shoulder height.

Backyard: Where you ride often—never defecate there.

Baffle: Sound deadening material inside a muffler that quiets the exhaust noises.

Bike Count: To stem the tide of the so called "popup clubs" some councils require a minimum number of motorcycles to be in a MC before they will allow it to start up in their region. MC numbers are proven when the MC undergoes a bike count of its members; usually with all members present on their bikes.

Black Ball List: A list enacted by an MC coalition or council. It is directed at non-compliant MCs that serve to notify other MCs not to support the "black-balled" chapter nor allow it to participate in any coalition authorized Set functions.

Blockhead: The V-twin engine Harley, 1984 – 2000.

Boneyard: Salvage yard for used bikes and parts.

Brain Bucket: Small, beanie-style helmet (usually not Department of Transportation (DOT) approved).

Broad: A female entertainer for the MC. She may be a dancer or at times a prostitute.

Broken Wings: A patch meaning the rider has been in a crash.

BS: bullshit: NONESENSE usually vulgar: to talk foolishly, boastfully, or idly: to engage in a discursive discussion.

Burnout: Spinning the rear wheel while holding the front brake. (Conducting burnouts while visiting another MC's clubhouse is disrespectful as it brings complaints from the neighborhood and invites unwanted police attention. Make trouble in your own neighborhood and be respectful with noise and other commotion while visiting others.)

Cage: Any vehicle of four or more wheels, specifically not a motorcycle.

Cager: Driver of a cage. (Usually, cagers are thought of as dangerous to bikers because they do not pay attention to the road.)

Chopper: A bike with the front end raked or extended out.

Chromeitis: A disease associated with a biker that cannot seem to buy enough aftermarket accessories (especially chrome).

Church: Clubhouse ("Having church" or "going to church" is referred to as the club meeting at the clubhouse).

CLAP: Chrome, Leather, Accessories, Performance

Clone: A motorcycle built to resemble and function like a Harley-Davidson motorcycle without actually being a Harley-Davidson motorcycle.

Club Name: Also known as a handle. A name given to a MC member by his brothers most often based upon his character, routine, quirks, and/or a noteworthy event that happened in the MC of which that member played a part. This is usually a name of honor and often indicates the personality one might expect when encountering that member. This name is generally accepted with great pride by the member and is a handle he will adopt for a lifetime. For instance, I once became annoyed with a member of the Black Sabbath Atlanta chapter for giving me a hard time when I needed him to break into my house and get the keys to my trailer so he could rescue me from the side of the road in Little Rock, AR nine hours away. He gave me so much grief about my trailer registration, working condition of my signal lights, and notifying authorities before he would break in my place that I frustratingly named him "By-the-Book", instantly changing his name from "Glock." By-the-Book so loved his new name that when he later departed the Mighty Black Sabbath M.C. Nation, he took his name with him and is still called By-the-Book to this very day. It is an honor for the MC to name you and quite improper for you to name yourself.

Club Hopping: The frowned upon practice of switching memberships from one MC to another. Traditional MCs have low tolerance for bikers who "club hop" as this phenomenon breaks down good order and discipline in MCs. In fact, this was seldom done in the early days. Most coalitions and councils regulate club hopping and enact vigorous laws against it. Often, OMCs refuse to allow former members to wear another MC's colors after serving in their OMC. An MC should generally ensure that a club hopper waits at least six months before allowing them to prospect for their MC unless the former President sanctions the move.

Colors: Unique motorcycle club back patch or patches.

Crash Bar: Engine guard that protects the engine if the bike crashes.

CreditGlide: A RUB's Motorcycle.

Crotch Rocket / Rice Burner: A sport bike.

Counter Steering: Turning the bike's handlebars in one direction and having it go in the opposite direction. All bikers should learn this maneuver for safety.

Custom: A custom-built motorcycle.

Cut: Vest containing the MC colors. The name comes from the practice of cutting the sleeves off of blue denim jackets.

DILLIGAF: "Do I Look Like I Give A Fuck?"

DOT: Department of Transportation.

Drag Bars: Low, flat, straight handlebars.

Evo /Evolution®: Evolution engine (V-Twin, 1984 – 2000).

Fathead: Twin-Cam engine (V-Twin, 1999 – Present).

Fender / Fender Fluff: A female passenger who is not an Old Lady but simply a lady a biker has invited for a ride.

Flathead: The Flathead engine (V-Twin, 1929 – 1972).

Flash Patch: Generic patch sold at meets and bike shops.

Flip: Occurs when an OMC takes over a less powerful OMC or 99%er. This can occur against that MC's will and could be violent. The less powerful MC will flip from their colors to the dominant MC's colors.

Flying Low: Speeding.

Forward Controls: Front pegs, shifter, and rear brake control moved forward (often to the highway pegs).

Freedom Fighter: An MRO member dedicated to preserving or gaining biker's rights and freedoms.

FTA: "Fuck Them All."

FTW: "Fuck the World" or "Forever Two Wheels."

Get-Back-Whip: A two-to-three-foot leather braid with an easy release hard metal clip that can be attached to the front brake handle or the clutch handle. Often it contains a lead weight at the bottom of the braid with tassels that just barely drag the ground when the bike is standing still. This ornamental decoration can quickly be released to make a formidable weapon to be used to slap against offending cages that invade a biker's road space (to include breaking out the cager's windows). Either end can be used in an offensive or defensive situation. The Get-Back-Whip is illegal in MANY states.

Hard Tail: A motorcycle frame with no rear suspension.

Hang Around: The designation of a person who has indicated that he formally wants to get to know a MC so he can begin prospecting for them.

HOG: Harley Owners Group.

Independent: A biker who is not a member of a MC, but is normally a well-known, accepted individual of local Biker Set (of a higher order than a hang-around).

Ink: Tattoo.

Ink-Slinger: Tattoo Artist.

KTRSD: "Keep the Rubber Side Down" Riding safely and keeping both tires on the road instead of up in the air—as in having a wreck.

Knuck/Knucklehead: The Knucklehead engine (V-Twin 1936 – 1947).

LE/LEO: Law Enforcement Officer/Official.

Lick and Stick: A temporary pillion back seat placed on the fender through the use of suction cups.

MC: Motorcycle Club.

MM: Motorcycle Ministry (Also known as 5%ers).

Moonlight Mile: A short adventure with a lady friend away from camp.

MRO: Motorcycle Rights Organization. These organizations seek to protect the rights and freedoms of bikers (i.e., ABATE, BOLT, Motorcycle Riders Foundation, American Motorcycle Association, MAG, etc.).

MSF: Motorcycle Safety Foundation.

OEM: Original Equipment Manufacturer.

Old / Ole Lady: Girlfriend or wife of a biker, definitely off limits!

OMC: Outlaw Motorcycle Club.

OMG: Outlaw Motorcycle Gang.

On Ground: Refers to showing up on or riding a motorcycle instead of showing up in or driving a cage.

On Two: Refers to showing up on or riding a motorcycle instead of showing up in or driving a cage.

Pan/Pan Head: The Pan Head engine (V-Twin, 1948 – 1965).

Patch: The back patch is the colors of a MC.

Patch-Over: Like club flipping a patch-over occurs when a MC changes patches from one MC to another. This is acceptable and not looked upon unfavorably in most cases. 99%er MCs patch-over MCs they acquire instead of "flipping" them because 99%ers do not enforce territory. This will be a peaceful gentlemen's agreement that happens unremarkably and without incident. 1%ers flip MCs.

Pillion Pad: Passenger Seat.

Pipes: Exhaust System.

PRO: Public Relations Officer.

Probate/Probie/Probationary: A member serving a period of probation until he is voted into full patched (full membership) status.

Probation: The period of time a Probie must serve before full membership is bestowed. This is the time distinguished from being a hang-around because the member is voted into the Probie status and is permitted to wear some form of the MCs colors. The Probie is also responsible to follow the MC's bylaws.

Prospect: A member serving a prospectship until he is voted into full patched (full membership) status.

Prospectship: The period of time a Prospect must serve before a vote for full membership is held. This is the time distinguished from being a hang-around because the prospective member is voted into the Prospect status and permitted to wear some form of the MCs colors. The Prospect is also responsible to follow the MC's bylaws.

Rags: Club colors or a Cut.

Rat Bike: A bike that has not been maintained or loved.

RC: Riding Club. A group that rides for enjoyment (perhaps under a patch), but members do not incur the responsibility of brotherhood to the level of a traditional MCs, modern MCs, or OMCs. Members generally purchase their patches and do not often Prospect/Probie to become members. Rides and runs are generally voluntarily and there is no mandatory participation. RCs are still required to follow MC protocol when operating on the MC Set and would do well to know the MC laws and respect them so as not to wind up in any kinds of altercations.

Revolution™: The Revolution engine, Harley-Davidson's first water-cooled engine (V-Twin, 2002 – Present)

RICO Act: Racketeer Influenced and Corrupt Organizations. Initially, these laws were passed for law enforcement to combat organized crime such as the mafia. They were quickly used to prosecute OMGs, OMCs, and some 99%er MCs.

Riding Bitch: Riding as the passenger on the back of a bike.

Road Name: Also known as a Handle. A name given to a MC

member by his brothers and is most often based upon his character, routine, quirks, or a noteworthy event that happened in the MC of which that member played a part. This is usually a name of great honor and often indicates the personality one might expect when encountering that member. This name is generally accepted with great pride by the member and is a handle he will adopt for a lifetime.

Rocker: Bottom part of MC colors which usually designates geographic location or territory, though other information may be contained there such as the word "Nomad."

RUB: Rich Urban Biker.

Rubber: Tire.

Rubber Side Down: Riding safely and keeping both tires on the road instead of up in the air—as in having a wreck.

Run: Road trip "on two" with your brothers.

Running 66: Though rare it is sometimes necessary to ride without the MC's colors showing (also known as "riding incognito").

Shovel/Shovel Head: The Shovel Head engine (V-Twin, 1966 – 1984)

Shower Head: The new Harley-Davidson V-Rod motorcycle motor.

Sissy Bar Passenger Backrest.

Slab: Interstate.

Sled: Motorcycle.

Softail®: A motorcycle frame whose suspension is hidden, making it resemble a hard tail.

SMRO: State Motorcycle Rights Organization. Same as an MRO except defined by the state in which they operate, (i.e., ABATE of Oklahoma, MAG of Georgia, etc.).

Straight Pipes: An exhaust system with no Baffles.

Tats: Tattoos.

Tail Gunner: The last rider in the pack.

The Motorcyclist Memorial Wall: A biker's memorial wall located in Hopedale Ohio where the names of fallen riders are engraved for a nominal fee (www.motorcyclistmemorial.com). Memorial bricks may also be purchased to lie at the beautiful site.

The Motorcycle Memorial Foundation: The foundation that operates the Motorcyclist Memorial Wall. P.O. Box 2573 Wintersville, Ohio 43953.

Thirteen ("13") Diamond Patch: This is a patch commonly worn by some Outlaw MC Nations. The "13" symbol can have several meanings referencing the thirteenth letter of the alphabet, "M," standing for Marijuana, Methamphetamines, Motorcycle, or the original Mother Chapter of a MC. In Hispanic gang culture, "13" can represent "La Eme" (Mexican Mafia).

Three-Piece Patch: Generally thought of as being OMC colors consisting of a top rocker (name of MC), middle insignia (MC's symbol) and bottom rocker (name of state or territory MC claims). Not only OMCs wear three-piece patches, but new 99%er MCs should stay away from this design and stick to a one-piece patch.

Turn your back: A show of ultimate disrespect is to turn your back on someone.

Twisties: Section of road with a lot of increasing, distal, radial turns.

Vested Pedestrian: Is a person who is in a MC and wearing colors but does not own a motorcycle. Often thought of as a person who has never had a motorcycle, rather than someone who may be between bikes for a short period of time (i.e., a month or two).

Wannabe: Someone that tries to pretend to be a part of the biker lifestyle.

Wrench: Mechanic.

XXF-FXX/XXFOREVER – FOREVERXX: Patch worn by MC members to represent their total commitment to the MC and every other member of that MC. XX stands for the name of the MC (i.e., Black Sabbath Forever Forever Black Sabbath).

◊◊◊

About the Author

John E. Bunch II 'Black Dragon' rode on the back of a Honda Trail 50cc for the first time when he was six years old. Instantly, he was hooked! His mother could not afford to buy him a motorcycle so he borrowed anyone's bike that would let him ride- on the back roads and farms all over Oklahoma where he grew up. When he was fourteen his mother bought him a Yamaha 125 Enduro, cashing in the US Savings Bonds his father had left him. By the time he was seventeen, his stepfather, J.W. Oliver, gave him a Honda CX500. He was known throughout the neighborhood as the kid who always rode wheelies up the block (16th street and Classen), and as the kid who always rode wheelies with his sisters, Thea, and Lori, hanging off the back. He took his first long distance road trip at seventeen riding from Oklahoma City to Wichita, Kansas to visit his aunt and uncle. He knew then that he was born to distance ride! The nomadic call of the open road in the wind, rain, cold, heat—under the stars were home to him.

In the late 1980s, he found himself a young submarine sailor stationed in San Diego, California. He got into trouble on the base with a Senior Chief who gave him and his best friend an order they refused to follow. The white Senior Chief did not want to see the young black man's career ended over insubordination, so he did Bunch an extreme favor. He sent him and his insolent friend, Keith (Alcatraz) Corley, who was similarly in trouble; to see African American, then Senior Chief, George G. Clark III, instead of to a Courts Martial. Senior Chief Clark threatened Bunch and Corley with physical violence if they did not obey the white Senior Chief and worked out a solution that saved both of their careers. Later, Clark invited them to 4280 Market Street when he discovered Bunch had a love for motorcycles. Bunch walked into the mother chapter and was blown away to learn that Senior Chief Clark was also known as 'Magic', former President of the Black Sabbath Motorcycle Club Mother Chapter. His insubordinate ways were not quite behind him, so it took Bunch several years to actually cross over as a full patch brother known as 'Black Dragon' in the Black Sabbath Motorcycle Club Mother Chapter.

In 2000, Black Dragon began advising writer/filmmaker Reggie Rock Bythewood, who co-wrote and directed the Dream Works movie Biker Boyz. Black Dragon went to Hollywood and worked as the Technical Adviser on the film. Biker Boyz has often been credited with re-birthing the African American MC movement in the United States.

In 2009 Black Dragon brought the Black Sabbath Motorcycle Club to Atlanta, GA as President and an Original Seven Atlanta founding member. He suffered his first setback in Atlanta during a coupe that cost him the Presidency of the Atlanta chapter in December 2010. In February 2010, he was elected to the Office of National President and began his nationwide march to spread the Black Sabbath Motorcycle Club from coast to coast. By 2011, the Black Sabbath Motorcycle Club became the Mighty Black Sabbath Motorcycle Club Nation with chapters from the West coast to the

East coast.

Black Dragon has published several biker magazines including:

Urban Biker Cycle News, Black Iron Motorcycle Magazine, Black Sabbath Motorcycle Newsletter, and the popular blog *www.blacksabbathmagazine.com*. In 2013, Black Dragon wrote the first MC phone app, *"Black Sabbath Motorcycle Club"*.

Today Black Dragon is building a Mighty MC Nation that rides cross country year-round, rain, sleet, or snow—where no trailers are allowed! Black Dragon currently serves the Mighty Black Sabbath Motorcycle Club Nation as a Senior Lifer.

Black Sabbath Forever Black Sabbath
A Breed Apart
Since 1974

www.blacksabbathmc.com

◊◊◊

A NOTE FROM BLACK DRAGON

Now what? You have read the book and you know the power of the information held within. I want you to know that you can help other presidents navigate their way through the murky waters of leading their beloved motorcycle clubs on the Biker Set.

If you were helped, educated, or informed by this book there are a couple of simple things you can do to join me in remaking the MC world through knowledge, experience, education, and love:

> 1. If you believe the President' s Bible has helped you then I ask that you spread the word by buying a copy for a president or a someone you think should be one.

> 2. Give President's Bible as a gift or setup a reading group to discuss how this book applies to the leadership of your MC. You can also write an honest review on social media, your blog, website, or on your favorite bookseller's website. There are countless ways you can help others by spreading this word. President's Bible is not just a book worth reading, it is a vision and a plan worth following for every President to contribute positively to their MC. It is a vision worth sharing.

> 3. Enrich other motorcycle clubs by buying this book for your brother and sister MCs on the set with whom you share alliances. Imagine if other Presidents could have the benefit of the knowledge you have attained.

> **Thank you for your support!** Send me an email anytime with questions, improvements, or your best president's tales!

About the Cover

"Death of a President is Delivered by a Thousand Back Stabs"
Commissioned by: Black Dragon Created by: Chainz President/Founder Nut Basketz MC

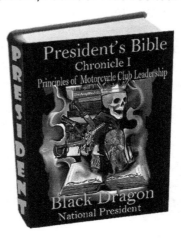

The job of President is the loneliest one in the MC. He must be tireless and resolute in his duties. He must be resourceful and giving. He must never think of himself instead concentrating constantly on the WeMC and the welfare of his brothers and the extended family. And after he has given has all and spent himself on the altar of MC sacrifice—most often he will find he is disillusioned, abandoned, abused, and unappreciated. He will indeed discover that he is dying a sad death—the death of a thousand back stabs, wounds that pierce down to his very soul.

Still, he gladly accepts his fate. He would do it again choosing his exact same steps! For he was a leader and will always have been and will forever BE!

They called him Prez! Or National! Or Regional! Or State Boss! And he answered their calls until he was no longer capable. And he forgave the backstabbers who finally gobbled him up.

John E. Black Dragon Bunch II
Lifer
Mighty Black Sabbath MC Nation
A Breed Apart
Since 1974
And Still Strong...................................///

About the Cover Artist

Chainz Prez Nut Basketz MC

What would you want your legacy to be if you died tomorrow? What would you be remembered for and by whom? Did you live the life you wanted? Did you touch the souls of the people around you and do everything you could to help yourself and your family?

From a young age I've been through detention centers, prisons, foster care homes, and more. My mother was in and out of prison my entire life for prescription forgery, which is how I got put into the foster care system. How does someone learn to cope with everything that life throws at them? For me it was bikes, music, and my art.

I got my first bike when I was 14 years old. It was a UM twin 250 sport bike. When I was 17 years old, I sold that bike and bought a GXSR 750. A week later I slammed it into a mailbox going 100 mph. That experience turned me away from bikes for about ten years. During that time, I was focused on my art and music. However, my brothers Greg, Whiskey, KO, and Kountry all got bikes and begged me to get another one so we could all ride together. I ended up getting a GSXR 600. From there KO and I started going to meets, talking to members from different MC's, including KJ from Barebones MC, and we decided to start our own club. About a year later, in 2019, we got ourselves in a situation that brought us in front of the Outcast MC Nation Atlanta chapter, and they patched us, the Nut Basketz MC, in as a support club.

For us the Nut Basketz was more than just a motorcycle club, it was a representation of not only mine, but all of my members' battles with mental health issues and served as a way to cope with them. The name came from a term to describe mental health patients, so called "Nut Baskets". I have Paranoid Personality Disorder (PPD), my brother is schizophrenic and has manic depression, and many members of my club and their families deal with their own mental issues, including depression and anxiety. So, we started the club to be a positive aspect to help us escape all the negativity that we have lived and fought through, and to help others that deal with the same things we have suffered. We started riding for charities, donating to hospitals, and working to aid and bring awareness to the mental health community and those suffering within. I have even used my gift to design club patches and artwork for other motorcycle clubs.

Being the President of the Nut Baskets MC has helped me grow up mentally and learn how to deal with massive amounts of responsibility. It taught me how to make decisions that affect the club and all of my brothers as a whole. It taught me how to sacrifice and I learned how giving of yourself makes you stronger. While being a full patch brother in the club is amazing it has definitely been a rollercoaster of ups and downs. We have lost brothers, gained new brothers, dealt with issues from other clubs, and all-in-all the club has taken over my life. Once, it almost cost me my life.

Last year I was riding my sport bike and I hit an oil spot which sent my bike out from under me and pinned my leg to the concrete, snapping it in half. This experience made me rethink a lot, including cruisers vs. sports bikes. Even with this having happened, I do not regret my club at all. It has been one of the main things in my life that has helped me make it through.

Through all if this I never once stopped working on my music and art. When I was 12 years old, I was sent to the Marietta (Georgia) Youth Detention Center where I saw some of the other kids giving each other stick and poke tattoos. I could always draw pretty well so I decided to give it a try and within no time I was the best in there. When I got out, I started tattooing myself and all of my friends in the neighborhood and everyone tried to get me to quit, even my foster parents tried to get me to quit by threatening to get me in trouble with my probation officer but not even that stopped me. I kept pushing and pushing to be even better. By the time I was 15 years old my foster dad had given up on trying to get me to quit and actually bought me my first machine kit off of eBay and told me if it keeps me out of trouble, he would support it. From then until when I was 18 years old, I tried to get an apprenticeship with a shop, but no one wanted to take me. But that did not stop me from progressing.

I was completely self-taught and fresh out of prison in Ohio when I moved back to Georgia at age 20 and tried out at my first shop, Naked Guns. They hired me on the spot, and with no equipment to my name. I tattooed somebody for a tattoo kit and continued to work there until they moved locations and rebranded to Insane Asylum Body Art, for about a year. I then worked at two shops— Unique Ink, Black Ink, and even out of my home. During this time, I was going in and out of jail, getting into drugs, and in a very toxic relationship for about seven years which really took a toll on my mental health. I went to prison three times, once for violation of street gang terrorism, second in Ohio for a gun charge, and third for a trafficking charge, which I beat but still got sent to prison for a probation violation. Through all of this I was still tattooing in and out of prison. Life was definitely a little rough.

However, things started to change when I met my wife, Ashley. I got sober, had my son, Loucious, and my daughter, Indikah, and started working at Ink Paradise. At Ink Paradise I started going to conventions and got well known in the tattoo industry, success started rolling in. My motto became, "My art means a lot to me so if I can design something that makes you happy, it makes me happy."

Around this same time, my music career took off from an MGK diss I posted on YouTube during his and Eminem's feud. From that I got a distribution deal with Sony for a year and am now talking with other labels about going major. While this was the first time my music really started to get popular, I have been rapping and writing music my entire life. I started Anxiety Music in 2014 which is just another example of how I cope with my own battles with mental health.

I had been following Black Dragon, in fact my entire club followed him for quite some time. We had an opportunity to meet him at an Outcast MC Nation Atlanta chapter function on Juneteenth and we were thrilled to meet him. He graciously took pictures with us and took time to speak with us and answer questions. When he discovered I was an artist he surprised me with a request to do the cover of his book President's Bible Chronicle I Principles of Motorcycle Club Leadership. I could not believe he was going to give me, a guy he did not even know, an opportunity to do the art on the most ambitious book he had ever written. But I told him what I tell everyone, "My art means a lot to me so if I can design something that makes you happy, it makes me happy." He described his concept to me and when he saw what I created he howled! The rest is history.

I am Chainz President/Founder of Nut Basketz MC Atlanta. If you are ever in the area and need a tattoo hit me up. Follow me on Instagram and check out my music, the links are below. If you have a mental health issue you are not alone. Get some help because it is out there for you. Ask me, I will never mind helping you out and guiding you to where you need to go.

Forever yours,
Chainz

@Blackinkchainz
@officiallychainz
@nutbasketz_mc

JBII

Buy Prospect's Bible

More from John E. **"Black Dragon"** Bunch II

Bunch Media Group LLC.

Prospect's Bible
Amazon #1 Best Seller

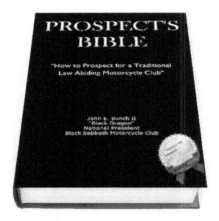

Learn how to prospect for
a traditional MC!
Order 24 hours per day
www.blackdragonsgear.com
Available from Kindle, Amazon.com, and retail bookstores.

Buy Sergeant-at-Arms Bible

More from John E. **"Black Dragon"** Bunch II

Bunch Media Group

Sergeant at Arms Bible
Amazon #1 Best Seller

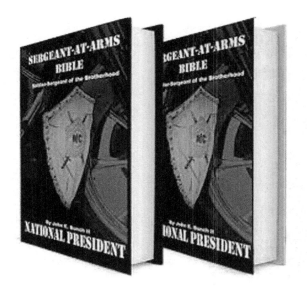

Learn how to be the Sergeant-at-Arms for
a traditional MC!
Order 24 hours per day
www.blackdragonsgear.com
Available from Kindle, Amazon.com, and retail bookstores.

Buy Public Relations Officer's Bible

More from John E. "**Black Dragon**" Bunch II

Bunch Media Group

Motorcycle Clubs Public Relations Officer's Bible
Amazon #1 Best Seller

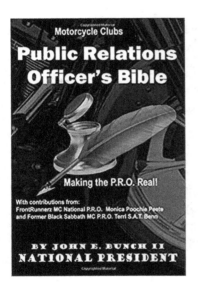

Learn how to be the Sergeant-at-Arms for
a traditional MC!
Order 24 hours per day
www.blackdragonsgear.com
Available from Kindle, Amazon.com, and retail bookstores.

Made in the USA
Columbia, SC
11 January 2023

10089024R00245